# Praise for *America the Principled*

"Full of optimism for what our nation can become . . . a rejuvenating read!"
    —**Wendy Kopp,** president and founder, Teach for America

"Kanter combines tough analytical skills with practical strategic steps to create a better, more decent world."
    —**Warren Bennis,** distinguished professor, University of Southern California, and author of *On Becoming a Leader*

"A patriotic call to excellence from a woman who has lived the American dream and achieved excellence. Kanter's pep talk to America is brimming with optimism at a time of so much pessimism. Restoring American confidence will not be easy, but Kanter provides a road map to success."
    —**Alan M. Dershowitz,** Author of *Blasphemy: How the Religious Right Is Hijacking the Declaration of Independence*

"Rosabeth Moss Kanter's *America the Principled* is a book of heart, soul, and substance, brimming with practical ideas for restoring the idea and practice of community. It's a powerful palliative for America the Disconnected."
    —**Arianna Huffington,** founder and editor, HuffingtonPost.com

"Rosabeth Moss Kanter is not only a Harvard professor with a capacious mind, she is also a national leader with a noble heart. Here she brings both to bear in thinking through our current troubles as a people and how we can fix them. Every presidential candidate should read this book: It is brimming with smart ideas. If we did only half of them, the country would get back on a winning streak—and be a lot happier, too!"
    —**David Gergen,** editor-at-large, *U.S. News and World Report* and White House counselor to four U.S. presidents

"Brilliant and inspiring ideas that will help get America moving in the right direction. This lively, must-read book offers fresh, clear thinking about how we can recapture American traditions of openness and opportunity."
    —**Cathie Black,** president, *Hearst Magazines*, and author of *Basic Black: The Essential Guide for Getting Ahead at Work (and in Life)*

"Rosabeth Moss Kanter urges America to restore itself by investing in its own people, retreating from right-wing fundamentalist ideologies, and returning to open society principles. A must-read for anyone seeking an optimistic response to our troubled times. This is a terrific book."
> —**Norman Pearlstine,** senior advisor, Carlyle Group, former editor-in-chief, Time Inc., and former managing editor, *Wall Street Journal*

"This is the business version of *The Little Engine That Could*. Dr. Kanter never gives up—here is her positive, optimistic strategy for America. I love this book."
> —**Donna E. Shalala,** president, University of Miami, and former U.S. Secretary of Health and Human Services

"A timely and timeless book on innovative leadership in America . . . a powerful and compelling analysis of the American tradition of optimistic leadership striving toward the path of creative thinking in a global economy . . . America the Principled is a tour de force and a must-read for corporate America, government officials, and everyday citizens."
> —**Charles J. Ogletree Jr.,** Harvard Law School professor and director of the Charles Hamilton Houston Institute for Race and Justice

"What's most appealing about Rosabeth Kanter's new book is her optimistic look at the future and how America can get back to being its 'better self.' Perhaps best of all is that it won't be as hard as many might think, especially now that we have her pragmatic six-point program in hand."
> —**Alberto Ibarguen,** president of the Knight Foundation, and former publisher of the *Miami Herald*

"A robust vision for national renewal in the twenty-first century, one anchored in our unique strengths as a people."
> —**Marc Freedman,** founder and CEO of Civic Ventures, and author of *Encore* and *Prime Time*

# America
## the
# Principled

## Also by Rosabeth Moss Kanter

Confidence: How Winning Streaks & Losing Streaks Begin & End

Evolve!: Succeeding in the Digital Culture of Tomorrow

Innovation *(co-authored)*

Rosabeth Moss Kanter on the Frontiers of Management

World Class: Thriving Locally in the Global Economy

The Challenge of Organizational Change *(co-edited)*

When Giants Learn to Dance

Creating the Future *(co-authored)*

The Change Masters

A Tale of "O": On Being Different

Life in Organizations *(co-edited)*

Men and Women of the Corporation

Work and Family in the United States

Another Voice *(co-edited)*

Creating and Managing the Collective Life

Commitment and Community

# America the Principled

## 6 Opportunities for Becoming a Can-Do Nation Once Again

Rosabeth Moss Kanter

CROWN PUBLISHERS

NEW YORK

Published in the United States by Crown Publishers, an imprint of the
Crown Publishing Group, a division of Random House, Inc., New York.
www.crownpublishing.com

Crown is a trademark and the Crown colophon is a registered trademark
of Random House, Inc.

Library of Congress Cataloging-in-Publication Data

Kanter, Rosabeth Moss.
  America the principled : 6 opportunities for becoming a can-do nation
once again / Rosabeth Moss Kanter.—1st ed.
      p. cm.
Includes bibliographical references and index.
  ISBN 978-0-307-38242-9
  1. United States—Economic policy—2001–2.   2. Community
development—United States.   3. Social values—United States.
4. Technological innovations—Economic aspects—United States.
5. Leadership—United States.   I. Title.
HC106.83.K36 2007
338.973—dc22      2007024635

ISBN 978-0-307-38242-9

Printed in the United States of America

Design by Joseph Rutt

10  9  8  7  6  5  4  3  2  1

First Edition

*To Matthew and Melissa,*

*who have tied the knot, and*

*for whom I wish the joys of summer year-round*

# Contents

# America
# the
# Principled

# Seasons of Opportunity

*"Now is the winter of our discontent . . ."*
—WILLIAM SHAKESPEARE,
opening line of
*The Tragedy of King Richard III*

Years ago, I discovered a truth about success in work and in life. Opportunity is a great motivator. People put in the effort today because it leads somewhere—because it helps them get closer to realizing their dreams. The expectation that there are open doors, clear paths, warmer weather, and brighter prospects ahead keeps people going during even the darkest days of the coldest winters. But closed doors and limited options depress aspirations. Without opportunity, people cannot prosper. When people close their minds, fearing the future, they fail to learn how to master new challenges. Closed doors also permit mischief to take place behind them that can distort outcomes. And when countries and companies alike systematically close their doors, they erect barriers to problem-solving and allow a few to succeed at the expense of the many.

Once widely admired as the land of opportunity, America could instead be closing it down—unless we create a positive agenda to renew the American spirit. Americans were once known as a people who responded to circumstances, however seemingly adverse, by saying, Yes, we can. The grim opening years of the twenty-first century, however, have been the winter of America's discontent, when anxieties are so chilling, stresses so burdensome, and major institutions so discredited that it is tempting to retreat behind closed doors. Terrorism, economic recession, corporate scandals, and war have dampened the national mood, despite a recently booming stock market that reached new highs. The 2006 elections shifted national power and perhaps mood, and notes of hope sounded by candidates for public office resonated with the public. But grim realities come to mind quickly, as seemingly intractable problems appear daunting.

Consider these six opportunity-constraining issues that must be faced if we are not to be frozen into perpetual winters of discontent:

- For all the talk about the centrality of innovation to the economy, science has been under political attack (whether the issue is biology or global warming) and forced to compete with religious ideology. Too few young Americans achieve excellence in math and science, let alone pursue careers in science and engineering. Furthermore, advanced technology is used only sporadically in two sectors critical for America's economic future: health care and public education.

- For many middle-class families, the burdens of daily life seem more onerous, and even well-educated professionals struggle with issues of work and family, loss of job security (they are not the unemployed but the "uneasily employed"), and a continuing gender gap.

- Corporate financial scandals have caused business leaders to fall precipitously in public esteem and have given zealous prosecutors and regulators an easy target—at the same time that top executive pay has swelled to many hundred times that of the lowest-paid worker. But ending wrongdoing is not enough; many stakeholders demand even higher standards. What more should companies be doing to become good corporate citizens?

- Mistrust of government is at an all-time high, and unfortunately, contempt for government or subversion of its powers is prevalent at the highest levels. As the disturbing events surrounding Hurricane Katrina made clear, it is difficult for government to perform effectively, even in basic areas such as public safety and response to natural disasters, without a view that public service is an honorable vocation for the most competent.

- The prevailing political ideology that opened the twenty-first century is xenophobic and isolationist, viewing other countries primarily as threats, failing to maximize the value of our national diversity as a nation of immigrants in forging connections to competitor nations (such as China and India), and missing opportunities to cultivate new kinds of leaders who invest in their people.

- As Americans separate into antagonistic ideological camps, we struggle to find common ground and the sense of community that once made "one nation" (under whatever one believed in) the strongest country on earth.

This book offers a positive agenda for dealing with these issues by returning to core American principles. We can use these principles to move forward toward new solutions—in the best American tradition of optimistic leadership for innovation. In that tradition, there is better weather ahead.

That tradition of looking forward to a brighter future has been threatened by negative voices reminding people of threats, not opportunities, and causing them to slam doors on one another. Our can-do nation is being overrun with can't-do/better-not-try pessimists. If "bleeding heart liberals" were once a political caricature accused of too much compassion and wanting to give away too much, today the caricature might be "bleeding ulcer conservatives," who suffer from too much bile because of the things they hate.

Events of the 2000s (terrorism, corruption, war) partly account for this tragic style of thinking. But right-wing fundamentalist ideologies play a large role in shaping a zeitgeist that threatens to make the land of the free and the home of the brave into the land of the screened and the home of the scared. Popular discourse is peppered with images of disaster that are the stuff of tragedy, and our stock of comedy has been depleted. Poking fun has given way to poking huge holes in the social fabric through seemingly endless negativity. We have lost a collective sense of humor, which would allow us to laugh at our pratfalls, correct them, and move on to a happy ending. I call it our "gross national comedy deficit."

A belief that disaster looms seemed to surround America in the opening years of the new century. Popular television programs, beginning with *Survivor*, portray life as a Darwinian jungle of scarce resources in which only some are fit to survive. Struggle-to-the-death metaphors underlie all the knockoffs of *Survivor*, including the career struggle-to-the-death of *The Apprentice*. Comedian Steve Harvey, who made the switch from sitcom to reality show, told a reporter, "People want to see other people fall on their faces. No matter how much your life sucks, 'At least I'm not that guy.' " It is indeed a tragedy when people feel better off only if someone else is worse off.

Comedy, in contrast, is sunnier. It involves ludicrous juxtapositions without destruction of the underlying possibilities for improvement. We need comedy to help us understand that things aren't always as they appear, that they can shift shape or form, that there are opportunities for change, and that we're not stuck inside past decisions.

What worries me about the wintry chill of a comedy deficit is that it reflects a dangerous shift in national mind-set from the optimistic to the apocalyptic, from American dreams to collective insomnia, and from a world of promise to one about to end. A surprising proportion of American religious believers view the end-of-the-world-as-we-know-it as foreordained. But fundamentalists are not the only apocalyptic thinkers who think that the-world-as-we-know-it is doomed. Global changes are often described in dire apocalyptic terms: that the American "empire" is about to fall, that there is an inevitable clash of civilizations between Muslim nations and the West, and that China and perhaps India will take over the world and take all the best American jobs.

Laugh and the world laughs with you, the saying goes. But there's nothing funny about grim battles to be the survivor. We won't lighten up until there is a new vision for America—for our responsibilities at home and our role in the world—that makes us believe again in happy endings, not end games. We need a change of seasons, from winters of discontent to summers of more open doors.

## Toward a Vision for a Positive American Future

America can restore its strengths as the world-respected land of opportunity by returning to open-society principles. An open society invests in people and new ideas, rewards talent and hard work, values dialogue and learns from dissent, operates to high standards with transparent information, looks for common ground, sees problems as opportunities for creative change, and encourages those who are fortunate to help others get the same chance, because service is the highest ideal. With such standards in mind, America the Beautiful can return to its admired role as America the Principled.

Enduring American principles can help unite a divided country and, it is hoped, heal a troubled world. This book takes off from the challenge of the current century: that the global playing field is increasingly level and that America can no longer assume unquestioned superiority or domination. Ensuring continuing national strength requires investments in people and institutions rather than fearmongering or saber rattling. To deal with the six challenges that form the chapters of this book, we can focus on the ingredients that can maintain America's economy and quality of life:

- Widening the net of prosperity by spreading innovation and the opportunity to participate in the "white coat" economy and life sciences revolution of the twenty-first century

- A new social contract based on real family values, with fair and flexible workplaces that are productive while also attentive to the needs of families and women

- Values-based capitalism, with companies that are responsible and go beyond the letter of the law to provide motivating and satisfying work and contribute to solving social and environmental problems

- A new commitment to government as an instrument of public interest, replacing contempt with competence

- Grass-roots engagement by ordinary American citizens to help those enlightened leaders in other countries who empower their people to build their economies

- A community ethos of caring about others, and a program of national service to unite people behind common purposes

In this book, I lay out a positive management agenda for America that speaks to (or chastises) national leaders and deals with matters of concern to average Americans in their work, family, and community lives. It is an agenda that gives each of us something to do, whether as leaders or followers, in whatever sector we operate. We need to govern our activities, inside and outside of Washington, by a set of core principles that can keep us innovating and make the world respect us again.

This perspective comes from my work as an entrepreneur, Harvard professor, business consultant, corporate board member, political activist, adviser to government, community leader, and media commentator. My lifelong mission has been to enhance the effectiveness of large systems by enhancing the effectiveness of the people in them—in essence, to organize and empower people so that they can take positive actions that make a difference in the world and in their lives.

I began my career by studying American history; my doctoral dissertation focused on the leadership and organizational dynamics of nineteenth-century religious and secular utopian communities, often founded by immigrants who came to the United States because of its promise of freedom and limitless room, geographical and mental, in which diverse groups could express themselves. They were trying to construct perfect societies in microcosm, and I deconstructed their designs to identify what worked and what didn't work. I noted how much the human spirit craves social bonds and higher purpose, but I saw clearly the limits to authoritarian modes that suppressed individuality in the name of orthodoxy. That was particularly important to me as a woman who wanted to break barriers so that I could practice my chosen profession without being confined to the social category into which I was born.

My research and scholarship have always been accompanied by practical action, whether I was founding a business or consulting to business. I have always traveled widely internationally and domestically. Sometimes I felt I was following in the footsteps of French aristocrat Alexis de Tocqueville, who wrote about his long tour of America in the nineteenth century, in being an anthropologist of American culture and, indeed, of the many countries in which I have had consulting work. I sit with national leaders and CEOs at conference tables and conferences, and I talk with average people in many walks of life as part of formal research or out of personal interest, and I do so through nonprofit and community service activities. In recent years, I have paid particular attention to current events and spoken with people across America about them, writing a stream of newspaper and magazine columns that directed my thinking toward some of the ideas in this book. But it took a lifetime to gain the knowledge to write this book and simply state my views. (Of course, I also built on research studies—mine and those of others. Key notes can be found at the back of the book.)

For several decades, I have worked with major corporations and organizations in every sector—banking, health care, education, software, food and consumer products, media, social service, and so on. Though passionate about thinking globally and building bridges across cultures, I am deeply committed to my country and what it has stood for. I have brought to my engagements ideals of fairness, justice, equal opportunity, inclusion, open communication, transparency, generosity, and social responsibility that are also classic American values. I have learned that these are not simply ideals but excellent management principles capable of bringing about substantial changes in people, organizations, and social systems. I have seen firsthand in exemplary companies that values and economic growth are compatible and that empowering people can enhance business success and build social capital that provides a favorable context for spreading the benefits of that success. It is no accident that management philosophies grounded in such values guide many business enterprises across the globe and that, for most of the twentieth century, leaders everywhere turned to Americans to teach them.

Of course, enduring principles must confront new realities. These include technology and the importance of the Internet, global economic competition and its impact on labor markets, a resurgence of religious faith, the crisis of climate change, and other contemporary issues. But these twenty-first-century challenges should not and must not be excuses for subverting or diverting principles that have made America the land of opportunity, the place with open doors. Indeed, where people have been taught not mere prudence but outright fear, mistrust, anger, and prejudice, they have found their opportunities and their well-being reduced. Where people have closed their minds, they have lost the chance to convert change from threat to opportunity.

The six chapters that follow describe major challenges and offer directions for taking action, guided by the values that have made us great. As former President Bill Clinton is fond of saying, "There's nothing wrong with America that can't be solved by what's right with it." An open society is key to economic opportunity and personal well-being, an idea recognized by financier George Soros, creator of the Open Society Institute. Clearly, there are trade-offs, and not everyone is the immediate beneficiary of change, as recent debates over immigration policy illustrate. But I will argue that the principles of an open society make it easier to deal with difficult problems involving conflicts of interest in a way that is more likely to minimize short-term losses and maximize long-term benefits.

I hope that the facts, figures, ideas, stories, arguments, and personal experiences in this book of commentary will appeal to concerned citizens and leaders in all sectors who want to reclaim and take advantage of American ideals to restore the American dream, not only within our borders but also, when added to other nations' own dreams, throughout the world.

America, at its best, has as its centerpiece a universal vision, driven by a promise to care about others, however remote, and to help them gain their own unique freedom. America is a country that should give a damn, wherever these ideals are being violated, not because they are automatically America's business but because America is one country whose history makes clear the power of those ideals in practice. Our great power can be turned to great purpose.

How do we open those doors we've closed in the winter of our discontent and move on to the promise of summer? In the passage from *Richard III* that starts this chapter, Shakespeare went on to write that winter became "glorious summer" when the right leadership appeared.

# ONE

# Securing the Future

## Innovation and the White Coat Economy

The fourth-floor walk-up on a crowded inner-city street might not be the first place you would look for a future scientist whose work will create American jobs. But something special about the education of children in Union City, New Jersey, drew me there to see Robert and his family in 1998. Five years earlier, in 1993, Union City had created Project Explore at the Christopher Columbus Middle School, the latest incarnation of a run-down parochial school that the public school district had purchased recently. The Columbus name was a deliberate signal that discovery was the mission. Robert was one of the fortunate first beneficiaries of new technology-enabled teaching that emphasized team-based exploration, not rote learning or received wisdom. And he was on a path to be among the scientists and engineers who could maintain America's lead in innovation.

Just across the Lincoln Tunnel from Manhattan, Union City was then the most densely populated city in the United States, with 42,000 residents per square mile. In the schools,

92 percent of the students were Latino and 75 percent did not speak English at home. The city was known as one of the nation's most impoverished communities, with 30 percent of its residents living below the poverty line. School buildings had broken panes of glass, windows that didn't open, one set of encyclopedias in the mostly empty libraries, and many fewer textbooks than children, so the students had to share. But it was assumed for years, the superintendent had told me, that these urban children were not capable of learning, anyway. Robert and his 134 classmates, who started with Project Explore in seventh grade, would prove those low expectations wrong. And as they continued through school, they would tell their stories to President Bill Clinton, Vice President Al Gore, congressional leaders such as Newt Gingrich, and distinguished visitors from around the nation and the world.

I was there on a gloomy winter day in 1998 with a camera crew. After climbing the stairs to Robert's apartment, I passed through the narrow sliver of rooms—kitchen, parents' bedroom, and sister's bedroom, each opening into the next, train-style—to reach Robert's computer command central at the end of the line. The state-of-the-art desktop computer, which the family could never have come close to affording, was a donation from Project Explore's corporate partner. I perched on the edge of Robert's narrow bed while the animated high school junior showed off his Web prowess: the sites he had built and the research ideas that he had generated and was enthusiastically pursuing with other students. He was also well into his college applications.

Later we sipped coffee and tea with his beaming and hospitable parents around the small kitchen table, which doubled as living room and guest seating. Robert's parents had moved to Union City from Central America a decade earlier, never dreaming that their son would be part of a significant educational innovation. His mother was a hairdresser and his father a skilled factory worker, and until Project Explore, both had been taking any other work they could get so they could save enough to leave Union City. The thought crossed my mind that Robert's mother's employment was undoubtedly more secure than his father's, as manufacturing jobs were starting to flee America and the alarm was sounded that those with poor educations would be stuck in low-wage service jobs. I also thought that Robert's parents were wise to promote his dreams of studying science and someday starting his own technology-based business.

Today, Robert and his Project Explore peers, many of them once destined to be high school dropouts, are college graduates. Some have master's degrees; others are enrolled in Ph.D. programs. They have attended Yale, MIT, and numerous other top-tier colleges. Overall, the number of Union City students enrolled in highly ranked colleges grew tenfold when the Explore students finished high school, and now every student is expected to be on a college track. Their teachers were appropriately surprised and impressed. "I couldn't believe these low-performing kids were producing honors-level work," one told us.

When Union City began to plan its remarkable experiment in school reform in 1989, the digital age was barely under way, and the district was the third-worst-performing in the state, failing on forty-four out of fifty-two indicators. But enlightened public officials saw the potential for innovation to transform their community. Mayor Robert Menendez, who was later elected to Congress and then the U.S. Senate, brought to the new school superintendent, Thomas Highton, an advocate of collaborative learning, a potential partnership with Bell Atlantic (now merged into Verizon). Bell wanted a test site to understand the potential of DSL networks; Union City's density made it feasible, and the school connection made it socially desirable. The renamed Columbus School was wired, and 135 entering seventh-graders and their teachers were given home computers and Internet connectivity. This also gave Highton a tool to use to prod teachers to adopt new collaborative and theme-based learning that stressed student research.

Bell Atlantic's biggest fear was a lack of digital content to send over the networks the company was testing in Union City. Luckily, the coming of the World Wide Web in 1993 solved that problem. The second-biggest fear was that the poor Hispanic inner-city children would steal or damage the computers the company was donating to them. But on the contrary, the gifts were treated so respectfully that students like Robert learned to repair computers for other students rather than bring problems to the attention of school officials. The fees Robert earned went straight to his college fund.

Technology was the catalyst for change, and a public-private partnership got it moving, but teachers, students, parents, administrators, and corporate partners attribute the success of Robert and his peers to three elements that reflect bedrock American principles:

- The students were launched on a journey of discovery, crossing new frontiers. They were taught to be scientists, creating and testing hypotheses and exploring new arenas for discovery. Nothing was off-limits. Even the devout Catholics in the group felt that they could raise questions and poke at scientific frontiers. Yet while feeling free to reject orthodoxy, the students were unfailingly polite and respectful.

- They were taught that knowledge did not end with the pages of a book or with the limits of their teachers' brains. They worked in self-managed teams. Marjorie Zacagna, then head of the English department at Emerson High School, where the Explore students went after middle school (taking principal Bob Fazio with them), recalled: "I was running late to class, walked into the room, and all my kids were already busy working with their collaborative learning groups in front of the computers. In twenty-four years of teaching, I had never seen anything like it."

- They became teachers themselves. Margaret Mead once said that America was the world's first example of a culture in which the young taught the old—in which children often learned new ways before their parents and passed them on. Union City's version of children teaching their parents was called Parent University. In training sessions held before school, after school, and on weekends, all to accommodate working families, the children taught their parents computer skills. Parents brought those skills to their workplaces and testified to the positive impact on their jobs and earnings. Within the schools, Project Explore students shared their knowledge and computers with other students, changing the culture and achievement levels of the whole school.

In 2003, we visited Union City again, in Thomas Highton's last week as school superintendent before his retirement. In 1989, when he started, Union City had one of New Jersey's highest student-transfer rates. Now the schools were so popular that they suffered from overcrowding; at Emerson High, even the faculty dining room was turned into a classroom. A National Science Foundation grant helped support technology internships, college visits, and ventures such as Project Smart, which paid students to design websites with new curricula for the schools. "The technology has made it cool for these urban children to be smart!" exclaimed an Emerson teacher.

This success story is about an educational innovation using a technological innovation that is spawning innovators likely to produce further innovations—a virtuous chain and a necessity for securing America's future in a highly competitive world. The last I heard, Robert was planning to apply his tech skills to health care, specializing in biomedical engineering.

I can't predict what Robert or anyone else will discover, but I can predict that the awakening of scientific imagination in young people will produce many discoveries holding promise for our future. Here's an environmental example. Under an MIT-sponsored program called InvenTeam, a group of chemistry students at New Hampshire's Merrimack High School began to develop a solar-powered biodiesel processor to produce clean-burning biodiesel fuel from discarded vegetable oil from local restaurants. They undertook tests of whether this biodiesel fuel could run school buses. And vowing to waste nothing, the students made soap out of glycerin by-products from the processing to sell to raise money for their project.

A nation whose prosperity depends on innovation should attract more people to the innovation game and forge close connections between innovation and better lives for all citizens.

## American Inventors and American Principles

Clearly, innovation is back in the buzz. Never a fad, but always in or out of fashion, innovation is currently top of mind for government policy, business strategy, and even pop culture.

If you have any doubts about the pop culture side of this,

tune in to *American Inventor*, the prime-time television show from the producers of *American Idol*. Inventors of everything from "the wacky to the heartwarming" (its website says) can compete to invent the next Rubik's Cube or Cabbage Patch Kids dolls, which might be a restroom door clip, an umbrella that's easier to close, an electronic word game to teach reading skills, or a double-traction bicycle. Finalists get $50,000 to develop their product while competing for the $1 million prize and the chance to get rich by finding investors for their idea.

*American Inventor* is just a caricature, especially compared to a search for truly significant discoveries such as search engines, cancer cures, or hybrid cars. Still, invention and discovery, pop or esoteric, enables America to produce opportunity for a good life.

This chapter offers an agenda for ensuring that America continues to lead through innovation. Our economic security depends on this. If we are to create jobs when other countries have cheaper labor, we must have smarter labor, and we must be the leaders in new discoveries that we use to generate jobs in America. Even our future homeland security depends on innovation to make us energy-independent in an environmentally friendly way—innovation such as the development of alternative energy sources and more energy-efficient technologies.

Innovation thrives on traditional American values of openness, tolerance, broad-mindedness, and inquisitiveness. It stems from investments in fertile environments in which ideas can grow and people can gain the skills to imagine and develop them. However important in the past, this is even more important for the future. The central driver of the economy, I propose, has already moved from manufacturing to services, from blue collar to white collar. Now the economy is starting to shift from white collar to white coat—that is, creating value from endeavors in which discovery and invention, particularly in the life sciences but also in other areas of technology, play a larger role. But I will also argue that, in recent years, America's strength in innovation has been jeopardized by attempts to close minds, as evidenced by the stem cell research controversy and by failures to invest in critical educational institutions at every level that produce scientific talent. I will end with a proposal for a national effort to enlist schools, hospitals, and communities as innovation zones, much like the Union City experiment. We must bring every part of America into the innovation mainstream.

## Open Markets, Open Borders, and, Above All, Open Minds

The 2000s have brought a variety of economic worries—as every decade does. The "what keeps me up at night" list for the new century includes rising dependence for energy on unstable and troubled parts of the world, continuing high and escalating costs of occupying civil-war-torn Iraq, ongoing terrorism uncertainties, a ballooning federal deficit mortgaging the future, and the increasing cost of higher education that puts college out of reach for many families, eroding one of the key foundations for prosperity. There are fears that India will steal high-tech jobs and that China will conquer manufacturing. In some areas, American job creation has been anemic, while India cannot find talent fast enough—Indian outsourcers to whom American companies outsource work are now outsourcing some of that work back to American engineers in America, if you can follow that ironic chain.

The best way to alleviate American worries is by supporting the foundations of American resilience and job creation: open markets, open borders, and open minds. The first two are fraught with caveats and sometimes require modest fences to protect our interests. The third is more basic and more important in the long run. Open minds embrace new ideas that build innovations.

If there is a magic bullet that creates jobs, it is innovation—new ideas that open new business (and life) opportunities. Fresh ideas are the lifeblood of job-creating entrepreneurs. Innovation is America's strength in global competition; we are not the lowest-cost nation but the one with the best and latest innovations. Innovation also protects against uncomfortable change. Wherever brainpower is nurtured through investments in education and scientific research, new industries arrive as old ones disappear. In the higher-education-intensive Northeast, textile and shoe manufacturing were replaced by computer manufacturing, then software replaced hardware, and today health sciences herald a new innovation wave. In earlier research, I identified three prototypical ways that regions can succeed in a global economy: as *thinkers* (dreaming up new products or processes), *makers* (handling manufacturing or logistics), or *traders* (doing the deals and moving the goods that connect regions). More than ever, the American economy depends on thinkers to create the well-paid jobs of the future.

Thinking about new ideas through basic research is an essential component of national competitiveness. Federal funding can produce breakthroughs that only later are commercialized by private-sector entrepreneurs; the Internet derived from the defense-related federal Arpanet. Cisco CEO John

Chambers has given many an impassioned plea for a federal initiative to get the country wired for broadband—an effort akin to rural electrification in the 1930s (which brought modern opportunities to every corner of the country and readied the nation for industrial production), the interstate highway system in the 1950s, or the space program in the 1960s. It hasn't happened yet. Of course, other industrialized and emerging countries spend large amounts for government-sponsored projects, and those do not always bring expected results; French-government-subsidized Airbus has been out-innovated and out-competed by Boeing, the American private-sector behemoth. America's openness to mobility of people as well as products produces advantages. America won World War II with the help of technologies from top scientists fleeing repressive Nazi Germany.

Open markets built the United States of America in the first place. The United States has been dubbed the world's first common market of separate economic regions. Boundaries of states do not determine the flow of goods and services, though regions anchored by a metropolitan area increasingly compete with other economic regions for jobs and people. (Will the next Silicon Valley be New York's Silicon Alley, Seattle's Silicon Forest, Denver's Silicon Mountain, or Phoenix's Silicon Desert?) Open markets furthered America's fortunes more recently. The economic boom of the 1990s was energized by the opening of markets in Asia and Eastern Europe as political barriers fell. An estimated 30 percent of the rise in the U.S. economy after 1993 was trade-related.

Moreover, new science- and technology-based companies were then and are now "born global," developing their ideas for world markets from the start. The 1990s boom was also propelled by Internet-centered technologies that raised productivity and inspired entrepreneurs. Later, globalization enthusiasm was tempered by terrorism fears and trade woes, and the 1990s stock technology bubble burst; but e-mail, e-commerce, and mobile communications are now firmly established. After licking their wounds during the recession of the early 2000s, American companies have accelerated their push for innovation.

## Imagination Moves Economies: Kaleidoscope Thinking

I don't know if faith can move mountains, but I do know that imagination can move economies. Innovation relies on entrepreneurs and mavericks who see the possibilities of new technologies and challenge orthodoxy. High levels of innovation are associated with a restless curiosity, openness to ideas from unexpected sources, permission to slaughter sacred cows, and an optimistic belief in the potential for change.

I call the mind-set required for innovation "kaleidoscope thinking." It's the best way to think about innovation—as a means to change patterns in sometimes unpredictable ways (at least at first, until they become the norm).

Kaleidoscopes work the way our brains do when we dream or when we have creative breakthroughs. A kaleidoscope is a device for making patterns. If you shake it, twist it, or change the angle or perspective of it, the same fragments form an entirely different pattern. Often it is not reality that is fixed; it is our view of reality. Minds can become closed to even modest changes if rituals and rules require only one correct pattern. Kaleidoscope thinking is even farther out of the box than out-of-the-box thinking; boxes are rigid structures, whereas kaleidoscopes permit vast numbers of possibilities.

Thus, innovators question the status quo. They imagine how things could be, rather than feeling stuck with today's options. Every new idea starts out as someone's silly thought—silly only because previously unthinkable. I picture people in Kitty Hawk, North Carolina, a century ago, taunting the Wright brothers because they thought that their idea would never fly.

Innovation flourishes where there are continuing conversations leading to unpredictable connections and combinations of ideas. Innovation is the result not just of analysis (rational problem-solving) but also of interpretation (exploring and making sense of ambiguity). In new areas of technology, the innovation process is likely to resemble improvisational theater—a process of unfolding discovery that led to the Sony Walkman or Apple iPod. There is a theme rather than a fixed script, and the actors in the innovation drama learn as they go, playing off the reactions from the audience to improve the product (or in tech-speak, "rapid prototyping"). In today's digital age, innovations also spring from communities of interest finding their own solutions, such as the now-established open source software, which derived from a social movement of sorts led by Linus Torvalds, the original author of the Linux operating system, from Helsinki, Finland.

Diversity of ideas is essential for innovation-seeking economies because new ideas arise from unexpected places and challenge conventional assumptions. It is difficult for orthodoxies to be maintained when constantly confronted by a mix of people from different backgrounds and with a clash of perspectives. This is why the idea of the "creative economy" is currently popular among economic development officials around the world—mix in a few musicians and performing artists, and scientists and engineers will be more innovative, they think. But I think that the presence of colleges and universities is even more fundamental.

Quality-of-life amenities are assets for regions dependent on brainpower, but even more important are social institutions dedicated to innovation: universities to spawn advanced ideas, encourage learning, and seed networks of talent and other mechanisms to commercialize ideas, including access to capital and affordable space. Silicon Valley's superior performance in growing new technology companies in the 1980s and 1990s compared to Massachusetts's Route 128 high-tech corridor adds a dimension: the importance of open human networks for the free exchange of ideas. Massachusetts's high-tech firms were more likely to be involved in large federal contracts, especially defense, which made them more closed environments, so that even the innovative companies faced inward and restricted the flow of ideas. As a result, they fell behind more dynamic California companies, whose ideas were likely to be part of a more public conversation. In California, it was common for roaming "knowledge nomads" to hop from company to company in search of the next new tech environment, sprinkling ideas across companies. Mobility and open conversations stimulate innovation.

## Orthodoxy Versus Creativity

Tolerance, broad-mindedness, and open-mindedness are not only great values; they are smart economics. In contrast, pushing orthodoxy over inquiry is anti-innovation. That's why anyone concerned with securing the future should also be concerned about the battle between science and religion.

Recently, when I was speaking in Silicon Valley, executives

asked me if America was losing confidence. That week, as if to answer them, the most popular national television program was a religious drama about the end of the world. That same wonderful week also brought accusations that then–Senate Majority Leader Bill Frist was pursuing a "religious war" over federal judge selections by portraying Democrats who blocked the president's nominees as "against people of faith," as a *New York Times* editorial put it.

The far right has made a practice of trying to close minds, often on religious grounds. Georgia, whose low educational rankings among the states have worried the leaders of Atlanta's high-tech companies, averted near-disaster recently when state officials reversed plans to restrict teaching of evolution and other key concepts in physical and biological sciences. But restriction is already trumping science. A University of Minnesota biologist found that about 15 percent to 20 percent of the nation's high school biology teachers teach creationism, and at least twenty-four states have been dealing with this issue, as biblically rooted creationism tries to fly under the pseudoscientific flag of intelligent design. Federal judge John E. Jones III, an independent-minded Republican, called intelligent design disguised religion (he also called it "inane") in ruling against it in Pennsylvania. Kansas overturned a previous school board decision to require it. In 2006, the Ohio state school board argued about whether to add a critical analysis of evolution to the science standards. Meanwhile, the religious right argues for its positions on freedom of speech grounds, saying that speech shouldn't be denied to those espousing "biblical morality."

It's one thing to be critical of "different" ideas. It's another to forbid people to think them in the first place. That's the threat posed by right-wing religious orthodoxies—our kaleidoscopic brains will get locked into one set of "correct" beliefs, stifling innovation. The tension is not between religion and science per se. Both can contain rigid assumptions, and both can support the search for insight. There are scientists of faith, and there are deeply religious people who value science. The real tension is between orthodoxy and creativity.

Some types of values open dialogue, but others attempt to close minds. Science is not just another body of opinion, and the process of discovery (the scientific method) is not a matter of listening to inner voices without empirical observations. When science is manipulated or ignored in the interests of holier-than-thou political posturing, a great deal is jeopardized, including national economic security and health. This is especially clear around America's next frontier, the life sciences.

## Shoot-out at the Life Sciences Corral

Praying for a miracle cure? Or praying to stop it? Sometimes that's what the stem cell debate seems to come to.

In 1998, the first human embryonic stem cells were isolated by scientists at the University of Wisconsin and Johns Hopkins University, ushering in a new range of possibilities in the life sciences. Stem cells are the basic building materials for the human body: "blank" cells that have the potential to develop into any type of cell in the human body, such as nerve cells, heart cells, and kidney cells, once they receive a specific biological signal. If stem cells could be harvested before this point, they could be steered toward becoming certain types of cells, providing great potential for curing diseases. For example, if scientists could grow nerve cells (by determining the process of manipulating stem cells into nerve cells), they might be able to repair brain cells damaged by Alzheimer's or Parkinson's disease or replace injured spinal cord cells in a paraplegic.

Sounds like a miracle? Not so fast. The religious right claims that stem cell research is wrong because it destroys human life (since harvesting a stem cell has generally necessitated the destruction of an embryo). Also, one of the simpler ways to grow transplantable replacement tissues from the new cells would require a patient to be partially cloned. Some argue that stem cell research is taking valuable research money from other areas of medical research. And while stem cell research contains very high potential, no cures have yet been developed from it. But the potential is there, and so is the religio-political noise. It is appropriate to raise ethical questions and set guidelines, but much of the controversy involves attempts to suppress science to further the agenda of the radical right.

In August 2000, the National Institutes of Health issued guidelines, supported by President Bill Clinton, that allowed federal funding of embryonic stem cell research. In February 2001, after one month in office, President George W. Bush put a hold on federal funds for stem cell research. A few months later, Senator Bill Frist (R-TN), a physician, and Senator Orrin Hatch (R-UT), a vocal abortion opponent, called for limited federal funding for stem cell research, but within ten days, House Speaker Dennis Hastert (R-IL) and other Republican House leaders came out in opposition to federal funding for research. On August 9, 2001, President Bush declared that federal funds could be used to support research only on cell lines that were already in existence on that date (while states retained the ability to appropriate money for research or to restrict it). Right-wing religious conservatives wanted to ban all research, so this compromise drew measured praise from scientists. But they cautioned that Bush's limitations would slow down the pace of research. Among other things, disputes reigned over how many approved lines actually existed (the Bush administration said about sixty; scientists later estimated twenty to twenty-two). Many of the approved lines proved to be contaminated, and some contained genetic mutations, making them unsuitable for research.

States sprang into action. In 2002, California passed a law allowing research on embryos, including the use of cloned embryos, but prohibited reproductive cloning to create stem cells. Two years later, in November 2004, 59 percent of California voters voted for Proposition 71, which called for spending $3 billion over ten years on stem cell research (the first Americans to vote for science with their pocketbooks), although legal challenges from the religious right later put the funding on hold. Also in 2002, New Jersey Governor James E. McGreevey signed a law permitting research and use of human embryonic stem cells, germ cells, and human adult stem cells from any source, and in June, legislators passed a state budget that included $9.5 million for a newly chartered Stem Cell Institute of New Jersey. By 2005, the New Jersey allocation had risen to $150 million, and Connecticut lawmakers approved $100 million in funding for stem cell research over ten years in an effort to help the state's biotech industry compete with California and New Jersey. Illinois, divided into Chicago versus the Bible Belt, faced more resistance from legislators but dedicated $10 million by executive order of the governor, while Maryland's legislature authorized $15 million.

Congress got the message. Republicans, including Frist and Hatch, broke ranks with their president and proposed a variety of measures to loosen restrictions, despite Bush's continuing opposition and stated willingness to veto legislation. It didn't move the president. As he had promised, the stem cell bill received his first veto in July 2006.

Meanwhile, in a bid to replace America as the world center for life sciences, Britain announced major initiatives for stem cell research. The United Kingdom had long included biotechnology and life sciences on its agenda as industries to build for the future. Since 1990, the government allowed research using embryos remaining after assisted reproductive procedures. A new interpretation of the 1990 law in 2001 expanded this to include many types of basic research. Though allowance for cloning was being challenged by several groups, in 2004 the Newcastle Center for Life was granted one of the first government licenses to clone human embryos in order to extract stem cells for research purposes. The United Kingdom also established a Stem Cell Bank, open to domestic and foreign scientists, and a ten-year plan for public and private research funding.

Singapore launched a major biotechnology initiative in 2000, after the electronics industry that had helped transform it into a rich nation faced declining returns. Singapore's explicit strategy was to lure top international talent while developing a homegrown core of young scientists, many of whom were sent for education to America on government scholarships. By the spring of 2006, Singapore had already spent $4 billion and committed another $8 billion through 2010. A self-enclosed, state-of-the-art, ten-acre science city called Biopolis was constructed to house governmental research

institutes, biotech start-ups, and global drug companies, including Novartis's tropical disease research center—and it is
surrounded by housing attractive to foreigners and an arts
community in rehabilitated pre-1950s buildings. I first heard
about Biopolis when I was asked to join an advisory panel,
and I had a long personal tour in 2006. It's impressive.

In late 2005, the Singapore Stem Cell Consortium was
launched, with a $45 million commitment. Two of America's
most prominent cancer researchers, Neal Copeland and Nancy
Jenkins, who had worked for twenty years at the National Cancer Institute in Maryland, rejected offers from Stanford and
packed their bags for Biopolis. Another prominent scientist
who had left the National Cancer Institute a few years earlier
waxed eloquent to the *New York Times* about how Singapore
welcomes new ideas. Academic freedom is a key factor in attracting top talent. This is Philip Yeo's view, and Yeo should
know. Chairman of Singapore's Agency for Science, Technology, and Research (STAR), he was the force behind much of
Singapore's economic development strategy for decades, as I
learned when I met with him in the STAR offices in 2002.

And guess who else is eager to beat America in life sciences
research? Iran. Yes, Bush's axis-of-evil Iran. A country ruled
by religious orthodoxy has found expedient ways to exempt
science from religious strictures. This fundamentalist nation
that once lost about 15 percent of those with college or graduate education to the United States, according to a 1990 International Monetary Fund study, is investing not only in
nuclear research but in health initiatives such as therapies for
drug addiction and prevention of heart disease. A striking
photo in the *Boston Globe* in August 2006 depicted white-
coated scientists working on embryonic stem cell research

with government funding and freedom at the Royan Institute in Tehran. The country's leaders might be closed-minded in most respects, but perhaps they are not stupid about technologies for the future.

If Iran can, why can't we? At least a little faster?

## The Emerging White Coat Economy

The stem cell controversy is significant because the life sciences promise to be both life-saving and job-creating. The health sector is the next big American frontier.

The U.S. employment profile has become less blue-collar and even more white-collar, with some pink collars in the mix. Millions of manufacturing jobs have been lost in the Rust Belt and now even in the Sun Belt, where many northern companies set up shop and foreign companies located their plants, such as BMW in South Carolina, and Mercedes in Mississippi. The construction trades are the one remaining source of America's blue-collar job growth. Jobs in services have burgeoned, such as in retail, leisure, and hospitality, but the job market has also grown in education and health.

Increasingly, the American workforce is not just white-collar; it is white coat. Engineers, scientists, and health professionals in lab coats are important creators of the next new thing. The life sciences have become a much more important part of the research-and-development mix everywhere, forming a core element of national competitiveness strategies in Asia and Europe. Knowledge is developing so quickly that about two-thirds of all U.S. postdoctoral fellows are in the biological, medical, or other life sciences. Between 1995 and 2004, the number of doctorates awarded in engineering,

math, computer science, and physical sciences fell, while doctorates in biological sciences grew. Emerging fields such as
neuroscience, biological immunology, cell biology, and bio-
metrics accounted for most of that growth. (Of course, one
national priority is to ensure that it is as easy to find nurses as
waitresses and science teachers as retail clerks.)

Among the twelve largest American export categories,
pharmaceutical products have been the fastest-growing, more
than doubling from $10 billion to $21 billion between 2000
and 2005, up from $2.7 billion in 1990. The category that in-
cludes medical and surgical equipment also grew significantly
between 2000 and 2005 (from $45 billion to $55 billion in
exports). Export growth reflects strength that keeps American
jobs in America.

My home state of Massachusetts is a bellwether for this
transition. Health-related products were the fastest-growing
category among commodities exports by dollar value between
1996 and 2005. Medical and surgical instruments, the largest
export in 2005, nearly doubled over the decade. Pharmaceutical products jumped more than tenfold to become the fourth-
largest export category. In contrast, the biggest declines were
in photographic goods and industrial machinery, a category
that includes computers. The Massachusetts Biotechnology
Council had about 100 member companies in 1995, but by
2006, it represented nearly 500 companies engaged in drug
discovery and in biotechnology and pharmaceutical research.

One of the characteristics of the emerging white coat
economy is the central role played by large not-for-profit
organizations (especially hospitals, colleges, and universities),
nonprofit research laboratories, and the complex public-
private partnerships that are woven through the tapestry con-

necting basic science to small start-ups and large established firms. In contrast to those information technology ventures that were at first home-garage-based, such as the famous development of Apple Computer and IBM's equally famous effort to duplicate a garage-like environment in creating its PC in Boca Raton, Florida, the life sciences flourish in laboratories and require highly trained professionals not only for discovery but also for testing because of the risks to human subjects. Hospitals and universities that house such labs are largely nonprofit. These star charities are financed through philanthropic dollars in addition to fees for services, government grants, and corporate R&D funding. Their prestige and academic freedom attract talent, and those talented people in turn enrich knowledge.

It is important to maintain the public character of these institutions so that they do not become captive to commercial interests and place restrictions on the flow of knowledge. The role of these nonprofits is increasingly recognized in regional strategies that once were consumed with courting large corporations. For one thing, universities are themselves acting as catalysts for development, creating large science and biomedical complexes to attract researchers and the companies interested in that research. More important in the long run than big companies are big ideas. The latest hot properties are research labs, not company headquarters or manufacturing facilities. While losing corporate headquarters, Massachusetts has gained research-and-development centers, which require many thousands of white coats. For example, Swiss giant Novartis moved its global research center to the Boston area, hired physicians and scientists from the teaching hospitals, and set up collaborations with small companies to solve big problems, such as pandemic flu vaccines through a partnership with Alnylam, a small biotech firm.

Continuing public investments in higher education, science and engineering, and the life sciences in particular must be a national priority. States cannot make up for federal reductions in research funding, even though California, Connecticut, New Jersey, and Maryland are trying in the case of stem cells. The federal government needs to meet the challenge, making the R&D tax credit a permanent benefit for stimulating innovation and fully funding the national institutes that support the most promising ideas. As long as American thinkers develop knowledge that others want, the economy will be strong. Of course, that proposition assumes sufficient numbers of American thinkers in the science and engineering talent pool.

## Who Wears the White Coat?

Global competition for foreign students has increased in the past two decades, eroding America's lead as the advanced knowledge destination. Although the United States remains the predominant desired educational location for foreign students, accounting for 40 percent of internationally mobile students in 2004, American universities now account for only about 22 percent of science and engineering doctoral degrees conferred worldwide, a slip over the past twenty years. By the late 1990s and early 2000s, the number of science and engineering doctorates awarded leveled off or declined in the United States, the United Kingdom, and Germany, but the number rose in China, South Korea, and Japan.

Even more alarming statistics, as we think about the American future, are these: Opportunity-seeking people all over the world want the best and latest technical knowledge from the United States, but do American students? Foreign nationals accounted for almost a third (31.6 percent) of all science doctorates and nearly two-thirds (60.3 percent) of engineering doctorates conferred by U.S. higher education institutions in 2003. If U.S. permanent residents are taken out of the pool, foreign students on temporary visas accounted for 27 percent of science doctorates and 55 percent of engineering doctorates that year. Foreign science and engineering graduate students rose from 19 percent to 27 percent of the total between 1983 and 2003. The number of doctorate recipients with science and engineering postdoctoral appointments at U.S. universities more than doubled in the past two decades, but noncitizens accounted for most of the increase, representing 58 percent of the postdocs in 2003.

In 2004, over 40 percent of the foreign students came from India and China, with another 14 percent from South Korea and Taiwan. Some of these foreign students are already permanent residents, others might want to stay in the United States, and still others might maintain ties with American institutions, including multinational corporations. That's the silver lining in a very threatening cloud that could rain on America's prosperity if we stop investing in advanced skills.

## Healthy, Wealthy, and Wise

One change in America since Benjamin Franklin declared that "early to bed and early to rise makes a man healthy, wealthy, and wise" is that sheer industriousness is not enough (as I show in the next chapter) and that Yankee ingenuity requires the discipline of acquiring advanced knowledge. Yet too many American students are late to bed and late to class (as evidenced by some college guides ranking the best "party schools").

Higher skills translate into higher wealth, better health, and greater longevity. This fact of individual fortunes is also reflected in geographic clustering around centers of both education and prosperity. The states with the highest personal income per capita are also the places with the highest percentage of people over the age of twenty-five with college degrees, and, not surprisingly, they are found in the higher-education-intensive Northeast corridor. In 2005, the U.S. average income per capita was $34,586, but for the highest-ranked state, Connecticut, the figure was $47,819, and in the second-ranked state, Massachusetts, personal income per capita was $44,289, just ahead of New Jersey. West Virginia, Mississippi, and Arkansas anchored the bottom in both college education and income.

But overall prosperity masks widening inequalities. Zoom into Massachusetts, for example. The gap between upper-income and lower-income families has widened more in Massachusetts than in any state except Arizona and New York. Over the past decade, incomes for the highest-income families grew almost five times as fast as those for low-income families. Between 1990 and 1992 and 2001 and 2003, the ratio of income of the top 20 percent to the bottom 20 percent grew from 6.7 to 7.3.

Inequality shows up in another way: a racial gap. Although the life sciences are more woman-friendly than other technology areas—life science firms are more likely to have women on the board of directors, and Susan Hockfield, a neuroscientist, is the first woman appointed president of MIT—the same cannot be said for people of color. The "white" in America's white collars and coats is an unfortunate reflection of reality; opportunities in science and engineering have not crossed the race barrier. Robert and his peers in Union City are an exception.

Numerous programs like those in Union City have been created to entice minority youth to become interested in math and science and to steer them toward opportunities in life sciences and health. Such programs include vacation camps, internships for high school students, mentoring programs, and college scholarships, and one example is the Biomedical Sciences Careers Program started by Harvard Medical School's dean for diversity, Dr. Joan Reede. Meanwhile, here's a thought-provoking observation: In affluent areas, special math programs already exist, but it's striking to see the profile of those who take advantage of them. One after-school and Saturday voluntary math program in a Boston suburb, which serves several hundred children from K–12 schools, was started in 1998 by Russian immigrants (presumably to get math enrichment for their children). The most common participants are not African Americans or Hispanics but children of families with origins in India, China, and Israel.

Ambitious immigrants and second-generation hyphenated Americans recognize the importance of math and science. But other things must be done to make science cool on the street. There is peer pressure on some black students who try to excel; they're told they are "acting white" and encouraged by peers to give up on school.

Even if we get more children interested in math and science, who will teach them? This is a big question not just for minorities but for the entire U.S. public school population.

Jobs requiring science, engineering, and technical training will increase by 51 percent through 2008. This increase could lead to 6 million job openings for scientists, engineers, and technicians. In order to prepare today's young people for these careers-of-tomorrow, more than 260,000 new math and science teachers are needed by the 2008–2009 school year. The situation is already dismal. In 2000, nearly all of the largest urban school districts noted an immediate demand for science teachers and mathematics teachers. Even those who are employed are not always qualified; about 37 percent of high school math teachers and 31 percent of science teachers lack a major or certification in their field.

One innovation-conscious corporation is stepping in to help fill the gap. In January 2006, IBM began a program that should become a national model: Transition to Teaching. Transition to Teaching, which IBM hopes other companies will emulate, is aimed at encouraging the development of 100,000 new science and math teachers from among maturing technical professionals. Departing IBM veterans with degrees in science or math who are interested in teaching can remain at the company for up to three months while they student-teach or engage in coursework and receive up to $15,000 from IBM as reimbursement for associated tuition and costs. In 2007, California added state funds to grow this idea, calling it En-corps.

Immigrants and foreign students are replenishing the American science and engineering talent pool because U.S. secondary education is not doing its job with respect to math and science education and motivation. Something is preventing American youth born in the United States from flocking to the new frontiers of science and engineering. Investments in education should remain on the agenda—especially in promoting math and science excellence. I wish we could motivate girls and boys across races and ethnicities to develop their talents by giving all middle school students the equivalent of a white lab coat that would start them off on a journey of discovery, just as the Union City students did when they received their computers and home networks.

## Technology and the Health Care System

The implications of the new life sciences are still emergent (as are financial payoffs from early-stage biotechnology investments), while information technology (IT) now infuses every part of life. We must nurture the first—the basic sciences—but we also must apply the second, IT, to improve health care. Recently, in the name of national security, many Americans found that technology was being used against us, for surveillance. Instead, it should be better deployed *for* us, in areas vital to our future economic security: health and education.

As everyone who has a brush with the health care system knows, it's enough to make you sick. The Institute for Healthcare Improvement, a Boston advocacy group with national reach, announced its "5 million lives" campaign in December 2006 because approximately 5 million people are harmed in the United States every year by avoidable medical errors or infections that occur in hospitals.

I don't have a problem with the dedicated doctors and noble nurses on whom we depend for care, although I wish there were more of them, as shortages loom. I'm not criticizing pharmaceutical companies, which have gone overnight from the world's most-admired companies to being viewed as greedy price-gougers preying on addicted citizens, akin to the tobacco industry. My quarrel is not with the financing of health care, either, though there's plenty to complain about, with so many uninsured Americans.

My gripe is with the health care *system*. Maybe it comes from waiting in endless lines to get "admitted" to the hospital for routine tests (does one have to "apply"?), only to repeat the same information to a serial claque of clerks. Maybe it was the struggle to get Medicare payments for my Alzheimer's-afflicted mother-in-law who couldn't speak for herself—when it took endless hours to find her records and then fill out new form after form. Or maybe it was the unnecessary death of a valued community member (ironically, a health reporter for a major newspaper) who was accidentally given four times the appropriate dose of medication at a leading hospital.

Delays, duplication, errors, and neglect—these can cause rather than ease suffering, raising human and financial costs. Recent studies show that clinicians spend only 16 percent of their time in direct patient care, but 60 percent of their time seeking information—including test results, medical histories, and even the current location of their patient in the hospital. "Close to one-third of the $1.6 trillion we spend on health care goes to care that is duplicative, fails to improve patient health, or may even make it worse," Senator Hillary Rodham Clinton wrote in the *New York Times Magazine*. The prestigious Institute of Medicine has reported that about 55 percent of preventable deaths are due to medical errors, many associated with faulty information transmission, such as prescription mistakes. While some large and well-funded hospitals are pioneers in using technology to improve quality and reduce costs, other hospitals are barely scratching the surface. On the cost side, clerical armies processing paper account for a high proportion of budgets. Wasteful duplication, such as reentering information sent electronically into an incompatible database, could be eliminated. One suburban hospital has as many as 150 different databases that don't talk to one another.

Transforming the way the health care system handles information can save time, money, and lives. Smart use of information technology could be one factor that might make health insurance more affordable for practically all Americans; electronic claims filing alone could save a minimum of $70 billion over ten years. At Washington Hospital Center (WHC) in Washington, D.C., and throughout its parent, the MedStar Group, one of the nation's largest hospital networks, information networks have saved lives and money, among many other benefits.

As part of turning around WHC's emergency department from the city's worst to its best, Dr. Craig Feied set out in 1996 to create a kind of air traffic control system for health care dubbed Azyxxi: to make all existing data, including scans of handwritten paper, ubiquitously and instantly accessible through any device. Dr. Feied, a spritely man who favors bow ties and mixes complex data displays with cartoons in his lectures, created his system on a stealth basis. He used a small group with minds more open than the hospital's information technology department and spread his system by word of mouth. Physicians discovered for themselves how much time they saved and how much they could improve patient care— e.g., by getting the results of a brain scan on their handheld devices wherever they were in minutes instead of waiting four hours for someone to carry records from one place to another and track them down.

With a minimal investment, Dr. Feied's Azyxxi system improves quality of care. Doctors and nurses can view orders, lab results, and x-rays in real time and instantly access old lab results, diagnoses, or x-rays. Records of previous visits reveal patterns and problems that might go undiagnosed in a single visit. Instantly available images save the lives of patients with critical injuries such as brain traumas. Physicians can click through a patient's medication history and then zap prescriptions instantly, reducing time lags and errors. And, a feature for which I am very grateful, any staff member can admit patients instantly using a handheld computer.

Between 1996 and 2001, the same number of WHC staff handled twice the volume of patients, up from 35,000 to 70,000 per year, while median time in the emergency department dropped from eight hours to just two hours. Patient satisfaction increased from the fourteenth to the ninety-ninth percentile among comparable hospitals. Such successes made WHC the preferred treatment center for victims of the September 11, 2001, Pentagon attack. A few months later, it became a national showcase for tracking information about the anthrax exposure. Then–Secretary of Health and Human Services Tommy Thompson recognized the enormous potential for public health from Dr. Feied's system. Azyxxi can pinpoint outbreaks of diseases down to neighborhoods and streets, providing early warning of potential health disasters.

All the problems of health care financing and delivery will not be solved by sprinkling computers everywhere. But there is great potential for improving care through better information. A national health information network proposed by Congress would store data from electronic medical records (anonymously) to see what works and what doesn't, giving medical professionals an alternative to self-interested studies by drug companies and medical device makers. Health economists disagree about whether this would save money or increase the demand for health care once it is known what treatments are efficacious. But "increasing demand" is economist code for improving lives through better health care. Better health brings benefits to people's lives and to economies—as French scientists found in using statistical models to argue for the expansion of AIDS drug donations in Africa, in which a small investment in health brings big payoffs in economic opportunities.

It's said that knowledge can make us free—but only if information gets to the right people at the right time. That's true for health, and it's also true for the other major social institution underlying a white coat economy, education.

## Educators Need Tools

The great American educational paradox is that we have the world's best higher education but a disgraceful decline in K–12 public education.

Consider the tools disparity. Duke University now supplies every freshman with an Apple iPod to download audio content for courses. This move signals another technology advance for higher education beyond the now-ubiquitous notebook computers carried by college students. At the other extreme, California recently settled a class-action lawsuit accusing the state of denying poor children in public schools adequate textbooks, among other deprivations. An estimated 1–2 million California students lacked books to use in school or to take home for homework. In poor urban districts elsewhere, where basic tools are not provided, teachers must buy pencils, notebooks, and marking pens from their own funds. Without tools, can we expect children to learn and achieve?

Like book-deprived children, educators themselves often lack tools—especially tools for making necessary changes. Public schools must become the beneficiaries of information network innovations. This is not an argument for computers in the classroom, which have been oversold and underused. Many schools in many states are wired and have access to computers for classrooms, but technology is not yet used to provide teachers with information they need to help students with specific skill deficiencies or to give teachers on-the-job mentoring. Teachers and principals need data and tools that can improve their own effectiveness in teaching children to learn.

The 2001 federal No Child Left Behind Act (NCLB) imposed harsh sanctions on low-performing schools, as measured by test scores, attendance, dropout rates, and suspensions. Identifying troubled schools is a first step in ensuring accountability and provoking change. But NCLB set new requirements without new resources, because it was never fully funded. Just as schoolchildren cannot be expected to make progress without tools for learning, school leaders cannot be expected to make improvements without tools for change. Change requires more than slogans, unfunded federal mandates, or abandonment of the public system. For example, the $745 million promised to Memphis for school reform following the passage of NCLB became more like $50 million. By 2003, Memphis's Booker T. Washington High School, considered a school of last resort for students ineligible for specialized schools, appeared on the dreaded list of low performers despite an enlightened principal who improved teaching, attracted national grants, and encouraged college aspirations. Those on "the list" face extra scrutiny, reports, and time-consuming meetings. Punishment for poor performance means taking time away from improving performance— a classic Catch-22.

As a solution to failing schools, NCLB offered conversion to charter schools—quasi-independent start-ups freed from some bureaucratic constraints and thus free to innovate. But charter schools are not always the cure that proponents promise. Studies of the achievement of their students show mixed results; some outperform students in regular public schools, but others, on average, perform no better. The innovation promised by charter schools is under way, including experiments with longer school days or missions that motivate high achievement (like arts or science emphases), but such innovation is not making its way into regular public schools fast enough.

Public education faces a leadership crisis. Superintendents turn over at an alarming rate. School districts with a principal vacancy report a shortage of qualified candidates. A Massachusetts Department of Education study of eight of the state's lowest-performing schools found not just poor teaching but a leadership vacuum—principals didn't monitor teachers' work and didn't help teachers to improve, and district officials didn't initiate improvement efforts.

Technology isn't a cure-all, but it has the potential to provide solutions to problems such as teacher preparation and development, measuring performance, and English immersion. West Virginia demonstrated substantial gains in math scores in a single school year in schools that used online lesson plans and Internet tools created in a public-private partnership with IBM. The opportunity for teachers in schools that were geographically isolated to exchange ideas and teaching practices electronically, coupled with new lessons developed by experienced teachers to meet state standards, helped transform classroom practices and boost the achievement of underperforming students.

School districts in Georgia accelerated progress at systemic reform by drawing from a suite of Web-based leadership tools with help from the nonprofit Georgia Leadership Institute for School Improvement. Having tools for change readily available helped Georgia leaders such as Sharon Patterson, superintendent of Bibb County schools, identify neglected areas and guide her staff to change unproductive policies.

Superintendent Scott Cowart in Monroe County adopted a weekly initiative tracking sheet, among other management tools; Ann Procter in Walton focused on training to make teachers passionate about raising student achievement. Online tools permitted frequent assessments and updates, automatic project tracking, and widespread sharing of information about successful practices, a spur to innovation.

Better leadership and better tools can combine to produce striking improvements. A new principal armed with tools turned around a Tennessee elementary school that was failing to educate neighborhood kids from disadvantaged backgrounds. Because the school also had a magnet program that attracted motivated students from other areas, overall test scores and dropout rates looked satisfactory. The previous principal coasted because no one examined the breakdown to see that only the magnet students were doing well, and school board–mandated evaluations of teachers were often neglected. The new principal set higher standards for teachers, supported by extensive data analysis and performance reviews, including purchasing a commercial evaluation tool that he helped them learn to use. Teachers who had thought their students were achieving good results could see which students had not progressed since the previous year and build individual improvement plans. He also tore down the "do not enter without permission" sign that had appeared on his predecessor's door and invited widespread dialogue that was supported by frequent teacher e-mail exchanges. Standardizing daily class schedules opened regular time slots for groups of teachers to share best practices and access model lesson plans on the Web. Technology alone didn't do the trick, but it was part of a culture of innovation brought by a new leader, and openness to innovation changed the school. For example, after establishing a parents' resource center, the principal encouraged 150 fathers to form a volunteer security team for the beginning and end of the school day.

Reform without resources is a waste of time, just as resources without reform are a waste of money. Valuing education means ensuring that educators are well equipped for improvements that build high performance. Perhaps back-to-school should become forward-to-school. Forward-looking Americans should commit to outfitting students and educators with the best and latest tools for K–12 schools everywhere. Then we could all look forward to higher achievement, with no school left behind.

## Communities as Innovation Showcases

When Cory Booker, a thirty-seven-year-old former Rhodes scholar, was elected mayor of Newark, New Jersey, in May 2006, the city's first new mayor in two decades, one of his first

moves was a call to black leaders to support innovation. Another early step was to invite Stanley Litow, Robin Willner,
and others from IBM's corporate community relations staff to
discuss how to create integrated solutions to improve schools,
health care, and job prospects simultaneously.

Here's an idea to toss around in Mayor Booker's kaleidoscope—or the kaleidoscopes of other civic leaders and elected
officials in America's cities and towns. Imagine that visitors
from around the world are enticed to some of America's formerly most-distressed neighborhoods to see the latest, hottest,
most-promising applications of technology demonstrated in
public schools and health centers. Alternative energy is in use
right there, primarily biofuels and solar power, but no idea is
too small to be tested, including experimental treadmills on
sidewalks to spur exercise and reduce obesity while powering
small generators. Health information networks ensure state-
of-the-art care while researchers set up laboratories in the
neighborhood, and white coats are indeed the middle school
uniform of choice. Software firms vie to have satellite offices
there so that they might learn from community residents.

A fantasy? That's no more science fiction than visions of
dark doomed cities. Public schools and health centers could
become beta sites for America's newest technologies, show-
casing ideas of the future while improving communities. I envision a national effort to find the right settings in which
integrated solutions are all applied together.

The vehicle could be a series of officially designated innovation zones, in which public-private partnerships would
demonstrate the applications of technology to transform communities. Companies, or not-for-profit organizations such as
hospitals, would be stimulated to develop still more innova-

tions in response to the special difficulties of distressed or disadvantaged neighborhoods. Social needs would be top items
on the corporate innovation agenda.

Like empowerment zones offering economic stimulus packages to attract jobs to distressed neighborhoods, innovation
zones could offer benefits to early investors, attracting private
investment with a modest sprinkling of public monies. Incentives could include the following:

- Federal or state planning grants and assistance with
  securing matching funds

- A "social R&D" tax credit

- Co-investment by local governments or school systems
  from their technology budgets

- Relationships with some of the region's best brains, who
  would willingly join advisory groups for significant social
  innovations

- User groups available for trial runs and feedback on
  rounds of prototyping

- The chance for companies to show off their innovations to
  customers and visitors and gain abundant publicity

Candidate communities for innovation zones would have
to demonstrate their willingness to be a learning laboratory—
to collect data, assess progress, implement changes in their
own practices, and welcome observers, researchers, and visitors who come to learn. There would be safeguards against
exploitation, so that community members would be partners,

not guinea pigs, and corporate partners would have an obligation to teach and give to the community.

New public-private partnerships could blossom in innovation zones. Please recall the story with which I opened this chapter. Verizon's predecessor company, Bell Atlantic, invested many millions of dollars to turn around the Union City, New Jersey, schools through the use of information networks linking school and home because the company wanted a test site to demonstrate the potential of DSL. Then-Mayor Robert Menendez, now a U.S. senator, wanted to make Union City the first wired community and transform its failing school district. The resulting technology innovations catalyzed other change. Teachers improved their effectiveness, parents became more involved, the district attracted other private and public resources, and student achievement soared.

So imagine the possibilities. Perhaps a telecom or cable company with broadband capabilities teamed up with, say, a community health center to wire a low-income urban neighborhood for high-speed networks or install ubiquitous wi-fi hot spots connecting state-of-the-art health care applications in one system. That network could be used for physician-patient e-mail dialogues that would shorten office visits, e-mail reminders to take medication, patient-directed home-to-lab tests, or timely interventions based on the aggregation of formerly separate data. The health center could cut administrative costs by reducing paperwork and accelerate revenues by billing third-party payers faster. More people could be served more efficiently. The neighborhood would be healthier. Physicians would want to practice there. High school students could get great jobs in science. All that, and more, could stem from defining neighborhoods as innovation zones.

Bringing the white coat economy of invention, discovery, and advanced skills home to the neighborhoods, with health and education central to their vitality, would be good for the economy and good for people. It would renew America's strength as the land of opportunity and a world center of innovation. It would stimulate the children in those neighborhoods to become our white coat innovators of the future.

## The 3T Innovation Agenda: Talent, Technology, and Truth

This chapter has revolved around 3 T's that can secure the American future.

### 1. Talent

Educating American children and youth in math and science is vital to national security (of all kinds). Other nations are now competing to be leaders in the development of advanced knowledge that was once dominated by the United States, and while legal immigrants enrich our mix, we should not rely on foreign nationals who might take knowledge with them when they leave the country. Increasing national funding for science and engineering, with an enriched pool of scholarships, fellowships, and assistantships, is essential, but that doesn't mean that American students will take advantage of this. We need to begin a white coat campaign in the early grades and make schoolchildren proud to wear that coat. Mentoring programs that match students with scientists need to be enlarged. The teacher shortage should be addressed by finding new pools of talent, such as experienced engineers and scientists near retirement who want to contribute to schools if they can get credentials and placements. Better science and math education will benefit the nation even if not every child is destined for college.

## 2. Technology

Technology can constrain or empower. Rather than being used to invade people's privacy, technology should be applied to improving their lives. In health care and education, tools and networks to increase access to information can help care providers and teachers improve outcomes. National campaigns to encourage the building of information infrastructure should include incentives to develop technology innovations in the social sector. A national health information network could improve public health. Investments in tools for educators could pay off in better teaching and learning. Social needs should be turned into innovation opportunities; modest national and state incentives, such as my innovation zone proposal, could transform distressed areas into beta sites and showcases.

## 3. Truth

Since innovation starts with discovery and interpretation, has an improvisational element, and cannot be totally planned, the best guarantee of innovation is informed and open minds. Innovators challenge received wisdom and conventional assumptions, like shaking a kaleidoscope, and they flourish when orthodoxies are not allowed to stifle new ideas. The best test of an idea is whether it remains true after experimentation and observation. It is important to ensure that science—the quest for empirical truth—is not held hostage to religious or political ideologies. Ethical questions, especially in the life sciences, should be raised in a spirit of fact-based inquiry. To support American ingenuity, national leaders should encourage tolerance for one another's ideas and openness to new possibilities. To help new ideas surface in public conversations, rather than being sold to the highest commercial bidder too early in the process, leaders should promote generous funding for higher education and basic research.

These principles can ensure that the can-do spirit of innovation can flourish, to make America secure for years to come.

# Pursuing Happiness

## Work, Family, and the "Woman Question"

Have you noticed that baby names come in waves of re-markably similar choices? That must be why I met so many Sarahs in my conversations throughout America. Three stories in particular reflected the current state of work and family in America. I call their stories *A Tale of Three Sarahs.*

Sarah I is a former future hospital CEO of America. She is now so far off track she will probably ask me not to mention it again, but for a while she was introducing herself by parodying Al Gore's joke that he is "the former next President of the United States." Sarah I's intelligence shines more brightly than her sleek blonde hair. She was educated at one of America's best universities, earned an M.B.A. at another school known for its dedication to nonprofit management, took a highly paid job at a prestigious global consulting firm working on health care issues, and strategized about how to move into position to someday lead a great teaching hospital, her lifelong dream. Sarah I knows she is privileged, knows that she worked hard to earn top degrees, and knows that she could have done anything. But what she is mostly doing now is driving her three children, ages three, seven, and ten, to all the extra lessons and tutoring they can manage and having lunch and book discussions with her equally well-educated stay-at-home-mom friends. Despite living in a western state with a flow of immigrants seeking work, she has had constant nanny problems when she has tried to take on a part-time project with local community hospitals to keep her hand in the management game. Forget full-time work, she proclaims; that's impossible until the kids are much older. Her second husband (her last husband, she jokes) is a senior executive well positioned in the next race for CEO of his company; he feels compelled to cut vacations short, work through holidays, and arrive home after the children have had dinner.

Sarah II is a caretaker. Her day job at the cubicle outside of a corporate lawyer's downtown office pays well for what used to be called clerical work and allows her to go home (theoretically) at 5:00 P.M., but she must sit in the office all day. Evenings and weekends are filled with her unpaid caretaking job. She runs errands and cooks for several elderly relatives who have been plagued by a series of medical emergencies but refuse to move out of their houses. Every Sunday, she fills their freezers with the healthy meal packages she has prepared all weekend. Evenings, she cleans their houses and hers, visits with them, shops, and handles life's other necessities, like the occasional haircut. The rest of the family would like to help, they say, but they work hard, too, to make ends meet, and anyway, Sarah II is the oldest, and she always takes responsibility. Her kind, caring husband can't help much because he works all the time. He is employed at a bank and moonlights with a partner running a small repair business (and doing many of the repairs and deliveries himself, at night) because the family needs the extra income for medical expenses, although they still can't afford round-the-clock care to substitute for Sarah II's ministrations.

Sarah III is a juggler who so far—knock on wood, she gestures—feels that she can just about have it all. Almost. That's because she is employed by one of the handful of progressive companies creating mobile workplaces of the future. Based in the Midwest, Sarah can use her home and her car, as well as the company's sleek high-rise tower, as her office. Equipped with a laptop computer and a cellphone PDA, she has the freedom to work anywhere and anytime she can plug in. Since the company's customers are global, she sometimes has middle-of-the-night conference calls, but her husband understands because he works for the same company. She still feels some limits, however. Recently a few senior managers have told her that they are counting on her for bigger responsibilities (they emphasize diversity, and Sarah III is a woman of color) and that she has a chance to do things that other women cannot. That makes her feel that she carries the future prospects for all women on her shoulders, so she feels pressure to spend more time in the office and less time working at home. As a result, she has put her two young children in day care (on company premises), but she still feels stressed. Sometimes she envies one of the company's high-ranking Asian executives, a legendary woman whose husband cheerfully answers to the title "Mr. Mom."

Sarah III is well aware of how lucky she is, even though nearly every family event she remembers has been interrupted by a work task or two. But noting that the single mothers from her old neighborhood have it much worse, Sarah III told me that she wonders what is meant by all the rhetoric among politicians about "family values," when she thinks they don't care about her family needs. Certainly she doesn't want her children exposed to sleazy websites, so she uses blocking software, but she is adamant that she doesn't want the government making decisions for her about character. She'd rather see a big push to change the workplace. Meanwhile, she wonders about that "pursuit of happiness" promise following "life" and "liberty" in the U.S. Declaration of Independence.

The dilemmas of the three Sarahs reflect an American paradox. We applaud individual achievement against all odds but fail to put in place the social and community supports that could shift the odds to make it possible for more people to earn a living without sacrificing having a life. Think of the opportunities we would have if the two were combined.

## What Are Family Values?

Family values make it possible for people to earn a living and care for families—both. These values help men and women exercise choices about how to organize their lives to balance personal with occupational responsibilities. Innovation and the white coat economy require a large pool of talented people who can be productive without burning out.

National health and prosperity depend on ample opportunity for all people to develop and use their talents, while ensuring that their children have the same opportunity to thrive. That requires adequate wages, affordable health care, and attention to the organization of work. It includes rights for divorced fathers to care for their children and opportunities for working mothers to combine family time with employment. But the extreme right wing has hijacked the term "family values" and used it to justify censorship, control over women's bodies, stereotypical gender roles, and a weakening of equal-opportunity policies.

As long as family is considered women's domain and women are defined by their gender, we will fail to live up to the true meaning of family values. Unless we address these issues, we will suffer as a nation: There will be more stress and vulnerability for families because of parents' work, or there will be a waste of talent when parents choose to opt out completely because they want to be with their children and cannot find a middle ground. The innovation economy could sputter.

Four significant issues represent opportunities for change:

- **Workload** Too many Americans face the double stress of overwork and job insecurity.

- **Work versus family** The legacy of industrial-era separation of employment from family life still shows up in rigid gender roles and difficult balancing acts.

- **Gender gaps** Despite strong female educational attainment, gaps continue to show up in wages as well as attitudes about "women's place" or women's inevitable choices.

- **Stereotypes** Lingering social norms and roles that are still too rigidly defined could reverse progress if right-wing ideologues convince the terrorism-fearing public to allow suspension of liberties.

In recent decades progress has been made toward helping Americans pursue happiness by balancing personal and work lives, but not enough. To explore the problems, I will draw on evidence from national surveys, international comparisons, my decades of workplace observations, the treatment of high-profile cases such as Carly Fiorina and Martha Stewart, a science fiction novel, and discussions with women determined to combine work and family as well as employers determined to make that possible. To find solutions, we must think about work and workplaces in imaginative new ways and take advantage of twenty-first-century tools.

## Gone Fishing? The Work-Life Balance Joke

A former investment banker, a man behind some of the largest corporate mergers of our time, told me this story of an American executive and a Mexican fisherman.

> A business executive with an M.B.A. was on vacation in a coastal village in Mexico. He decided to hire a boat with a guide to take him fishing. He was referred to a local fisherman and given directions to the outdoor café where the fisherman had a drink with his friends in the evening. The executive found the fisherman at the café and made a deal. Early the next morning, they hit the waters. The fish were biting, and there was an abundant catch. By noon, the American was still reeling them in, but he noticed that the fisherman had put away his rod. When the executive inquired, the local explained that he had caught enough fish to feed his family.
>
> The businessman decided to use his M.B.A. smarts to

help the poor fisherman. "If you caught more fish," the American told the fisherman, "you could sell the surplus at a profit." "What would that mean?" the fisherman wondered. The businessman replied, "You could invest your profits to buy a second boat, and you could hire someone to catch more fish. You could sell even more fish and make much more money." The fisherman looked interested in the idea of making more money. So the executive continued, "Your second boat would help you finance a whole fleet of boats. You could move to Mexico City and head a big company. You would get wealthy." The fisherman liked the idea of getting rich. He asked, "What would happen then?" "That's the best part," the business executive answered. "You could retire, get a house by the ocean, fish as often as you want, and go to a café at night."

The former investment banker who loved this joke had traded seventy-hour workweeks on Wall Street for a sailboat and seaside home while still young enough to enjoy them. Clearly, work-life balance is not just a women's issue, nor is it code for child care and housework. It is also clear that the highly affluent can buy themselves any kind of luxury, or balance, they desire.

But a balanced life is elusive for too many working Americans, and that hurts them and their families. Overwork can be driven by financial needs, personal ambition, or subtle employer pressures. Whatever the cause, the signs are that work is making it difficult to manage the rest of life. Numerous national surveys report that many Americans are not taking their full allotment of vacation time. For example, a May 2006 poll found that 43 percent of respondents had no vacation plans—even to hang out at home, let alone go fishing in Mexico.

## The "Uneasily Employed"

We shouldn't forget about the problems of the unemployed, but perhaps those most in need of a vacation from stress are the people whom I call the "uneasily employed"—people working hard but with less and less to show for it. Some of the uneasily employed are educated professionals with middle-class jobs who appear on the surface to be successful. Yet even these so-called gainfully employed feel that they are slipping rather than gaining because of rising health care costs, energy-price increases, or fees for formerly free public services, such as national parks or arts programs at their kids' schools. They worry about the next paycheck—its size and whether there will be one.

During my recent travels, I had the opportunity to speak with people from all walks of life who make up the ranks of the uneasily employed. Their stories, and the questions they readily asked a stranger, add to the picture of stresses faced by my three Sarahs:

- **Squeezed professionals** Advanced degrees do not insulate people against uncertain times. John, an Ohio lawyer turned cable television talk-show host, said his current job was shaky, and he was too old to hang out his shingle as a lawyer, especially when local law firms were downsizing. Anyway, he faced ageism in the media and a reduction in local programming because of media consolidation. So he asked me whether he should try real estate—but then, what would he do about health insurance? Linda is a Florida teacher with a master's degree who is married to a police officer. The couple wanted to move to a community with better schools for their children, but their combined salaries wouldn't cover higher housing costs or longer commutes, and they weren't sure he'd keep his job if they moved out of the city where he worked. Sam, a primary physician who had once been at the top of the heap because his ethnic group valued doctors above all, merely sounded demoralized, but he said he wished he had also studied business.

- **Reluctant consultants** I met a surprisingly large number of people who were peddling multiple business services and handed me several business cards, reflecting their various offerings. Bob, an involuntarily retired manufacturing executive at a once-highflying Midwest corporate giant, cobbled together a set of writing, speaking, and management-coaching assignments. Supposedly conducting an interview with me, Bob didn't ask me questions; he asked for referrals. Carmen, an enterprising woman in Texas, offered personal-assistant services for other solo workers. One of her employers had arranged for us to meet; Carmen wanted to know if I could steer her toward a "real" job.

- **Stranded techies** Silicon Valley was once the epitome of the American dream. Computer programmers and engineers felt they had been promised that they would always be in demand at high wages. Unfortunately for Dan, a California systems engineer accustomed to company-hopping for the best opportunities, his most recent hop was to a declining telecom, where he worked on temporary contracts and without benefits. He complained that he and his wife couldn't buy a house, and now that their kids were getting a little older, they were running out of space in their rented condo.

Middle-class families are increasingly pinched by high costs of housing and health insurance, and so they must spend more time at work. Catastrophes hurt these families, Harvard law professor Elizabeth Warren has shown, because they are already working to the max and have no one to turn to and no time left for additional jobs should disaster strike—a danger especially for the uninsured or poorly insured. Dependent on two incomes, sometimes from more than two jobs, they cannot afford to cut work hours, and they certainly cannot afford to get sick. But long hours bring stress that can cause more serious illnesses; U.S. and Japanese workers who work more than fifty hours a week have been found to have much higher rates of hypertension. Long commute times compound the work hours problem. So do anxieties about job security in companies with recent layoffs. Workplace stress from any source is associated with higher-than-normal blood pressure even while sleeping.

One big issue is control, not just time. Younger workers increasingly demand flexibility. At least, they are somewhat less likely to work themselves into a frenzy than their elders—or they have not yet joined the sandwich generation in needing to care for both young children and aging parents. Younger workers are less likely than those between ages forty to fifty-nine to say that they are chronically overworked. If younger workers are more likely to protect their lives outside of work, that's a harbinger for the future and a wake-up call for companies.

At companies that offer flexible arrangements, many fewer employees say that they are chronically overworked. That's the good news. I'll say more about flexibility and how it can be attained later in this chapter. The bad news is that flexible schedules are widely viewed as a begrudging accommodation for women with children. Even in companies building flexibility into their work cultures, women are much more likely than men to take advantage of parental leaves, reduce their work hours, or opt for flexible schedules.

It seems that work lives with greater balance will take hold only when men demand them, too. I'm tempted to joke that the next time a business convention overrun with male executives needs a speaker, it should get a Mexican fisherman—but that would be too glib for such a serious issue. Instead, we should look at the system. Let's go back to assumptions that derive from the industrial age, and then we will go on to challenge them, as we consider work arrangements better suited to the twenty-first-century digital age.

## Getting Beyond the Myth of Separate Worlds

If people cannot take time for a vacation, no wonder there is a problem with time for family. Let's not make the problem more difficult to solve by continuing to see family life as primarily the responsibility of women.

The industrial era of the last century separated work from family and segregated children from adults. As the population moved from rural to urban areas, employment was formed around industrial, not agrarian, rhythms. The separation of work and family found its ultimate expression in the "organization man" and the accompanying "feminine mystique" of post–World War II suburban legend (and the titles of two best-selling books of that time)—that is, rigid gender roles that confined men and women to stereotyped positions. In popular lore, men were the breadwinners too absorbed at work to have meaningful relationships with their families, while women served as unpaid family workers. Cookie-baking stay-at-home moms were the ideal, as Hillary Clinton made clear by rejecting this expectation on the presidential campaign trail in 1992. She lashed out at critics of her high-powered legal career by wondering what they expected her to do—stay home and bake cookies?

A few decades ago, I called this the myth of separate worlds because it was more symbolic than real. The myth forced people in each world to act as if the other did not exist. While in the workplace, it was important to pretend that families were irrelevant. As long as men with wives at home dominated important positions, companies could enforce a strict separation of domains.

Numerous social changes helped undermine the myth of separate worlds. The dramatic rise in women in the paid workforce starting in the 1960s brought family issues to the forefront. The baby boom generation that began to enter the paid workforce in droves in the 1970s brought a different set of values from their suburban parents. Numerous changes in families were also a concern, with a rise of single-parent households, dysfunctional family systems among segments of the poor, and children ill-prepared for school achievement. And work itself was beginning to change, as the industrial era was passing into a postindustrial information age that brought "knowledge work"—less observable, more portable, demanding of mental energy, and capable of being performed anywhere at any time.

Today there are signs of change that can be good for working parents and their children. These signs include a child care industry with high-quality providers and professional training, an after-school movement to add enrichment activities to the school day while ensuring children's safety, and increased benefits for working parents offered by major employers. "Work/life balance" is the new buzz-phrase. *Working Mother* magazine honors the best companies for working parents, and balance issues are included among screening criteria for *Fortune*'s 100 Best Companies to Work For, making policies friendly to families an arena in which companies compete. The gender-neutral cubicle culture of the comic strip character Dilbert replaced the organization man as the caricature of stifling work to ridicule.

In general, policies and practices have lagged behind the changes in individual lives. Experiments with flexible work hours, or "flex-time," repeatedly demonstrated the benefits to workplace productivity—for example, fewer distractions as workers did not have to worry about coming in late if taking children to school, or less absenteeism when parents didn't have to take an entire day off just to manage a midday parent-teacher conference or child's dentist appointment. Yet, despite the evidence, companies were exceedingly slow to let go of control of the structure of the workday, and even where such policies exist on paper, middle managers sometimes undermine them in practice by favoring employees who work the old-fashioned way. Affordable high-quality child care is not available to some of those who need it most, and there are not nearly enough public schools with longer school days to accommodate working parents.

Tens of millions of people cross the moat between work and family every day. Some get caught in the swamp. Working family members juggle the demands of spouses, lovers, children, parents, bosses, colleagues, customers, vendors, and clients. They determine how to allocate their attention, even when they have little control over their time. Issues spill over from one realm to another. It is difficult to motivate and retain employees without seeing that their relationships outside of work affect their performance on the job. Elder care has joined child care as a cause of stress and lost productivity. Working parents often cannot take time away from work to attend school conferences with their children's teachers, even though parental involvement is considered key to student achievement. You'd think that time for parents to show up at occasional school meetings and events would be a no-brainer employment benefit in light of the amount of corporate concern about the quality of public education. But it isn't.

In some cases, changes to help balance work and family have been met with countertrends. "Anti-parent" and "child-free" movements argue against special privileges and employment benefits targeted at those with children. Longer life expectancies and lower birth rates make the time spent raising children a shorter part of most lives and thus make family issues salient to smaller segments of the electorate—evidence of which shows up in the difficulties passing school levies in affluent towns such as Wellesley, Massachusetts. And on the home front, sociological studies show that the household division of labor has barely budged. Housework is still primarily women's work, and, as sociologist Arlie Hochschild memorably put it, working mothers work a "second shift" at home.

The moat separating work and family could use a few more bridges. One bridge would make it easier for women to navigate the swamp by closing the gender gap. That involves changing a set of lingering social norms involving women and then adding pillars to the organizational support system.

## The Gender Gap

Women are changing the face of leadership, and we should applaud that achievement. Germany elected a female head of state. In 2007, Hillary Rodham Clinton began a campaign to leap across the gender chasm separating the First Lady's office from the Oval Office. Nancy Pelosi is the first female Speaker of the House of Representatives, second in line to succeed the president. Prestigious universities such as Harvard, Princeton, MIT, and Brown have appointed women presidents, and now half the Ivy League has women at the helm. Miami–Dade County has had a veritable dynasty of effective female state attorneys, from Janet Reno to Katherine Fernandez Rundle. For several years both the sheriff and the police commissioner in Boston were women. *Sesame Street* introduced a new female Muppet star, Abby Cadabby, trying to make her both girlie and powerful. Talented women apply their talents to nearly every field of endeavor and often get higher marks for leadership skills than men on corporate performance appraisals. Young women have brighter prospects than the women before them; a recent study showed that women from the ages of twenty-five to thirty-four now earn eighty-six cents for every dollar earned by men, up from sixty-five cents in 1970. Women occupy top positions in business in record numbers, including heading eleven Fortune 500 companies. (Eleven down, 489 to go.)

So why is there still a women's issue in America, and what does that have to do with family values? Take a look at some international comparisons.

The World Economic Forum (WEF) recently released its first-ever report on the gender gap, ranking fifty-eight nations on five indicators of success in closing the gap between men and women in terms of education, health, achievement, and support for families. I was invited to present the U.S. perspective at a briefing at the New York Stock Exchange. That assignment was tough because my beloved America, which likes to be the best, ranked a dismal seventeenth. We lagged behind Nordic nations; behind Anglo-Saxon cousins New Zealand, Canada, Britain, and Australia; and behind much-maligned France. We landed barely ahead of Costa Rica.

In the WEF rankings, the United States shone in women's educational attainment—we have a comparatively high proportion of women with advanced degrees—and received good scores for economic participation and political empowerment. So we seem to be doing well in education and in opening opportunity at the top. Indeed, girls' education is in good shape; the new issue in schools is boys who act up and drop out. However, the United States ranked poorly on both economic opportunity and on health and well-being, dragged down by meager maternity leave and limited government-supported child care. And compared with other developed nations, America has high rates of teenage pregnancies and maternal mortality—which is particularly shocking given our relatively large number of physicians. We are doing poorly for our women in the middle and bottom.

Some problems of opportunity that persist include the following:

- **Sticky wage discrimination** Despite progress for younger women (who now earn eighty-six cents to the average man's dollar), there is other evidence that women working full-time—not part-time, not on maternity leave, not consultants—still earn only seventy-seven cents to a full-time working man's dollar. U.S. employers pay hundreds of millions of dollars annually to settle sex-discrimination claims.

- **Educated professional women opting out** Sarah I is joined by a large number of her peers in being a former future CEO and now a full-time mother. Accurate data are scarce, but anecdotes are oft-repeated. A typical national headline: *Many women at elite colleges set career path to motherhood.* Some midcareer professional women are taking fertility treatments to give birth after the age of thirty-five, just at the time when employers want them to undertake greater responsibilities at work. Affluent suburbs teem with thirty-something mothers with M.B.A.s, J.D.s, and Ph.D.s who left partner tracks at investment banks or law firms to focus on their children. (That might be one reason that the wage gap widens after age thirty-four.) The problem is getting back in—or, to borrow Sylvia Ann Hewlett's metaphor du jour, "on-ramping" after having taken the career off-ramp. After a study found that as many as two-thirds of its women M.B.A.s were not in the workforce ten years after graduation, Harvard Business School began to develop special programs to help alumnae reenter the workforce.

- **Struggling single mothers** A whopping 29 percent of all new mothers are unmarried, and about half of unmarried mothers are poor, the Census Bureau recently reported. Washington, D.C., where national policy is set, has the highest rates of single motherhood nationwide, and 36.3 percent of all new D.C. mothers live in poverty. (Hello, Washington pols, are you listening?) The burden of single motherhood reflects the problem of fatherhood in the African American community, said by many analysts to be a legacy of failed Great Society welfare policies that provided disincentives for men to live with their children. These single mothers suffer when there are little to no maternal health services, affordable child care, and access to both training and jobs. Some of them might even have to work as nannies for those educated moms who can afford child care whether they hold paid jobs or not.

What's going on here? Is there a link among such disparate problems?

Some analysts say that women do not stand up for themselves (the thesis of economist Linda Babcock's book *Women Don't Ask*), arguing that the wage gap could be closed if women demanded higher pay. Former Massachusetts Lieutenant Governor Evelyn Murphy has created a national effort to start support groups in which women help one another develop strategies for changing their workplaces and getting equitable pay (the WAGE project, standing for "women are getting even"). I'm all for support systems and joint action, and some women might indeed get bigger raises. But I'm doubtful that just asking would do the trick for most women. Some of the problems are more deeply embedded in institutional assumptions and patterns—such as the assumption that women do the family work as their "second shift."

Another argument is that the childbearing years sidetrack women. Infants are undeniably attractive, even for those whose hormones aren't running in that direction. The late great anthropologist Margaret Mead once said that women want to be near their children not because babies cry but because babies smile. Finding more time to be with the children is definitely a choice that more women (and men) would like to make, income permitting. (Of course, there are also instances in which people use work to flee from unsatisfying families.) But it's not always clear what is pull and what is push. Sometimes women opt out because the job is dreadful and worth fleeing or because the work system is much too rigid to permit a daily or weekly balancing act. A former senior investment banker who loved her job but didn't want to miss every moment of her children's lives tried to continue part-time and failed because her peers persisted in interrupting her (unnecessarily, she thought) during her time out of the office.

Regardless of the choices women want to make, all women are handicapped by the fact that opting out of the paid workforce is an option for women much more than for men. David D'Alessandro, former CEO of insurance giant John Hancock, invoked the 80/20 rule to explain the problem. He told a group of high-powered women leaders at a recent lunch that women have come 80 percent of the way toward equal pay and leadership because of opportunity-enhancing programs and their own hard work. He argued that the remaining 20 percent of the path to top positions is plagued by subtle discrimination that takes place in conversations behind closed doors about which people to promote based on assumptions about future productivity. Male decision-makers, he said, assume that their best women will reduce their commitment because of family responsibilities. Companies pushing women out by failing to promote them provided a talent pool from which D'Alessandro fished for outstanding talent for Hancock.

In short, the lingering effects of a model of the division of male/female labor derived from the myth of separate worlds means that work and family issues have yet to be fully addressed—except, as D'Alessandro says, in whispered office conversations that sidetrack women.

Look at this another way: How would you complete this sentence? *If women ran the world* . . . For those not offended by the question (does it imply advancing one group at the expense of another?), answers are likely to invoke female gender stereotypes: e.g., *If women ran the world* . . . there would be fewer wars and more attention to human needs. But I ask this: If women ran the world, would running the world pay seventy-seven cents on the dollar? Now here's my serious answer to an unserious and loaded question: If women ran the world, then the world would have already changed to make it possible for more women to participate in running it.

Rather than force individuals to find solutions on their own, institutional change could open more opportunity for more people. Subtle social norms that block opportunity persist because there are too few women leaders to change the norms, and the gap between men and women remains because the organization of work needs some adjustments to permit balanced lives.

If America really lived up to the "family values" oft invoked by politicians, we would help our poorest women find economic opportunity (a great incentive for contraception) and not let our brightest women flounder on their own, forced to sacrifice careers and squander their education in order to choose to care for their children. Women have the talent, but institutional arrangements don't support them. I'm convinced, from years of consulting on human resource issues, that one of the reasons is that there are still not enough women in leadership roles to force a changing of assumptions and patterns. Until there are more women in leadership roles, it will be hard to close the gender gap, because the images of women will continue to reflect stereotypes that entrap and confine, rather than accurately reflect life possibilities.

## The "Woman Question": Equal Opportunity Prosecution and Conviction

As soon as the news broke about former Hewlett-Packard CEO Carly Fiorina's resignation in early 2005, reporters started asking me the "woman question." Was she booted because she is a woman? Easy question. No. The HP board of directors did its job by holding the chief executive accountable for the company's poor performance. Next question. Did she clash with the HP culture because her aggressive, risk-taking style, acceptable in a man, was not acceptable in a woman? Hmm. Let's pause to ponder that one.

Although gender did not get her fired, the media hullabaloo about her resignation was certainly gender-related. The woman question—did X, Y, or Z happen because she's a woman?—is a sign that not enough women are in any position yet to take women's presence for granted. Putting a woman on the spot and in the spotlight is inevitable when very few women occupy her position. Body type is the first characteristic that stands out because women are rarely seen in that particular role. As one of very few Fortune 500 woman CEOs, Fiorina would always have "woman" appended to her business title. Paradoxically, it's hard to be treated as an individual when you are out there alone.

Early in my career, I turned academic research into a semi-animated cartoon saga about this phenomenon. *A Tale of "O": On Being Different* described the fate of the single letter "O" in a group that consists otherwise of "X's." Plug any category into the O or the X role (gender, race, age, nationality) and what happens is similar, regardless of what makes the O "different." The only O, especially if the first of its kind to enter ranks formerly closed to it, is held to higher standards, evaluated against stereotypes of the "ideal" for its type, and put in the harsh glare of judgmental spotlights. The lone O receives disproportionate scrutiny. Even the smallest mistake is magnified and cause for alarm. The O carries an extra burden—to perform well and also represent all O's. O's who have made it into X-dominated groups must prove that they're exceptions to the stereotype of the usual O. Having just a few O's in positions of power doesn't produce pressure for change in the situation of most O's. The majority X's accept a lone O only if the O stays behind the scenes supporting them but does not try to get out in front.

This parable fits another high-profile case where the woman question was also asked. The Martha Stewart trial made it clear how far women have risen in the business world. Far enough to enjoy equal-opportunity prosecution and conviction.

Just as every board of directors and top management team is now incomplete without a woman or two, the lineup of recent business wrongdoers needed its token woman. When Martha Stewart's picture appeared daily next to the big-time corporate wrongdoers, the media could not be accused of gender bias—at least in that respect. I'm not questioning whether her prosecution was justified. It was; she was found guilty on the evidence. As the street saying goes, "If you do the crime, you do the time." Since the street in this case was Wall Street, the Stewart story took on epic dimensions as a tragic tale about hubris and humiliation. Stewart, who rang the bell to open the New York Stock Exchange when her company went public, was convicted of insider trading in stocks. Her legal crimes were itemized to the jury, but perhaps her larger mistake was violating lingering social norms by being ambitious and aggressive when many still clung to the ideal of woman as caretaker, more like Sarah II. Once Stewart was humbled in prison, she could be redeemed, because she now knew her place.

The Stewart saga will be fodder for business ethics classes for years to come, but I am concerned about another, more subtle story line: that women are more easily accused of the social "crime" of overreaching. The Martha-chat across the country seemed to reflect vestiges of ambivalence about women's achievements. When I heard people say that Stewart was getting what she deserved, they were referring to aggressive behavior, not to her stock trading sins. Was the Martha Stewart epic taken as a warning that women should avoid ambition? Stewart made it in a man's world—though, ironically, the world of perfect housekeeping that she invented has no men in it.

Women who veer too far from soft images can get hard treatment. Like hotelier Leona Helmsley, another high-profile woman business owner who served prison time (for tax evasion), Stewart was said to be difficult and demanding. But if being a tough boss were a sin, male management ranks would be depleted (more about that to come). Stewart dared to join the old boys' network that passes around favors and information, and that hubris was her undoing. She also made herself the brand, and that made her a target. A similar backlash confronted Fiorina from her first days as CEO of Hewlett-Packard, when she put herself into HP television commercials;

some said that "violation" inflamed the former board members who were behind the brief shareholder rebellion against the Fiorina-led Compaq acquisition and who ultimately led to her departure.

Equal opportunity may prevail in the courtroom, but it has not fully reached the boardroom. As long as women must meet higher social standards and are judged by whether they know their place, our system will operate justly by the letter of the law, but fairness in terms of opportunity will remain elusive.

My parable of the lone O among X's helps answer another big woman question du jour, courtesy of former Harvard president Larry Summers. Can women excel in science? Well, we won't know until we give them encouragement and the chance to try. Where only a few have made it, the rest too easily give up. Fiorina's fate (including her $21 million consolation prize for being fired) has little in common with the plight of large populations of women around the world except in this respect: Too few women in powerful positions make gender loom large in defining women's prospects.

What if the situations of women and men were reversed? To see what happens when stereotypes produce harmful generalizations, try the following tongue-in-cheek experiment.

## Are Men Fit to Lead? A Thought Exercise

Can men be trusted to be CEOs? What a ridiculous and offensive question. But if women are from Venus and men are from Mars, as a popular book has it, and if a proverbial Martian had landed on Earth in recent years, he would have had to wonder about his brothers in the executive suite. He might even have been forced to answer the "man question" about a number of former power holders:

- Are men too impulsive and too swayed by emotions to exercise good judgment? Romantic fantasies cost Harry Stonecipher his Boeing CEO job. It wasn't the fact of an affair with an employee that caused the board to ask him to resign; it was his impulse to send apparently torrid e-mails to his lover on the company network. Does that mean men are captive to their hormones?

- Do men have trouble with numbers? That was the essence of Bernard Ebbers's defense in the WorldCom corruption case. Ebbers said, in effect, that he had counted on the financial staff to give him the right numbers, and he never fully understood them. (He was convicted anyway.) Other CEOs on trial also invoked the "stupid defense"—that they were unable to understand the details of complex financial schemes foisted on them by their staffs. Should we start wondering if men can do math and give them remedial programs?

- Do men cling to relationships and have difficulty letting go? Maurice Greenberg was relieved of CEO duties at insurance giant AIG after nearly forty years at the helm. He held on despite regulators' investigations of whether the company manipulated its books to mislead investors. Is that a sign that men hang on to dead relationships too long?

- Do men talk too much? Eason Jordan resigned as chief news executive at CNN following a flap over his off-the-cuff remarks at the World Economic Forum in Davos in January 2005 about the U.S. military targeting journalists or jeopardizing their safety. From my third-row seat, I felt the shock waves when he went on and on about whether the U.S. military was responsible for deaths of journalists in Iraq. Why did he run off at the mouth? Is that a male propensity?

These men should be grateful for a few high-profile women who show that their failures of leadership are not a gender flaw. Men are not the only ones caught in financial messes (like Stewart), ousted for underperformance (like Fiorina), or accused of political corruption (like Mireya Moscoso, former president of Panama).

See how ridiculous and offensive it is to define men by their gender? Yet that is exactly what happens to women—but generally, as with Fiorina and Stewart, only when the stereotype is negative. I haven't heard it said that Anne Mulcahy is an effective CEO of Xerox because she's a woman. Stereotypes are pernicious and destructive. They are also contradictory. Will women bosses be softer and more nurturing because of women's "natural" connection to childbearing? Or will women at the top be tougher, to prove that they're one of the boys? Circumstances are often the determinant, not gender propensity.

Without greater opportunity for women to exhibit their individuality, the definition process could lead in a dangerous direction, one that takes right-wing caricatures of "family values" to a disturbing destination.

## When Anatomy Is Destiny: Fear-Driven Subservience

One particularly pernicious gender-coding trap involves the belief by right-wing religious fundamentalists that women should be defined by their reproductive organs. The idea that women's bodies should be public property was reflected in recent attempts to force women to undergo procedures for the benefit of fetuses. Consider this case, which was reported by the Associated Press. In Pennsylvania, Amber Marlowe, who had given birth to six babies weighing nearly twelve pounds each, was told by doctors at Wilkes-Barre General Hospital that her next baby must be delivered by Caesarean section to protect the fetus, even though Marlowe herself would face greater risks from surgery than from a natural birth. To force Marlowe into surgery, representatives of the hospital went to court to get legal guardianship of her unborn fetus.

Fortunately for Marlowe and her family, she had choices. She used another hospital for an easy natural birth. What if such choices should disappear?

Nearly twenty years before September 11, 2001, when a group of terrorists of the Muslim persuasion blew up America's illusion of invulnerability on our shores, Margaret Atwood spun a haunting dystopian fantasy about the transformation of the America of our era into a repressive theocratic nation called Gilead in response to attacks by Islamic fanatics. What Atwood imagined in her 1985 book, *The Handmaid's Tale,* sounds eerily possible: At some undefined time around now, the Army declared a state of emergency and suspended the Constitution after terrorist incidents in which the president was shot and Congress machine-gunned. The acts were blamed on Muslim fundamentalists, and the right-wing cabal behind the coup was ready with an engineered society that was implemented almost overnight—one built around women's subservience.

In Gilead, Eyes (watchers) and Guardians (police) kept people in line. Public entertainment consisted of religious revival meetings called Prayvaganzas and public hangings of the disloyal (Salvagings). Women were slaves who were made to wear burkah-like garments indicating which of four positions they occupied: Wives (the highest status), Aunts (elders who whip young women into conformity in Rachel and Leah Reeducation Centers), Marthas (domestic servants), or Handmaids (women of childbearing age assigned to households of male Commanders to have their children). Handmaids had no names or identity; their names changed with the men they served as breeders. The Handmaid who tells the story was known as Offred, since she was temporarily Fred's possession, living in his household.

Atwood described how easily this society came into being. It started with computerized banking systems, which replaced paper money with credit cards that happened to be gender-coded. One day, unexpectedly, all cards with an F for female were denied, and women could not buy anything anywhere. "That's how they were able to do it, in the way they did, all at once without anyone knowing beforehand," Atwood wrote. Women were fired from their jobs. Women could no longer hold property. Clothing was burned and uniforms issued. Newspapers were censored or shut. Potential Handmaids were sent to reeducation centers where writing was banned ("Pen Is Envy"). This was considered a privilege, since the alternative was a more repressive slave labor camp.

Some women in the novel were willing participants in this transformation toward oppression. They were the ones who stayed at home watching television, looking for direction. Roadblocks and national ID cards met with approval, a character said, "since it was obvious you can't be too careful." And nobody wanted to be reported for disloyalty. (By the way, women were not the only victims of the coming of Gilead. Jews were given their choice of converting or moving to Israel.)

In Gilead, Handmaids kept hope alive by passing secret messages, including a bit of make-believe Latin: *Nolite te bastardes carborundorum*—don't let the bastards grind you down. But fear, inevitably, does grind people down, in real life as well as in novels. It's interesting that the red of the Handmaids' robes matches Homeland Security's high-alert signal. When fear reigns, people go passive, reject change, and are willing to trade liberty for the illusion of security.

Let's not let fear, garbed in bright red, lead us too far to the right. To the right is the path toward Atwood's Gilead, the path away from the America we love.

## Diversity, Not Stereotypes

Anatomy should not be destiny; it should just be anatomy. Women, like men, come in all kinds of shapes and sizes, with a range of talents and ambitions. But one thing that women sometimes have in common is the vantage point of outsiders who have been excluded from public discourse.

When women are treated as a class, confined to limited roles, and excluded from the public debate, society suffers. In places where there is a sharp line between men's and women's roles, there tends to be more violence and less economic progress. And certain issues get handed over to women and neglected by men. In her book *This Was Not Our War,* Swanee Hunt, former U.S. ambassador to Austria, examined the war in Bosnia through the eyes of twenty-six Bosnian women. These women tried to prevent the war, held community life together during the war, and led grass-roots postwar reconstruction efforts. A male-dominated political hierarchy ignored them or treated them as "decoration." With so few women in the highest policy ranks, even the courageous women whom Hunt located became discouraged about their opportunity to make a difference. Hunt wants policymakers worldwide to hear women's voices.

Women's voices sing a variety of tunes in many different keys. For political heroines of war zones, peace is the issue. For welfare moms in inner cities, the issue could be public transportation. In Kabul, Afghanistan, and Cairo, Egypt, women's issues include garbage removal. In Africa, HIV-AIDS is a women's issue. At least, each is an issue for some women. Women do not vote as a bloc, share political beliefs, or all think alike. Any assumption that they do misses a pro-war secretary of state, an aggressive CEO, or a budding scientific genius.

Men don't think alike, either. What appear to be gender gaps will remain as long as societies make gender central to opportunities. Under those conditions, we cannot help but see gender first and individual talents or individual needs second. We will stop hearing the woman question only when there are more women in leadership and many more women's voices filling the air with productive ideas. An alternative to the career crunch for women who want to balance business with children is to start their own businesses.

## Hot Mamas: Breeding Businesses

A chorus of powerful women's voices sounded in Miami in 2006, during one of my cross-country tours to talk with a cross section of Americans about the issues that most concerned them. Even before I entered the ballroom of the Coral Gables Biltmore Hotel, I could feel the heat rising inside. The air-conditioning was on full blast. Yet pulses of warmth emanated from hundreds of high-spirited women business leaders. I was there to talk about confidence and success with members of The Commonwealth Institute (TCI), a national mentoring and networking organization that began in Boston to help entrepreneurial women grow their businesses. Enthusiastic chatter throughout the meal showed that the hunger to connect was stronger than the drive to eat. These women were passionate about their ideas and about translating them to the real world of business.

I have felt the heat at similar events nationwide. Women show up in droves to share tips, business cards, and innovative visions. Most balance families along with checkbooks. Kathy Korman Frey, who runs a Washington, D.C., consulting business while enjoying her babies, has dubbed such entrepreneurs "hot mamas." A Harvard Business School M.B.A., Frey represents many women with advanced degrees and fertile imaginations. She was sick of the media pounding on the difficulties of combining work and families. (She could chant that piece of fake Latin I mentioned earlier, *Nolite te bastardes carborundorum*—don't let the bastards grind you down.) To Frey, the path to balance is to start your own business, setting your own work hours and garb. Her business identifies and deploys female talent available for part-time projects.

According to one calculation, women entrepreneurs created more jobs in the early 2000s than the Fortune 500. They are certainly "hot." They melt myths, including the one that says women cannot juggle children and business. It is ancient history that Helen of Troy's beauty launched a thousand ships. Today, women entrepreneurs' brains launch a thousand businesses, with other women's help.

By 2004, women were majority owners of an estimated 6.7 million privately held firms in the United States with $1.2 trillion in aggregate sales and 9.8 million employees. In greater Miami, more than 76,000 women's businesses represented nearly 30 percent of all privately held firms. These hot mamas are ethnically diverse but share creative drive. Carole Ann Taylor, named one of Miami's top twenty-five black businesswomen, runs Little Havana To Go, a shop and e-tailer promoting Cuban American products. "Hot" is a good description of the delicious orange background and Latin music on her company's website. The founder and CEO of ClickPharmacy.com, Gloria Rodriguez markets products over the Web delivered by a network of local community pharmacies, leveraging her industry knowledge from years running a small pharmaceutical company. Some are "hot grandmamas," such as Ann Rosenberg, widow of Dunkin' Donuts founder Bill Rosenberg. She hatched the "Let's Make Wine" stores to enable consumers to select grapes and then bottle and label their own cases of wine.

Women entrepreneurs marry and have families, yet they form lifelong bonds with their businesses, too. Joyce Landry and Jo Kling repurchased their Meetings at Sea venture (cruises for corporate meetings and reward programs), which they started in Manhattan in 1982, brought to Miami in 1988, sold in 1998, and reacquired in 2005.

TCI founder Lois Silverman, a former nurse and a mother of two, founded CRA Managed Care to provide rehabilitation services under insurance contracts. She took her national chain public and now chairs the board of the hospital where she became a nurse. Silverman wants to help other women achieve similar success. TCI role models include Pat Moran, who runs the world's largest private Toyota distributorship, JM Family Enterprises (which is America's fifteenth-largest privately owned company, according to *Forbes*). Moran has three children, four grandchildren, and numerous grateful employees, as attested to by JM's place on *Fortune*'s list of the one hundred best companies to work for. Toni Randolph, another mother of a successful son, founded a private label manufacturer that includes Wal-Mart among its prestigious customers; she is an advocate for women of color. Other south Florida mentors include investment bankers, telecom executives, medical communication pioneers, and specialty-food magnates. They all want to open doors for other women to become business leaders. They feel that hot mamas will eventually change the corporate world, too, as they prove that a passion for business and a love for their families are compatible.

Across America, women entrepreneurs want the same things men want—access to capital, training, and markets. Big institutions, whether private firms or government agencies, can help them get access. In addition, women with businesses producing $1 million or more are twice as likely as male counterparts to seek advice from a mentor, and insist that they want to be taken seriously. That's where networks like TCI come in. They make it possible for hot mamas to meet one another and increase opportunities to cook for the kids at home and then create the sparks that keep the economy cooking. For hot mamas, family values include growing a business.

## Greedy Organizations or Enlightened Employers?

Today is "Take Your Dry Cleaning to Work Day." Or it could be, if you work for one of the companies that are trying to make life more convenient by offering prepackaged meals to take home for dinner and on-site laundries, banks, exercise rooms, pharmacies, and child care centers (on the first floor or next door). The office park is the new company town, offering everything except sleeping accommodations. (Some high-tech enclaves offer that, too, in the form of communal bunkrooms for 24/7 workers.) Workplace amenities and concierge services for the fortunate few are the new way to keep employees' personal lives going while they go all out for work.

This trend helps some people juggle their way across the family-to-work moat and back. But (a) just a small fraction of the workforce is helped, and (b) some critics think this makes it possible for employers to demand even more share of mind (and time) from employees who have now been relieved of the need to leave the workplace for anything. Are corporations that offer these almost live-in services enlightened employers or merely greedy organizations wanting to consume all of a person's time and attention? There are many professional firms (law, consulting, investment banking) that would like people captive 24/7, at the beck and call of clients; meal service is only one service they provide to ensure those impossibly long captive hours. Whether the new array of services under the banner of work-life balance supports families and personal life or just feeds greed is still an open question.

Sometimes the company is enlightened but particular managers are greedy. To some middle managers, split time means split loyalties. Though part-time or shared jobs might be options under company policy, in practice the viability of these options depends on the interaction between bosses or team leaders and team members. Managers and professionals in the middle ranks who are overworked and pressured for productivity themselves might not look favorably upon people they feel are not sufficiently available and committed—who are not only leaving work early but thinking of something else on the job. In practice, many people working what is called part-time end up spending more time focused on work than is required, but that time is unpaid and undervalued by bosses who are upset by the idea of employees giving less than their all. In practice, shared jobs have sometimes increased coordination time or have failed to become a norm because co-workers and clients don't set their expectations around knowledge of which member of the team is available when. Policies are only as good as the goodwill of the managers implementing them.

Some well-intentioned employers trying to help their employees with work-life balance have provided fixed days off, such as one Thursday per month. A high-tech company CEO complained to me that the company's policy of one day off after nine days of work (not including weekends) was interfering with productivity and was an administrative pain in the whatnot. But that company wasn't offering flexibility geared toward its employees' type of work and type of personal situation; it was simply substituting one form of rigidity for another. Similarly, another company took the popular step of offering Friday afternoons off in the summer. But while better than nothing, Friday afternoon did not always correspond to the timing of other obligations, such as orthodontist appointments. In some less-enlightened companies, rigidity sometimes forces people to take an entire day off just to make a one-hour personal appointment because it is easier to call in sick than try to get an exception to the rules.

## Portable, Virtual, Flexible: Nice Work If You Can Get It

There are some excellent models of flexibility in the business world. Deloitte & Touche, the accounting and consulting firm, has been honored by major magazines for policies promoting work-life balance, such as part-time work, flexible hours, and travel limited to no more than three nights a week away from home. At Semco in Brazil, a fast-growth company with over $160 million in sales that wants to be an international model, employees set their own work hours, bring children to their offices from time to time (there are playspaces), and come and go as they please. CEO Ricardo Semler calls this the "seven-day weekend."

IBM has broken new ground with its "dynamic workplace." Fixed offices and fixed work hours are disappearing—except as determined by the nature of the work, since there are still some jobs that require staffing a desk. Work is carried in laptops that can be plugged in at many stations at IBM facilities or used at home. Collaborative software, ubiquitous use of the Web, and cellphones connect people and permit them to self-schedule and make their own choices about how to meet goals. At IBM India, I met a thirty-something Harvard graduate and IBM star who picked one project at a time that she could complete largely from her laptop while her children were young, with the project rhythm determining when and where to meet face-to-face. At IBM Egypt, I talked with a set of women labeled "top talents" who were being groomed for significant positions, including working mothers who worked from home, virtually, several days a week. I also spoke with the first woman in IBM Egypt to bring her baby to work for breastfeeding.

Blackberries at the beach are no longer picnic items but the latest way to stay in touch, whether on the sand or at home. Even for those Americans who take their full vacation allotment, work comes along. Numerous national surveys show that a growing number of people spend time doing work and checking in with the boss while on vacation.

Technology makes it possible to work anywhere and at one's convenience. It also makes it possible to work all the time. We can ban usage of cellphones and Internet-connected computers from airplanes as a security measure, but we can't stop people from contacting the office. Nor would it be easy for one individual at a time to decide to be the only member of the team not available to the rest. Instead, we have to make sure that flexibility prevails and that people get the time they need for personal and family life when they need it, while not jeopardizing their opportunity for fulfilling and rewarding work.

## Toward a New Social Contract

Try to read this chapter during the holiday season, even if you can't afford to take a vacation. Holidays bring those joyous times of year when workplaces resemble the joke about Russian factory workers: "We pretend to work, and the bosses pretend to pay us." Alas, for those without secure employment, that's not funny.

Recall the old social contract regarding work: A person started his or her career as an enthusiastic young person who overperformed and was undercompensated; then, over the next thirty-five years, he or she rose to a position where he or she could underperform and be overcompensated—so it all evened out over the lifetime. This caricature of secure employment is just another joke.

The industrial-era bargain is going, going, gone. General Motors, once the icon for secure employment at the center of the industrial economy, slashed employee health insurance, while its suppliers sought wage cuts of as much as two-thirds.

The old industrial-era system assumed fixed employment, not mobility, with education and training primarily associated with promotion (and college tuition deductible only if improving skills in the present job). That system gave us employer-funded health insurance and pensions—benefits that were lost if the employee left. That era also produced legal definitions of full-time, part-time, and overtime that now seem quaint when work can occur anytime and anywhere linked by communications networks. And, of course, it reinforced the myth of separate worlds that limited women's opportunities to develop and use their talents.

Today, people have been cut loose. For some, this is liberation from indentured servitude; they set their own terms of work as self-employed "free agents." But most are simply adrift. For decades, some companies have tried to make people a variable cost by converting regular employees into independent contractors without benefits. The term *outsourcing* originally referred not to shifting jobs to China and India but to replacing permanent employees with temporary ones on someone else's payroll. By the 1990s, the temporary-staffing industry accounted for 10 percent of all U.S. job growth, despite accounting for only about 2 percent of total jobs. In 2000, Microsoft settled a lawsuit by "permatemps" (who claimed they were indistinguishable from regular employees) for $97 million, ending a dispute that started in 1992.

America needs a new social contract, with creative ideas that are good for people, families, and the future of a dynamic economy. This social contract would also help with the woman question by giving more choices to all my three Sarahs and to all women in the workforce. That deal could include the following:

- **Health care** Instead of demanding more from employers, including squeezing small businesses as some states propose, let's work toward universal tax-supported health care coverage. A recent Gallup poll showed that 79 percent of Americans want it, and 69 percent are willing to pay for it with higher taxes.

- **Lifelong learning** Imagine a GI Bill for veterans of industry wars that would pay for college after they suffer from corporate restructuring. Or Pell Grants (designed for young college students) extended to retirees who want education for a new career. Higher education builds skills that build the economy.

- **Savings** It's time for portable tax-advantaged savings accounts accessible at times of greatest need and matched by low-interest loans and employer contributions. People could draw funds when the family is growing, for education when changing fields, or to start a hot mama's business— and they could do so without losing tax advantages. This would supplement, not replace, Social Security.

- **Modular work** Full-time, part-time, and overtime, enshrined in wage and hour laws, are increasingly outmoded concepts that get in the way, when "full" means getting benefits while losing personal time and "part" means losing out. Work could be organized around projects and results rather than hours or days, as it already is in some organizations. The current system is dominated by on-off switches (employed or unemployed, full-time or nothing, on-ramping or off-ramping) rather than dials that permit many degrees between on and off. What if Americans could join the apocryphal Mexican fisherman that we met at the beginning of the chapter in deciding how many boatloads of fish they want to catch in any particular month? What if full-time jobs were divided into, say, five modules, and people could pick a workload for particular periods of time: from one to six? As long as the total number of modules over a defined number of years added up to four modules on the average, they could be eligible for full benefits.

- **Flex-year** Why stop with flexible work hours? Flexible work years could be made possible in many jobs. Some people want to pack more work into some times of year, less work into others. Parents of young children might want months off during their kids' summer vacation. Mature workers might want months off during the cold winter season. Home Depot is already allowing older workers to move from store locations in the North in the warmer months to store locations in the South in the colder months. Internet auctions could be used to match people with the schedules they choose, inside a company or within an industry. Continental Airlines created a website to enable flight attendants to trade schedules; sick days immediately decreased, and job satisfaction increased, making Continental an employer of choice.

- **A national sabbatical program** Taking those vacations to get healthy again would be a positive move. Going a step further, perhaps a longer stretch of time off from careers from time to time could become a desirable option for both men and women. Perhaps it would reconnect more men with their children and more women with the ability to reenter the workforce smoothly, since employers would develop mechanisms to ease the transitions. Some employers (including my publisher's parent company, Random House) now offer shorter versions of the sabbaticals familiar in universities, where faculty can be on leave, with full or partial pay, every seven years. This could go national. What if pension funds could be tapped for mini-retirements every seven years? The chance to take a breath, go to school, or spend an extended chunk of time with the children could become a universal program.

It is often said, but worth repeating: The purpose of making a living is to afford to make a life. In the land of opportunity, that's the true and enduring meaning of family values. All three Sarahs think so.

# THREE

# Growing Good Companies

## Can Values-Based Capitalism Replace Imperial Excess?

I first met fiery Eliot Spitzer in December 2003. He was New York State's zealous attorney general, directing most of that zeal toward prosecution of corporate misconduct. The occasion of our meeting was as participants in the closing panel in a human rights forum at the John F. Kennedy Library in Boston. The president of Starbucks and the vice chairman of Nike were on the panel, and I was the moderator, but Spitzer was clearly the attraction for the jam-packed room. Business leaders had come to the forum to find out what was on Spitzer's mind. Activists from nongovernmental organizations (NGOs) whose careers were dedicated to pushing, prodding, and protesting against multinational corporations were there to applaud Spitzer as one of their heroes.

In light of the increasing pressure on American companies to join the movement for responsible social and environmental practices, Kennedy Library president John Shattuck, a former U.S. State Department human rights official and ambassador to the Czech Republic, had convened the forum. The guiding question was whether large corporations could become part of the solution instead of remaining part of the problem. But in 2003, accounting scandals still dominated the news, Enron and WorldCom fallout had tainted even the best businesses, and the definition of "corporate social responsibility" seemed to be "staying out of jail." Fully 70 percent of respondents to a national survey taken at the time had indicated that they did not trust the word of brokers and corporations, and one-third said they had "hardly any confidence" in big-company executives—the highest proportion in three decades.

Before the program began, there was just time for a quick conversation with Spitzer. His piercing blue eyes took in the crowds as he joked about his popularity perhaps being higher among executives outside of his home state. It was hard to know what to expect from the panel, we agreed. The Starbucks and Nike executives were there as representatives of companies that had publicly embraced responsible conduct, especially with respect to third-world suppliers. But the activists were still gunning for them because the most visible companies with the highest aspirations were often the first targets of the NGOs.

As it turned out, the Starbucks and Nike executives had ample time to tout their various improve-the-world initiatives, from free trade coffee to changing labor practices in developing country factories, and to be applauded for them. When it was Spitzer's turn, he was polite regarding the two companies' well-motivated charitable and supply-chain initiatives, but he was firm and unwavering about the need for American companies to examine their most basic practices—from accounting to consumer marketing. No amount of good deeds or giveaways, he said, could make up for financial manipulations or business practices that were not in the best interest of investors and the public. Corporate social responsibility would be window dressing unless basic business practices improved. It was the case of the People v. Profiteers.

Eighteen months later, in June 2005, I appeared again on a program with Spitzer. This time it was a *Money* magazine summit high above New York City in the top-floor ballroom of one of Manhattan's most elegant hotels. Perhaps because of the audience and the setting or perhaps because times were changing, Spitzer balanced his expressed zeal for continuing prosecution of misdeeds with words of appreciation for a trend toward more responsible behavior. He said that he felt that the corner had been turned on corporate misconduct. It was time, he implied, to highlight *good* conduct and raise the standards even higher. He might have been thinking about IBM, Procter & Gamble, or Microsoft, which had woven community action to improve education into their corporate strategies.

I'm sure that the business leaders at the 2005 *Money* summit breathed a sigh of relief at Spitzer's balance and fairness. Their relief undoubtedly helped his career plans. In November 2006, Eliot Spitzer was elected governor of New York with a whopping 69 percent of the vote.

Many companies are indeed rising to meet expectations for good conduct, as corporate social responsibility increasingly becomes a boardroom preoccupation. But public expectations may be rising even faster, and there is not yet a national consensus about exactly what "good corporate conduct" means or what values should guide free market capitalism.

## The Corporate Conduct Continuum: From "Do No Harm" to "Do Lots of Good"

The land of opportunity depends on private enterprise to produce opportunity by innovating and creating jobs, and Americans increasingly expect that companies not only behave ethically but that they go beyond the letter of the law to help society, as Bell Atlantic (today's Verizon) did in Union City or IBM does through its dynamic workplace program.

The corporate good conduct continuum ranges from avoiding illegal, unethical, or harmful acts at the minimum to doing as much good as possible at the voluntary high end. The low standard is the domain of laws and regulation—Spitzer territory, we can call it. The other end signifies higher ideals. It is guided by publicity, reputation, and enlightened self-interest; the best companies are already well along toward being guided by values that encourage them to make a positive difference in the world.

This chapter addresses the whole range—from questionable actions that should be stemmed or sanctioned, through legitimate actions that produce by-products requiring attention, to positive actions that could make values-based capitalism the American way. In many instances, the intricacies of policy need to be worked out, but some important guiding principles—the route toward values-based capitalism—can be articulated.

Values-based capitalism is my catchall phrase for the wide swath from ethical behavior to above-and-beyond social contributions. It means being guided by standards and principles that are not reducible to economics. It implies responsibilities toward employees, customers, consumers, suppliers, communities, and the public that are shaped by social norms about appropriate, or better, treatment, even when there are no specific laws governing the relationships. Role model companies such as Procter & Gamble (P&G) and IBM have already made values, principles, and standards the core of their management controls. They are regularly taught in training programs, posted everywhere on the Web and in facilities, and used by people to guide decisions—as I saw when P&G managers in India echoed those in Cincinnati by reciting exactly which principles they used to guide the acquisition and integration of Gillette.

Excellent leaders in businesses with a tradition of meeting high standards steer their companies to contribute to society, above and beyond what is legally required—such as Procter & Gamble's A. G. Lafley or IBM's Sam Palmisano. But with prosecutors and the press focused on bad guys, segments of the public find it hard to imagine that there are any corporate good guys. Many still equate big business with bad business. On a 2005 national survey of confidence in leaders, business scored near the bottom (beating only government officials in lack of public confidence). Back-dating of stock option awards to make sure that option holders earn lots of money is just the latest in a series of unfolding corporate financial scandals. By late 2006, about 200 companies were either under investigation by federal authorities or conducting their own probes of this practice, and some executives faced criminal charges.

As certain failed corporate executives exchange pinstripes for prison stripes, gallows humor is tempting. Are CEOs becoming CETTs (Can't Ever Trust Them)? Only 18 percent of American opinion leaders surveyed about trust in institutions said that they find CEOs or CFOs the most credible source of information about companies; 58–68 percent place more trust in colleagues, family, and friends. Think about that one for a moment—your neighbor is a better source of business information than the leaders of the businesses themselves? Unless you live next door to Alan Greenspan, that statistic says a great deal about how strongly Americans feel that some corporate executives fail to disclose accurate information (i.e., fail to tell the truth).

Let's start with some of the problems that galvanize Spitzer and other prosecutors into action and make some Americans question whether corporations have consciences or values: the links between a culture of excess and excessively imperial CEOs. The issue is to define what is tolerable, what is appropriate, and what is excessive.

## America's Obesity Epidemic

Obesity is America's most important public health issue. Two-thirds of Americans are now classified as overweight or obese. So it was welcome news a few years ago when fast-food giant McDonald's eliminated supersized items to help Americans shed extra fat.

How does McDonald's former supersizing compare to other forms of obesity threatening to make us a dangerously unhealthy nation, such as supersized executive pay? McDonald's supersized fries weighed in at 610 calories, compared to 210 calories in the small package. That 3-to-1 fries ratio pales by comparison to the 282-to-1 ratio of CEO salaries to average worker pay. The CEO-to-worker wage ratio peaked at 531-to-1 in 2000, then fell back to the 1997 level of about 280-to-1 a few years later. Contrast that with the leaner 1982 U.S. ratio of 42-to-1 or the ongoing ratio in Europe and Japan of under 40-to-1. French women don't get fat, as the diet book title put it, and neither do French and other European executive paychecks. But staying thin in the wallet might not be fashionable in Europe much longer. By 2006, European CEOs were demanding bigger pay packages to prove that they're "worth" as much as Americans.

Excess is especially egregious when the pay is inversely related to performance—high pay for low service. Consider the obese $187.5 million deferred compensation package that disgraced former New York Stock Exchange CEO Richard Grasso felt entitled to get despite his failings at the helm. He was paid $139.5 million the year before his fall, and he then decided, under pressure, to forgo $48 million. Then–acting CEO John Reed demanded that Grasso return $120 million to the exchange.

Similar symptoms of America's obesity epidemic showed up in flabby morals and oversized egos of so-called leaders, such as Tyco's Dennis Kozlowski or the Enron bunch, who felt they could parade their excesses—from toga parties and $8,000 shower curtains to accounting tricks—with impunity. As in the case of the toga party, they were, literally, throwing their weight around.

Throughout the country, fat cats have been getting fatter. I am certainly in favor of more people attaining the American dream of affluence, but not when it means that the already-rich are getting even richer while the poor are getting poorer and the middle class is in decline. In 1989, the United States had 66 billionaires and 31.5 million people living below the official poverty line. A decade later, the United States had 268 billionaires and 34.5 million people living below the poverty line—about $13,000 for a three-person family. The top 1 percent of households had more wealth than the entire bottom 95 percent combined. One columnist did the arithmetic to show that the CEO of General Electric (a widely admired leader) earned almost as much in one day as the average U.S. teacher did in a year.

Supersized objects are the new status symbols of the wealthy, including light trucks and tank-like cars. These vehicles are gluttons at the energy table, sucking up high-priced gas and belching greenhouse gases. A *New Yorker* cartoon page satirized "Hummer Style" by imagining a series of enormous, overpriced, and ugly objects, such as the "Hummer vacuum cleaner," which is larger than the furniture and has no suction, or the "Hummer wallet," which has no place to hold anything and is too heavy to carry. Houses for the affluent have also swelled with supersizing. Families that are smaller than ever live in spaces that are larger than ever, as the platinum standard for luxury homes has come to include media rooms, gyms, or cavernous kitchens with six-burner restaurant stoves for people who eat out. On the resort island of Martha's Vineyard in Massachusetts, once known for fishermen's cottages and rustic woodland cabins, towns are considering whether to limit houses on relatively small lots to no more than 10,000 square feet—the equivalent of fifty rooms of ten-by-twenty feet. Some people are fighting this "restrictive zoning," which would limit their right to be ostentatious. Meanwhile, affluent suburbs nationwide have an affordable housing crisis, with the middle class squeezed out of home ownership. Teachers, police officers, and firefighters cannot afford to live in or near the towns they serve.

Then there's the obese federal debt. Many Republicans

were just as appalled as Democrats at the size to which it swelled in just four years—to $7.5 trillion, adding nearly $2 trillion of unnecessary pounds since 2000. And forget annual budget balancing. The $236.4 million annual federal budget surplus of 2000 became a budget deficit of $250 billion in October 2006, which reflected progress in weight loss, since the 2006 figure was half of the deficit two years earlier.

Will Americans slim down? For the health of the country, I hope so. And if ordinary Americans can learn to be satisfied on fewer calories and smaller servings of french fries, then the Richard Grasso types should be content as mere hundred-millionaires, CEOs should learn to enjoy a slightly smaller multiple of the pay of their lowest-paid workers, and the government should reduce federal debt by reducing supersized tax givebacks to the supersized rich. This diet still has a great deal of fat in it and ample ways to get and stay rich.

The one thing we had not seen by the time of this writing is leadership by enlightened CEOs to restore the good name of their profession. Giving back inflated bonuses calculated from discredited numbers would be a start. Why aren't the associations of corporate chieftains calling for innovative actions? *New York Times* columnist Gretchen Morgenson singled out former Pfizer CEO Hank McKinnell, who had chaired the pharmaceutical industry association, for failing to lead when he ignored a money manager's call to return to Pfizer's shareholders some of his estimated $65 million in total pay and a pension worth $83 million over a period during which shareholder assets dropped 43 percent. According to Morgenson, in April 2006, a few months before McKinnell was ousted (nineteen months ahead of his planned retirement), a watchdog group, Investors for Director Accountability, had urged shareholders to withhold their votes from four Pfizer directors overseeing compensation. McKinnell did nothing. And even excellent leaders in organizations with a tradition of meeting high standards, who also steer their organizations to contribute to society, are not speaking out about excess.

How much is enough? The answer is that we can't tell unless we have a chance to discuss it. That's a matter of values. Stamping out obesity wherever it is found—whether in our individual or our corporate bodies—should be the subject of a national conversation. The business press already issues regular reports on top executive pay and analyzes the correlation with performance, but often the matter stops there. Boards who make the compensation deals generally base their figures on "comparables" provided by compensation consultants; who these consultants are and what they are finding should also be disclosed. If CEOs can justify the wide gap between their pay and that of their lowest-paid workers to their shareholders and the public, then the more power (and money) to them. But unless national leaders put this topic on the agenda for public debate, we will never find ways to get the fat cats to slim down a bit.

## Business as the Last Monarchy: Imperial CEOs and the Problems of Empire

The pay gap is one manifestation of the rise of the imperial CEO over the past twenty-five years—the time when CEO pay started to swell far beyond that of ordinary workers. Imperial CEOs are supposedly a dying breed, as many big companies appoint "nice guy" CEOs who are more approachable and team-oriented than their predecessors. (They even answer their own e-mails.) But imperial CEOs are not disappearing fast enough.

I first encountered members of this class several decades ago, when I left school for the real world and started applying social science skills to business. The head of the largest subsidiary of a New York conglomerate had asked me to help "whip his management group into shape," which I thought meant team-building around shared goals and he thought meant public flogging (until we agreed on milder actions). "Business is the last monarchy," he frequently told his staff. He was Napoleonic in his short stature and big ego. For an important charity event at which he was being honored, I gave him a sterling silver ruler on which I had his monarchy slogan engraved. He liked the gift but missed the visual pun. (Postscript: He never did learn to be a team-builder and was ousted when a new owner bought the company.)

After the Enron implosion and other scandals, corporate chief executives seemed almost as likely to be featured in courtrooms as feted at charity dinners. That's an exaggeration, of course, but it shapes public perceptions. Both business leaders and members of the general public have attributed recent scandals to a general decline in values. But what angers people the most is seeing some executives enrich themselves while allowing their companies to decline.

Hiding bad news from stockholders and creditors while offering rosy forecasts to make managers look good is not a recent invention of Enron and Tyco in the United States or Parmalat in Italy or Royal Dutch/Shell in the Netherlands (whose chiefs overstated oil and gas reserves). In the 1960s and 1970s, "creative accounting" was found to be a factor in the bankruptcies of British companies. In 1994, at the start of

Continental Airlines' successful turnaround from financial disaster, the newly appointed chief operating officer was shocked to discover that the previous finance staff had inflated profit projections by plugging in overly optimistic revenue estimates, keeping hidden the fact that cash was overstated.

The arrogance of success is well known. Powerful people who are driven to turn their domains into empires begin to feel that they are above the rules, that what applies to ordinary people does not apply to them, and that they can use their power to suppress criticism and force their will on others, whether employees, customers, suppliers, or external watchdogs.

Consider the history of the Coca-Cola Company, holder of one of America's best-known global brands and a company whose outer successes hid questionable inner machinations. During one significant part of its history, vanity blinded Coca-Cola's leaders to vulnerabilities accompanying the unbridled exercise of corporate power. The Coke said to run in executives' veins went to their heads, and they became drunk with power.

Roberto Goizueta, who became chief executive in 1981, was much admired for moving the company close to its dream of "world domination." He took Coke to lucrative international markets and rewrote contracts to push the secret-formula syrup on increasingly captive bottlers, "launching an engine of wealth unparalleled in the American corporate world," as Constance Hays wrote in her book *The Real Thing: Truth and Power at the Coca-Cola Company*. Intense loyalty was demanded from everyone. Analysts were discouraged from publishing anything negative about the company. Goizueta worked out his bonus privately with a director, and enormous pay packages were presented to a compliant board as a fait accompli. Despite the New Coke debacle, he was "treated more like a pontiff than a chief executive," Hays wrote.

Then Goizueta died unexpectedly, and Douglas Ivester became CEO at Coca-Cola's zenith in stock price, market share, and prestige. Soon dreams of world domination became nightmares about world events. Far from controlling a submissive empire, Ivester found himself fighting wars of rebellion for which he was not prepared. He faced globalization woes (emerging market problems in Asia, devaluation of the Russian ruble); anti-American sentiment in Europe and unwelcome attention from European antitrust officials, egged on by Pepsi; and product safety issues, including the largest product recall in Coca-Cola's history after the illness of Belgian schoolchildren, which was eventually traced to contaminated shipping pallets. Ivester fumbled communication about the Belgian children with too little response, too late. Then he made another public relations gaffe when he touted technologically sophisticated vending machines that could raise prices when thirst increased. Under his watch, the company lost a race discrimination suit initiated years earlier, and Coca-Cola's highest-ranking black executive resigned as a result.

Viewed with today's post-Enron lenses, some practices associated with Coca-Cola hovered in ethical eyebrow-raising territory. The formation of a "super-bottler" in Coca-Cola Enterprises enabled the Coca-Cola Company to shift debt off its balance sheets, and though the company never owned more than 49 percent of any bottler, it exercised control through directorships. When an accountant at a small investment firm investigated these relationships, his boss stopped him out of fear of retribution. (That accountant's next target was Tyco, which later epitomized corruption under Dennis

Kozlowski.) The company also used its clout to get exclusive deals with retailers, a practice that sometimes crossed a legal line, as it was found guilty in a Texas antitrust suit brought by Royal Crown distributors. Coca-Cola bottlers were pushed to seek volume regardless of market demand or their own profitability because the company made most of its money from selling Coke syrup to the bottlers. Bottlers who had consolidated under Coca-Cola's influence felt the company had pushed them too far and started pushing back, whispering discontent to Ivester's detractors.

Boardroom maneuvering culminated in Ivester's removal after just over two years as CEO. Douglas Daft became chief executive in 2000, just as business conditions worsened. Hays described layoffs that were poorly handled, strategic floundering, a failed deal to buy Quaker Oats to get Gatorade, and the use of a feng-shui expert to bring better luck to headquarters. The one thing that Hays did not report executives doing was questioning their own practices with a dose of humility. Coke still made them drunk with power.

## Getting Drunk with Power Occurs Behind Closed Doors

Where was the impetus to change the organization from a closed empire to a more open, collaborative marketplace of ideas? Those who let power go to their heads are likely to hide their habit behind closed doors. If no one sees what they are doing, then perhaps they can get away with it.

Mistakes and problems are inevitable in complex enterprises. We shouldn't expect companies to be perfect, but we should expect them to catch and correct their mistakes quickly. Lapses from efficient, rational, law-abiding, virtuous, or otherwise functional behavior are a constant danger in organizations. Sometimes this occurs because of flawed people, but more often because of complex changes and ambiguous situations that require juggling competing demands (pay raises for employees or price cuts for customers?). When lapses or fumbles occur, denial is tempting, especially when people are pressured to promise strong results regardless of circumstances, and that's when those doors close and the power drinking occurs.

Fear of failure can lead to distorted numbers and ineffective actions. One example is "trade loading," also called "channel stuffing," a practice similar to Coca-Cola Company's demand that bottlers buy syrup whether they needed it or not. Producers of cosmetics, razors, or industrial diamonds would inflate sales at the end of a quarter by doing what it took to load up the trade—retailers or industrial customers—with excess inventory; lacking Coca-Cola's clout, they would discount heavily or add financial incentives, thereby undermining profitability. This made the problem worse in the next quarter; customers were fat with unwanted inventory, and anyway, they knew they could wait until that quarter's end for an even better deal.

In every sector, such cover-ups and downward spirals have become depressingly familiar. Mistakes and failures are covered up rather than confronted, information is distorted or restricted, communication becomes defensive, contact among organization members is minimized, and initiative shuts down, stifling dissent and problem-solving until it is too late. A small mistake for which a simple apology might suffice then mushrooms into a huge crisis.

Imperial CEOs flourish in a closed system lacking self-scrutiny, accountability, dialogue, and dissent. When those chiefs themselves do not break rules, they still create circumstances in which the people below them feel so desperate to please the domineering bosses that they cut corners, hide information, and make deals with the devil. The ultimate failure of leadership is that those at the top have stifled the initiative and innovation of those below. People begin to feel helpless to do anything to solve problems or influence change.

Transforming these sick systems involves more than improving governance at the board level; it involves changing the culture of the entire organization. That's Job 1 for leaders.

## Restoring Trust: A Promise Made Is a Promise Kept

Good leaders and good companies go hand in hand. Values-based leadership in an empowering system is not just a way to regain public trust; it is a better way to run a company.

Take the case of Gillette, where a new CEO shifted an escalating downward cycle of cover-up and passivity to a more productive culture of dialogue and innovation. Gillette had slipped from being on a winning streak to being in a decline cycle in 1996–1997. Earnings were flat and sales and market shares were declining in categories other than blades and razors. There were many reasons: the troubled acquisition of Duracell, uneven performance of product categories outside of shaving systems, unrealistic sales targets that led to costly end-of-quarter discounts, sloppy internal practices, and a confusing organization structure that made it easy to duck responsibility. Some of the company's historical strengths had become weaknesses, and the foundation for high performance had crumbled.

Jim Kilts was appointed chairman and CEO of Gillette early in 2001, the first CEO from outside the venerable consumer products company in over seventy years. On Kilts's first day as CEO, he convened his direct reports and made his expectations clear. Kilts described himself as open and straightforward—what you see is what you get. He said he was action-oriented, fair, but somewhat impatient. He wanted outstanding performance. He wanted integrity. He did not want competition among functions. Some of his words on that first day became slogans for the new Gillette culture:

- *Expect excellence; reward the same.*

- *Often wrong; never uncertain.*

- *Contribute before decisions made; support decisions once made.*

- *Don't make dumb mistakes, don't punish smart mistakes, don't make smart mistakes twice.*

- *Never overpromise, always overdeliver.*

- *A promise made is a promise kept.*

"If something bothers you, I want open dialogue," he told me that he said. "And I hate anyone saying 'Jim said' or 'Jim wants' as the reason for doing or not doing something. Things are done—or not—based on rigorous assessments and considered deliberation." How refreshing! How simple! Look at the facts, tell the truth, and run a company with integrity.

Kilts expressed his determination to set and achieve realistic targets. He outlined a disciplined process for setting annual and quarterly objectives and providing structured feedback through weekly operating committee meetings, quarterly two-day meetings away from the office, and weekly e-mail postings from the next layers of management around the world. Meetings, he said, would feature fact-based management, open communication, simplicity, and collaboration. Attendance was required, meetings would start on time, there would be no gossip, he wanted full attention and active listening, he strived for consensus, and he expected preparation.

Kilts's emphasis on honesty and integrity was manifested in his early actions. As CEO, Kilts was not afraid to say, "We were wrong." He reiterated the board's earlier decision to stop issuing earnings advisories before the end of a quarter (Gillette was one of the first U.S. companies to do so). And he told investment analysts that Gillette would lower its quarterly targets to make them more realistic. That was the shot heard round the world. Everyone in the company talked about it as a symbol of a new day dawning. I was told about Kilts's action in London, Singapore, Boston, and Shanghai.

Seeing Kilts stand up to Wall Street pressures was the moment that Gillette managers and employees believed a turnaround was possible. "I began to believe that Kilts had the courage to make the needed changes when he told us to forget Wall Street, we were going to deal with the trade loading," marketing executive David Bashaw recalled from his office at European headquarters. Over the next nine months, the company gradually eliminated trade loading, freeing resources to invest in improving the businesses. This also meant that Gillette's sales numbers were honest and accurate.

As financial and strategic problems too easily denied in earlier eras were confronted and solved, Kilts's emphasis shifted to what he called Total Innovation—empowering people to seek and implement imaginative new ideas for products or processes using the kaleidoscopic thinking I described in Chapter 1. In March 2004, I joined him at Gillette's first Innovation Fair to judge the winning exhibits from the twenty-five entries submitted by every department and business unit in North America. His behavior was strong and decisive, but decidedly not imperial—he was "often wrong, never uncertain," he repeated frequently, and he expected pushback from others. It was not accidental that Kilts was widely rumored to be the Coca-Cola board's first choice for a new CEO that could turn around the ailing company. He let it be known that he wasn't interested and that he would complete the job at Gillette.

## Leadership Can't Be Legislated

The essential task of leaders is to reinforce the foundations for confidence—to demonstrate that they will be accountable to and work with stakeholders more collaboratively and empower people inside the organization to speak up, speak the truth, and take initiative. For example, they can do the following:

- Model straight talk, based on facts and data

- Make information abundant and accessible

- Structure collaborative conversations with employees, customers, suppliers, investors, and the public

- Identify shared goals and joint definitions of success

- Open channels for new ideas and for communication

These behaviors and practices make it more likely that mistakes will be confronted and corrected, that people will speak up about ethical lapses, that cover-ups will soon be exposed, and that people in top positions will not be able to bend the organization to their will or use it for their own private purposes.

There is no way to legislate competent leadership—although I once suggested, tongue-in-cheek, as a member of a state commission reviewing antitakeover laws, that bad management could be made a felony. Of course, some aspects of poor management slide into the criminal because of laws against embezzlement or sexual harassment, to name just two. Union contracts, where they still exist, further constrain managerial behavior. But, for the most part, the market is supposed to reward good leadership and punish bad leadership, aided by the visible hands of boards of directors, who hire and fire CEOs and supposedly listen to market signals as well as obey laws. Those hands can be heavily influenced by two other public tools: disclosure and debate. Transparency—making information public—and airing issues in public forums are powerful forces for good conduct.

In fact, public discussion is exactly what ensued when Jim Kilts made his next moves after the turnaround period. Early in 2005, the Gillette board voted to sell Gillette to Procter & Gamble in a $57 billion transaction. Two complaints immediately surfaced in the press. The first, echoing the American obesity epidemic, was about the $153 million Kilts would receive upon change of control. This was definitely not a matter of Richard Grasso–style pay-without-performance. Supporters, including the legendary investor Warren Buffett, weighed in with praise for Kilts's un-imperial accomplishments. Under

Kilts's leadership, nearly $20 billion in shareholder value was added, and the stock price more than doubled; about three-quarters of Kilts's payout came from the rise in share price. *Chief Executive* magazine wondered in March 2005 if this was "the last great deal" for a public company CEO. Because of the media outcry and an investigation undertaken by Massachusetts Secretary of State William Galvin, boards of directors are likely to hesitate before offering CEOs luxurious life rafts for jumping ship by selling their companies.

The second complaint about the sale of Gillette to P&G involved the merger itself. What about the potential harm from the layoff of 6,000 employees from the combined entities? Legitimate business practices by ethical companies can still raise issues for the public. Corporate interests can clash with community interests.

## Elephants and the Grass Roots: Coping with Corporate Moves

"When elephants dance, the grass gets trampled." That African proverb could be an American business saying, too. After a pause in the early part of the decade, corporate giants began prowling again, hungry for acquisitions. Should the folks down at the grass roots worry about being crushed? Whether they should or shouldn't, they do. On a 2000 *BusinessWeek*/Harris poll, over 80 percent of Americans agreed that "business has gained too much power over too many aspects of American life."

The biggest retailers have been getting bigger. Federated (owner of icons such as Macy's and Bloomingdale's) bought May Department Stores (Lord & Taylor, Filene's, and others).

Drugstore chain CVS expanded its already-large chain by buying Eckerd. "As retailers swallow, manufacturers follow" is my newly coined business proverb. The prospect of giant chains getting even bigger provokes suppliers to follow their lead in seeking to get bigger to avoid losing power. Gillette executives cited the need for clout with gargantuan Wal-Mart and the need for wider distribution in emerging markets in China and India as reasons for the sale to Procter & Gamble. The combined company would be big enough to get better deals and have longer reach.

Size seems to be the law of the jungle, despite evidence that many mergers destroy value rather than create it (AOL–Time Warner, anyone?). Banks continue to consolidate; Citizens Bank CEO Larry Fish predicted that six big banks will soon dominate the U.S. market. Media conglomerates own local broadcasters and newspapers. The telecommunications industry is shaking down to just a few giants, with SBC's acquisition of AT&T and Verizon's of MCI. This merger surge derives from more than a herd mentality or an ambition to be king of the jungle. It reflects a long-term economic power shift from production to distribution. Companies with large distribution networks dictate terms to their suppliers and control the flow of goods and services to consumers.

Long-term economic logic might favor this process, but in the short term, much local grass gets trampled.

Let's start with consumers, whose purchases fill company coffers. Consumers hate mergers, *BusinessWeek* asserted in 2004. That's not surprising. In service industries, a change in company ownership potentially inconveniences each individual user of a bank account, e-mail domain, cellphone line, long distance plan, or discount card—not to mention losing neighborhood facilities. While waiting for services to improve, consumers bear the costs of confusion—and upgrades they might not want. Another grass-roots worry is rising prices if competition decreases. At a House Energy and Commerce Committee hearing at the height of telecom industry consolidation, U.S. Representative Edward Markey (D-MA) asked six telecom CEOs involved in three potential mega-mergers to guarantee not to raise postacquisition prices. No promises.

The workforce is often not happy, either. Falling U.S. job satisfaction involves widespread discontent across ages and incomes, to which merger angst contributes. Half of all Americans said on a survey that they were satisfied with their jobs, down from nearly 60 percent in 1995; only 14 percent felt very satisfied. In a related study, 40 percent felt disconnected from their employers, with 25 percent confessing that they were just "showing up to collect a paycheck." Mergers add uncertainty and anxiety that depress satisfaction. Some employees who lose their jobs in mergers pray for work and others decide to worship something bigger than business. After merger-related layoffs in a suburban high-tech corridor in Massachusetts, church attendance increased.

Community leaders deplore acquisitions that remove a local headquarters. In fact, they are wary of any corporate move in the era of global markets, in which companies become footloose and local fancy free, dispersing functions at will around the nation and the world. Being home to a large corporation brought benefits well into the 1990s because of what I term a "headquarters effect." Because of CEOs with public visibility, local loyalties, and decision-making clout, headquarters companies contributed disproportionate charitable contributions and civic leadership to their home-office cities. A division owned by a giant elsewhere does not have the same check-writing ability. Even individual employees contributed more per capita to United Way when working for companies with a headquarters in their city.

Today, the loss of headquarters is perhaps a bigger blow to the collective community ego than to the economy. Over the past ten years, corporate community service has become an ingrained expectation wherever a company has a critical mass of employees. Civic leadership is now part of the job description for local executives of global companies. Increasingly, companies disburse contributions to areas where they have employees and customers, not just where their top executives live. A Procter & Gamble veteran who moved to Boston to head Gillette's existing razors and blades business made a point of immediate lunches with local leaders to learn about their priorities and to pledge company support for local causes.

I am not a critic of all mergers, and I am a fan of some. I just deplore the way many are managed, especially when attention focuses on making the deal rather than on what happens afterward. Yet, some mergers do bring instant improvements. CVS enhanced pharmacies at former Eckerd stores and improved store layouts and inventory. Shinhan Financial Group in South Korea raised wages for workers in an acquired bank.

Opposition to mergers by local politicians is often misguided and futile. The Massachusetts official's probe of Gillette after the P&G sale announcement went nowhere; there were no legal trip-wires to be found. But although concerned citizens can't stop the elephant from mating or slow its movement out of the community, the people do not have to let grass grow under their feet, either.

Elephants are big enough to be visible targets for public outcries. In the digital age, the elephants pay attention to noises from the grass, especially as the noise is amplified by the Internet and echoed in federal legislation. Consider this example from Big Pharma, the giants in the pharmaceutical industry. Public outcry over direct-to-consumer (DTC) advertising of prescription drugs (costing about $4 billion that could be spent in more health-enhancing ways) led some companies to act in advance of legislation before Congress. The Pharmaceutical Research and Manufacturers of America created a voluntary advertising code, and Pfizer took a stronger stance, promising a host of changes, some of them defensive—the federal Food and Drug Administration (FDA) had halted Pfizer's "Wild Things" ads for Viagra. Pfizer promised to refrain from advertising new prescription drugs for at least six months (spending that time informing doctors) and to include in its DTC ads information about alternative treatments (such as diet or exercise) and more-detailed explanations of drug risks. Pfizer also agreed to submit its television ads to the FDA for review before airing and to match money spent on advertising specific drugs (well over half a billion dollars) on consumer health education. And Pfizer stopped advertising Celebrex after heart risks were linked to its class of painkillers.

To ensure that the giants don't trample the grass when they move in or out of a community as a result of mergers, acquisitions, or divestitures, people in local communities can take actions to make their views known and to strengthen their own ability to thrive with or without the footloose, ever-changing corporations. Consider these examples:

- Consumers can make noise at the first announcements and vote with their wallets if they feel that the merger will equate to higher prices.

- Workers can keep skills fresh and an eye on starting their own businesses to ensure that they are employable and perhaps even self-sufficient. Sometimes it's better to become a partner to a giant than an employee of one.

- Voters can insist on better programs to help with transitions and attract new jobs. Every community, whether Union City or Kansas City, should have a coherent plan for building on strengths, eliminating weaknesses, and investing in education and other ways to secure the future.

- Local nonprofits can develop innovations valuable outside their community that can attract nonlocal corporations to support them.

Above all, communities can encourage leadership from those more deeply planted than big companies: entrepreneurs (including the hot mamas I introduced in Chapter 2) and professional sectors such as education and health. A rich mix of talent, a solid business infrastructure, and a vibrant community can make any place a more attractive place for corporate giants to set down roots and fertilize the local grass.

We know what kinds of beasts the elephants are. That makes it even more important for the public—concerned citizens and civic leaders—to cultivate trample-proof grass.

A culture of corporate social responsibility can keep CEOs out of jail or mollify an angry public, but avoiding ethical lapses or refraining from offending public sensibilities is becoming only a minimum standard. Financial investors are joining customers, consumers, and the general public in holding companies to ever-higher standards. Fortunately, some companies are ahead of the curve.

## A Few Good Companies? Rising to Rising Expectations

Americans need many more examples of how business can make a positive difference—and even more businesses doing it. One source of role models is the Ron Brown Award for Corporate Leadership, given by the White House after a review of scope, impact, and sustainability. (I was a judge for the first seven years.) Here are some of the winners:

• IBM, one of the largest corporate elephants, was a two-time winner, first for workplace diversity and later for its Reinventing Education initiative, started in 1994 and reaching about a third of the United States and a dozen other countries, including Brazil, China, India, and Vietnam. Reinventing Education, described in Chapter 1, involves partnerships with public school systems to use technology to help solve such pressing problems as parent involvement in North Carolina, teacher support in West Virginia, or massive information needs in Broward County, Florida. IBM is also a perennial number one, or close, on *Business Ethics* magazine's list of the best companies in terms of ethics and integrity.

• Cisco Systems won for its Networking Academies, which teach information technology–related skills that prepare students in economically disadvantaged areas for jobs or higher education in engineering and computer science. About 10,000 Academies in 150 countries involve more than 400,000 students, who are taught in nine languages.

- BankBoston, now part of Bank of America, brought banking services back to inner cities, financing opportunities for poor people and new immigrants while educating them about money. Its network of community banks helps revitalize distressed neighborhoods, providing employment and hope along with reasonably priced loans.

- Timberland mobilizes employees, suppliers, and retailers for community projects in twenty-five countries, including global events on Earth Day. Saying that its shoes and boots help people "hike the path to service," the company gives employees forty hours a year of paid company time for projects of their choice and "service sabbaticals" for temporary assignments with nonprofit organizations.

Skeptics claim that such activities are self-interested. Of course they are. And they should be. Enlightened self-interest makes efforts sustainable because employees, customers, and shareholders reward good conduct with their loyalty. Over 90 percent of 25,000 citizens of 23 countries reported on a global Millennium Survey that they want companies to focus on more than profitability. In another survey, two-thirds of American consumers said they feel more trust in products aligned with social values.

Numerous investors also support social responsibility. Over the decade between 1995 and 2005, socially screened assets under management increased slightly faster than the broader universe of managed assets. Total social investment rose more than 258 percent, going from $639 billion in 1995 to $2.29 trillion in 2005. The universe of professionally managed portfolios during this same period increased less than 249 percent, from $7 trillion to $24.4 trillion. (During the 2001–2003 recession, social investment funds grew 6.5 percent, while professionally managed portfolios as a group declined by 4 percent.) Criteria for social investments included screens for alcohol, tobacco, gambling, defense/weapons, animal testing, environment, human rights, labor relations, employment equality, community investment, and/or community relations. Internationally, the Japanese Federation of Economic Organizations (Keidandren) features a Charter for Good Corporate Behavior. The Association of British Insurers, whose members control a quarter of Britain's stock market, asks companies to report on social, environmental, and ethical factors that might pose significant risks to short- and long-term value. The *Financial Times* called this a significant shift for investors who had traditionally seen social responsibility as an extraneous distraction. In South Africa, the Johannesburg Stock Exchange has called for "triple bottom line" reporting—financial, social, and environmental performance.

The standard for corporate conduct can be raised from "do no harm" to "do lots of good." Organizations associated with values increasingly gain goodwill benefits that contribute to financial performance, from brand enhancement to employee recruitment and retention. That's why Michael Ward marked his appointment as CEO of railroad giant CSX with a community-based strategy to improve the wrong side of the tracks. That's why "cause-related marketing" is a growing phenomenon, as companies parade their philanthropy and compete to ally with the best nonprofit organizations. But please note that some of the worst corporate crimes have been committed by companies with good track records of philanthropy. Neither corporate contributions nor individual donations should give executives a "Get Out of Jail Free" card—Eliot Spitzer's point on the panel at the Kennedy Library.

As parents know, you can't change behavior through punishment alone; you must also praise good deeds. The American public should want the good company models to spread—here and around the world. Awards and recognition can honor the exemplars, but such praise must be accompanied by disclosure to shame and shun the offenders.

A good starting point for positive action is provided by the companies that handle our money. Increasingly, it's not just the bills in our wallets that are green but the practices of the banks themselves—prodded by environmental activists and their nonprofit advocacy organizations.

## Mother Nature's Newest Helpers—the Banks

Protecting the environment can be fun. It's also good business. Mother nature—speaking through your friendly neighborhood banker—insists on it.

The fun part revolves around America's annual Earth Day, held in April for nearly forty years, but only recently a major community and corporate happening. By 2005, Earth Day had grown to become Earth Month. Activities that year began April 1 with the opening of Atlanta's "You Can't Fool Mother Nature" Art Show and ended May 1 with St. Louis's Earth Day Festival ("multicultural music and performers, local nonprofit organizations, educational displays, hands-on activities, art, green exhibitors, a peace garden, food and a whole lot of FUN!" proclaimed its website).

Fun is fun, but the biggest news of Earth Season is not the millions of people partying in parks. It is the millions of dollars that banks are dedicating to going green.

In 2003, ABN AMRO and Citigroup were among the first ten banks to sign the Equator Principles (EP), a set of voluntary environmental guidelines promoted worldwide by the World Bank's International Finance Corporation. Banks adopting the principles undertake to finance only those projects whose environmental and social risk comply with the criteria, restricting financing for projects with a negative impact on the environment, such as greenhouse-gas emissions or a reduction of biodiversity. In July 2006, forty large international banks signed a second, more stringent set of principles, EP II, which added labor practices and other social issues to the environmental screens and called for consultations with local populations.

"Just a few years ago, you would have been hard-pressed to find a banker and an environmental activist in the same room—much less agreeing on issues vital to the security and sustainability of our globe. Today you will find both," Citigroup CEO Charles O. Prince wrote after the release of EP II, describing his meetings with environmental activists Rainforest Action Network and Friends of the Earth.

The new spirit of partnership does not end disagreement, but it opens a channel for continuing pressure. The two environmental organizations talking with Prince were among the authors of "Principles, Profits, or Just PR?," a 2004 report by BankTrack, a consortium tracking the social and environmental impacts of the private financial sector. The report cited specific projects financed since the launch of the Equator Principles that contravened multiple EP standards, such as the $3.6 billion Baku-Tbilisi-Ceyhan (BTC) oil pipeline from the Caspian Sea in Azerbaijan to the Mediterranean in Turkey. In November 2003, cracks were discovered in the coating of sections of pipe yet to be laid—after an estimated 15,000 joints had already been buried in Azerbaijan and Georgia. Still, the criticism was accompanied by praise for the two U.S. signatories, Citigroup and Bank of America, for making environmental commitments that exceeded EP guidelines.

Green chic is the latest fashion. Numerous companies know that reducing waste, recycling materials, and avoiding pollution make economic sense. When Home Depot encouraged two of Chile's biggest loggers to stop buying land that is being deforested, the company pleased environmentally conscious consumers today and ensured a wood supply tomorrow. General Electric added "ecomagination" to its core business strategy in the 2000s, seeking innovations in terms of energy and the environment that would become profitable lines of business.

Banks add special clout to the socio-environmental agenda because the financial sector reaches across industries and has something everyone else wants: the money. By offering or withholding capital, banks rival governments in their power to shape business behavior. Cynics wondering if this is just window dressing should consider the case of ABN AMRO, a force behind the formation of the Equator Principles and a winner of international awards for its sustainability initiatives. Its subsidiary in Brazil offers one example of how the global bank has profited by becoming an environmental conscience.

Since 2001, ABN AMRO Real (formed when the Dutch bank bought Brazil's Banco Real) has built its business around socio-environmental responsibility, a position it took after more than a year of internal dialogue and conversations with NGOs. This necessitated tough decisions and trade-offs. Executives walked away from customers in military hardware or asbestos production and terminated some previous customers, including a lumber company working illegally in the Amazon.

They influenced change in the practices of customers and suppliers. Bankers helped a fish-harvesting operation in Brazil's coastal swamps minimize pollution and encouraged a motorcycle courier company to reduce emissions and adopt new practices to reduce accidents. New financial products focused on environmental improvements, such as commercial financing to treat effluents, control atmospheric emissions, or make environmentally oriented facility upgrades. Consumer loans were created to help people purchase solar-powered water heaters or convert cars from gasoline to natural gas.

Screening business customers on their environmental behavior strengthened the loan portfolio. "A company that treats its employees well and maintains a healthy relationship with the environment has a higher probability of being economically sustainable," a bank leader observed. The connection is not surprising. At ABN AMRO's global headquarters, corporate social responsibility originated in the "risk management" department.

Internally, ABN AMRO Real worked with Friends of the Earth and Ethos Institute to analyze and remedy its own environmental shortfalls, such as outdoor displays in environmental-protection areas or water for offices from an illegal artesian pond. Noticing a filthy, abandoned alley that sheltered thugs and drug dealers near its headquarters, bank leaders decided not to wait for police or city officials to act. Instead, the bank took responsibility for making the street safe and pleasant by creating a garden, replacing pavement and lighting and adding chairs and tables. "If each of us makes changes to the alley next door, we can change the world," an executive declared.

The payoff was a fast rise in the bank's financial performance, market position, and approval ratings. In 2004, ABN AMRO Real reached number fifteen on *Carta Capital* magazine's list of Brazil's most-admired companies, up from number 153 in 2003. On an internal survey, 93 percent of employees said that they were proud of working for the bank. On national surveys, the once-obscure bank rose to second in the percentage of customers of other banks who would consider switching to ABN AMRO. Many did. The director of one of south Brazil's largest advertising agencies, who was also president of two nonprofit groups, transferred the accounts of all three organizations to the bank after learning about its commitment to the environment.

Can the financial sector save the Earth? Can the private sector accomplish what politicians find difficult? Citigroup, Bank of America, and other prominent U.S. banks such as J.P. Morgan Chase are making commitments to environmental protection comparable to ones that the new Bush administration rejected in 2001, when the United States refused to sign the Kyoto Protocol, an accord to deal with global warming. This raises another question: Are financial and reputational incentives more powerful than regulations?

Ask Al Gore. The former U.S. vice president, an environmental enthusiast and now a movie star (thanks to his documentary *An Inconvenient Truth*), joined an ex–Goldman Sachs executive to start London-based Generation Investment Management, which invests in environmentally responsible companies. Kermit the Frog isn't the only one having fun being green.

## Making Values-Based Capitalism the American Way

Pushed by federal Sarbannes-Oxley regulations and nudged by negative publicity, corporate boards of directors are finally doing the right thing. More disclosure, firmer audits, and independent directors are required by law. Boards are also issuing tighter codes of conduct and holding CEOs accountable for performance, including firing them for lapses in ethics or judgment.

During one week of business infamy in March 2005, Maurice (Hank) Greenberg was ousted from AIG, the company he founded, by his board, and former WorldCom head Bernard Ebbers was convicted of an $11 billion accounting fraud. Fox News anchor Neal Cavuto asked me on national television whether boards are now too quick to terminate CEOs who crossed ethical lines but had done nothing illegal, such as Harry Stonecipher, whose romantic e-mails led to his ouster at Boeing (mentioned in Chapter 2). I replied that the CEO job is not a reward for staying out of trouble; directors, shareholders, and the public need confidence in a leader's judgment going forward. And those who get the biggest financial rewards should be held to the highest standards.

It is difficult and contentious to strike an appropriate balance between overly stringent regulation and overly zealous prosecution. We must proceed cautiously in loosening controls so that markets rather than politicians guide corporate conduct. We must debate what can and should be demanded of American companies—what is appropriate, and what violates our sensibilities and standards.

What those standards are derives from a public consensus about values and principles. Economic logic plays a role, of course, but quality of life is not reducible purely to equations, as the *Economist* said when it found the cost-benefit analyses of various actions to reduce global warming too equivocal to guide policy. The concept of sustainability has become a convenient way to talk about business actions today that do not destroy the basis for doing business in the future.

It takes leaders of good character—who exhibit humility rather than imperial arrogance—to guide good companies. But relying on individual attributes alone is insufficient. Good leadership is made possible not just because people have the right values, but because institutions have the right checks and balances, including abundant opportunities for dialogue and dissent. We can do the following:

- **Continue to demand transparency** Disclosure and discussion are among the best ways to steer business behavior toward high standards—and high standards include high performance. Hiding bad news undermines business success and hurts the economy. Good companies can provide plausible answers to the tough questions the press and the public ask. Give airtime to the NGOs that investigate; give equal time to companies to respond.

- **Keep score** Triple bottom-line reporting (financial, social, and environmental performance) is common in Europe, but at its infancy in the United States. Companies such as General Electric and IBM are issuing "corporate citizenship" reports and seeking standards for evaluating their performance against citizenship goals. Consumers can ask about every aspect of performance; investors can demand it. People should applaud the good companies, and vote with their wallets.

- **Use bully pulpits to push the highest standards** The United Kingdom has a minister for corporate social responsibility; in the United States, we prefer convening committees and councils with a private-sector chair, such as President Bush's corporate responsibility committee. In either case, public officials can make noise and broadcast a big message about what is expected. The stick of regulation can be waved in front of companies even when not being used to strike. The carrot of praise and publicity for voluntary compliance and above-and-beyond contributions can be held out frequently, and not just at annual award dinners. Political leaders can use their convening power to bring companies to the table to sign on to sets of principles in relevant areas, akin to the Equator Principles, which puts their commitments on record. And business schools represent another set of pulpits for educating future business leaders and rising executives about values.

- **Encourage local action** When the Chicago city council passed its own minimum-wage law for large retailers such as Wal-Mart, above the national minimum wage, the mayor (appropriately) vetoed it; but the action brought attention to public concerns about the discounter's employment practices. Communities can set standards and work with businesses to meet them. If communities are sufficiently strong in the assets world-class companies seek, such as human talent, communities can make their other values clear. BankBoston's inner-city banking initiatives were triggered by a Massachusetts report on racism and the failures of banks to provide services in poor neighborhoods; that one bank's response established financial services for neglected areas, which became a profitable business for the bank. And sometimes communities can act on issues without waiting for the government. California and Maryland did this with stem cell initiatives. Or consider that a coalition of U.S. cities committed to implement the Kyoto Protocol for environmental standards that the Bush administration refused to sign.

- **Expect politicians to raise standards to what the public wants** Politicians should not be creating standards to save money for an industry (a perennial consideration invoked around minimum wage, health benefits, or energy consumption). Higher standards can stimulate innovation because creative companies identify efficient new ways to meet them. And innovation, as we have seen, is the best way to secure the future.

# FOUR

# Restoring Respect for Government

## From Contempt to Competence

The horrifying pictures of mass destruction Americans saw in September 2005 came from the "Gulf War" that took place in New Orleans: looting and shooting in sewage-filled streets while dead bodies floated by and airports doubled as morgues. Behind this American nightmare was a failure of leadership, management, and ideology. Hurricane Katrina was the ultimate tragedy stemming from contempt for government.

An appearance of callous indifference is unbecoming in any leader, but even more so in an American president. When Hurricane Katrina struck, President Bush at first barely interrupted his vacation, and he later cracked jokes about partying in New Orleans. But the real leadership failure started well before Katrina: a lack of foresight to plan for the future—not to mention a failure to read and act on environmental reports and a failure to ensure help for disadvantaged fellow citizens.

Management failures abounded before, during, and after

the storm. "New Orleans is paying a deadly price for decades of mismanagement of the Mississippi River," the National Audubon Society president said. Despite well-known weaknesses in flood protection, Congress slashed $70 million from the Army Corps of Engineers' budget for the New Orleans district. Scientific reports were ignored, just as the Bush administration had earlier denied evidence about global warming and its consequences for storm frequency and severity. State and local government deserved their share of blame for ineffective actions.

After Katrina hit, chaos ensued. The Federal Emergency Management Agency (FEMA) was accused of an ineffective and even counterproductive response. FEMA's then-head Michael Brown was pilloried. He was an inexperienced manager who was sacked from his job running horse shows and who obtained the FEMA post through cronyism. FEMA was once an effective agency with pride in its mission and professionalism in its performance, but it withered under a crony manager and ultimately failed the public.

Katrina was a humbling as well as horrifying experience. Who could maintain that air of supposed American superiority and invulnerability afterward, when third-world countries (such as Sri Lanka) sent aid and lectured us on disaster response? Ideology-over-facts and competence-doesn't-matter also took a hit, as the results of neglecting scientific facts and engineering expertise were abundantly clear.

Trickledown economics theory was another Katrina casualty. The storm's human toll revealed large pockets of vulnerable minority Americans; trickledown started to mean the drip of flood waters, not a sound economic model. Ironically, the Census Bureau report on poverty was issued just as Katrina struck, disproportionately victimizing the poor. Over 23 percent of New Orleans residents lived in poverty, and nearly 86 percent of them were black. Nationally, we have endured the longest stretch of income stagnation on record. Income inequality was near an all-time high in 2004, with 50.1 percent of income going to the top 20 percent of households and 37 million Americans living under the poverty line. No wonder an estimated 100,000 people had no way out of New Orleans. Yet ideologues on the right in Congress argued for more tax cuts for the wealthy, opposed raising the minimum wage, and sought cuts in Medicaid, food stamps, and federal student loans during the same year that Katrina struck.

Compassionate individuals and organizations rallied. IBM made an immediate $1 million first-stage commitment, installing learning centers for displaced children in the Houston Astrodome and giving to FEMA the software and hardware to track fatalities and reunite families. AmeriCorps programs such as City Year (an urban Peace Corps) mobilized members for Gulf region projects and established a Louisiana site. But volunteerism is not enough; Habitat for Humanity cannot build a whole city's worth of housing. Only the federal government has the scale and resources to coordinate state and local efforts and invest in infrastructure, prevention, and preparedness.

Rebuilding New Orleans will require many years, decabillions of dollars, and a national conversation about priorities, there and elsewhere. The other rebuilding task might be even more difficult but is essential for America's effectiveness in the future: restoring respect for government, so that the best and brightest can ensure that whatever functions government performs meet the highest possible standards.

## The Vicious Cycle: Contempt Erodes Competence, Lack of Competence Encourages Contempt

The business of America depends on good government. Yet many people do not believe we have it or can get it. And a very large number don't want to pay for it, anyway. Performance failures have dominated the news, from ever-more-costly wars to disastrous disaster responses. Mistakes of this magnitude divert resources and attention away from investments that create opportunity in the future.

Contempt for government undermines its ability to protect all citizens. Good government should be based on facts. It should invest in maintenance of basic services, whether infrastructure repairs or public health, and be prepared for crises. Above all, it should attract the best and most professional people to public service. Unless we believe that public service is an honorable calling, we will never motivate talented people to join or achieve high performance. But none of that is possible unless those in positions of public trust carry out their jobs honorably, with respect for the institutions and the public they serve.

Confidence in public-sector leaders is low. Honorable public servants go unsung by "gotcha" journalism; abundant dishonorable actions saturate the media. A 2006 survey of the public's confidence in leaders in various sectors put federal officials near the bottom (just above the media, which held last place); state and local leaders generated only slightly more confidence. Lack of confidence in American government shows up in international comparisons. The United States was placed behind nineteen other countries on Transparency International's Global Corruption Index, which ranked 133 nations from the least to the most corrupt, based on surveys of business leaders, academics, and risk analysts.

Making the situation potentially worse is a shortage of talent to turn this around. Government faces a human capital crisis. The brutality of politics discourages potential candidates for elected office, and many incumbents run unchallenged. In the civil service, a wave of impending retirements will strip experience from many agencies. The pipeline at all levels of government is emptying, as I learned when I participated in a nonpartisan examination of the federal human capital crisis with Republican Senator George Voinivich of Ohio and other experts inside and outside of government. Graduates of schools of public administration have been flocking to private-sector jobs. Some prefer a different kind of government service: through consulting firms whose government practices have been growing. Others with a strong commitment to the public interest are becoming social entrepreneurs, starting or joining change-oriented not-for-profit organizations. Still others want to work for one of the crop of socially responsible companies I mentioned previously as an alternative way to contribute what they might otherwise have done through a government post. Money is not the sole driving force. Many people are turning away from government service because it has been discredited and disrespected.

By setting and enforcing standards, such as water quality, limitations on tobacco, speed limits, sanitary conditions in restaurants, food handling, or drug safety, government has played a role in the doubling of American life expectancy over the past century. Across partisan and ideological divides, the one function of government most people embrace is public safety. Even alone that requires highly professional government. Public safety was jeopardized in my hometown of Boston by construction defects in the tunnels of the Big Dig, the largest public works project in America—which ran years over time and billions over budget. It opened to great fanfare and leaks in the tunnels. In July 2006, portions of a ceiling fell out of a recently completed section, killing a woman, Milena Del Valle, in her car. Enough finger-pointing ensued to produce sufficient fingers to stem the leaks. One alleged culprit was a history of crony appointments of less-than-qualified people to head agencies overseeing infrastructure, such as the Massachusetts Turnpike Authority and Massport (whose crony-leader was replaced by a serious professional after the terrorist attacks of September 11, 2001).

## Governing Least: Best or Worst?

Some people think that these problems occur because government as an institution is inherently flawed. "That government is best which governs least" is a well-known American philosophy dating back to the origins of the nation. It can be found in Henry David Thoreau's classic essay on civil disobedience, but it was first said even earlier by Thomas Paine, author of *Common Sense*. Today, however, common sense would suggest that governing *least* governs *worst*. Bad government can actually add costs, increase dangers, and subvert or distort outcomes through abuse of public trust. We can argue about the optimal level of public services, but there is no doubt that effectiveness requires professional talent focused on outcomes with wide public interest in mind. That's why the Reinventing Government initiative led by then–Vice President Al Gore was an exercise in simultaneous downsizing and quality improvement—fewer people doing *better* work.

Around the world, governments have been reducing spending and privatizing public enterprises. At the beginning of the 1990s, government spending was no longer growing relative to the size of the economy in most developed countries. During that decade, government spending as a percentage of GDP fell in the United States, Canada, Britain, and Germany.

In the late 1980s and 1990s, euphoria about the triumph of global capitalism (since muted and even reversed in the 2000s, as I argue in the next chapter) was reflected in a glorification of business enterprises as a force for good and as a source of expertise that was lacking in a "less-professional" public sector that did not enjoy "market feedback." Interest grew in the private sector taking responsibility for problem-solving in the public realm. A deputy to a U.S. secretary of education said to me that problems of education required business involvement because "business is a neutral convener" (a somewhat startling statement given the legal mandate of corporations to be instruments of shareholders' interests, but a reflection of a ceding of community leadership to CEOs rather than elected officials). President Clinton declared that the "era of big government" was giving way to the "era of big citizens." The Clinton administration downsized government and rewarded businesses for their community responsibility through the Welfare-to-Work Partnership and the Ron Brown Award, and President Clinton frequently feted and touted social entrepreneurs serving community needs.

Markets and private-sector actions are important, but the argument for government rests on what economists call "market failures"—things in the public interest that wouldn't get done otherwise. The distinction between functions best performed by government employees versus those contracted out to private-sector providers is not clear-cut, as evidenced by the federal "in-sourcing" of airport security screening after the terrorist attacks of September 11, 2001, when this function was taken back from private vendors. While government does not have to do everything, it plays an important role in overseeing private action to ensure compliance with the law and responsibility for appropriate outcomes. Private contractors designed and built the Big Dig, but evidently public officials did not hold the contractors or themselves accountable. (Milena Del Valle's bereaved family brought suit against nine large private contractors in addition to the Massachusetts Turnpike Authority.) In contrast, the Massachusetts Convention Center Authority (on whose board I serve) replaced a crony appointee with an outstanding, experienced public manager before a new $8 billion convention center was built. In 2006, under professional leadership stressing accountability, this public authority settled a lawsuit against private contractors for design flaws that occurred under the previous administration, recovering $24 million.

Trust and performance are connected. If arms of government cannot attract, motivate, and retain the best people—and enable those people to perform their jobs to high professional standards untainted by politics—the public will suffer. If government agencies do not perform to high standards, they cannot attract the best people. Without getting into arguments about how to divide functions between the public and private sectors, I want to stress only that whatever functions various agents of government perform will not be handled effectively unless government itself is respected.

## Heading to the Right: Government as the Enemy

Throughout American history, there have always been scandals, violations of the public trust, and ineffective individuals and groups. But the costs keep getting higher and the missed opportunities more consequential. Why has so much gone wrong in the opening years of the twenty-first century? The current problem of good government is the culmination of twenty-five years of right-wing political ideology that has come to dominate American national politics. This ideology has made government the enemy. Not simply a flawed institution requiring better management, but the enemy of the people—so much so that even those seeking office, who hope to serve honorably, have had to run against government, with even the political insiders declaring themselves outsiders.

Asserting that government was the problem, some leaders set out to prove it by being lax about standards, appointing weak managers, and letting performance deteriorate. A related set of trickledown economic theories hatched in those years tolerated growing inequality and short-term consumption over long-term investment, neglecting both infrastructure and human services. Contempt for government made it possible to argue for tax reductions and starve essential services while borrowing heavily for favored projects, demonstrating hypocrisy that then fueled public cynicism about government—closing the loop of disrespect. As religious fundamentalism was added to this ideological package, science was dismissed as just another body of opinions ignorable by anyone speaking directly to God; facts—empirical truths and rigorously collected data—became irrelevant. This was accompanied by proclamations about America's self-evident superiority, a viewpoint that was used to justify a costly and unpopular war (later found to have been waged on false premises) and that displayed indifference to international cooperation.

When respect for the functions of government weakens, not only the truth suffers. So do many basic services, which are handled by people poorly equipped to manage them and cynical about whether that even matters. Some of the everyday things we take for granted can crumble, such as roads, bridges, tunnels, sewers, and, in the case of New Orleans, seawalls and levees. "It's your money," politicians leaning to the right have told voters as they curry favor by offering to cut taxes. "Yes," replied Massachusetts Governor Deval Patrick, a Democrat, in one of the debates culminating in his election in 2006, "and it's also your bridges, your roads, your schools, your parks, your clean air . . ." In recent years, some of the highest officials in the nation have manifested contempt for government in their words and deeds. Let's turn to some examples of what can go wrong when officials don't act as leaders.

## The Wages of Contempt: Setting the Wrong Tone at the Top

One of the fallouts of the period following the terrorist attacks of September 11, 2001, was a remarkable string of accusations of cynical abuses of power in and around the federal government. I don't know who did what to whom at the White House, the CIA, the vice president's office, Congressman Tom DeLay's campaign, the Defense Department's Abu Ghraib command, Guantánamo during Geneva Convention violations, or any of the others (name your favorite scandal). But from years of observing the corporate world, I do know about the causes of sabotage and abuse of power: If you have contempt for your place of work, then you feel free to trash it, subvert it, undermine it, and weaken it.

Contempt often starts at the top, when bosses believe their organizations are mere instruments of their own desires, to be exploited for themselves and their buddies. Cynicism spreads, reducing morale, depressing performance, and repelling the best people. A self-fulfilling prophecy is set in motion, whereby initial contempt is justified by subsequent failures—a classic losing streak.

Abuse of the power of office has occurred regularly in the opening years of the century. Of course, accusations are not proof, and indictments are not convictions—Americans are innocent until proven guilty. But a growing pile of indictments soon starts to stink. Some say the smell is a few isolated rotten apples spoiling the barrel. That was said about the torturers at Abu Ghraib. Until President Bush asked him to resign in late 2006, calls for then–Defense Secretary Donald Rumsfeld's resignation, on "the buck stops here" grounds that bosses are responsible for subordinates' actions, fell on deaf ears. An isolated rotten apple was what U.S. Senator John Cornyn (R-Texas) argued concerning indicted former Cheney chief of staff Lewis "Scooter" Libby. Cornyn told ABC's *This Week* that "any alleged wrongdoing is really confined to a single individual." Nice try, but not credible. The rot appears in the barrel itself, emanating from extreme right-wing ideology that holds government in contempt and then portrays it as ripping off taxpayers because it does not provide value.

Contempt for government leads to crony appointments, treating top posts as perks with no substance. Soon-forgotten Supreme Court nominee Harriet Miers is an example to add to the more consequential failure of former FEMA head

Michael Brown. Was she nominated because she was a loyal friend to the president? The scandal over the hiring and firing of U.S. attorneys under Attorney General Alberto Gonzales is another example. Contempt means feeling free to subvert the instruments of government to one's own ends—such as waging war on a flimsy, shifting pretext or getting rid of top officials because they're not ideological enough.

Contempt means not having to reach high standards. According to Associated Press reports, the Bush administration has missed dozens of post–September 11 congressional deadlines for developing ways to protect airlines, ships, and railways from terrorists. Even if the demands of Congress are excessive, an administration that campaigned for reelection on a promise to make Americans safer has failed to live up to its own highest priority.

The tone at the top has also tolerated disrespect of the worst kind, which fans partisan flames and threatens civility. Rodney Paige, secretary of education in the first Bush term, referred to the teachers' union leaders as "terrorists" and was not sanctioned. Vice President Cheney used a hostile, expletive-deleted phrase when he addressed Vermont Senator Patrick Leahy on the Senate floor.

Contempt in words and deeds makes it hard to attract the best people to public service and demoralizes talented professionals already there. How many bright college graduates will sign up for the CIA after suggestions of pressure to distort intelligence, capped by the outing of Valerie Plame? When leaders act to strengthen their organization, not sabotage it, others emulate that behavior. But when leaders put subtle pressure on those below them to subvert the mission, the results can be disastrous. Something like that could happen only when leaders put their own interests over the institution and distort facts to get what they want. Their cynicism infects the public servants below them.

Sometimes those in power don't even have to exercise it to abuse it. Here's another example, in the flawed intelligence that supported the case for the war in Iraq.

## Undermining Performance: Winks, Nods, and Destructive Workplace Pressure

The U.S. Senate Intelligence Committee's 512-page report on Iraq intelligence failures concluded that Bush administration officials made *no* attempt to coerce, pressure, or influence CIA analysts who provided flawed information about Iraq's alleged weapons of mass destruction (WMD) that supported the case for war. Democratic senators Jay Rockefeller, Richard Durbin, and Carl Levin signed a dissenting addendum to the report, arguing what most of us know from experience: It doesn't take a direct order from the boss for workers to see things the boss's way. Subtle cues can be significant influencers.

Who's kidding whom? Workers give top management the answer the boss wants to hear—the answer that will cover the big boss's you-know-what. And there was *no* pressure involved? Really? Administration officials stated publicly that Iraq had weapons of mass destruction before any meaningful intelligence analysis was conducted. (Did this public commitment turn the assignment from objective analysis into justification?) Vice President Cheney visited CIA headquarters several times before the war. (Did this serve as a reminder of who holds the power?) Policymakers apparently asked analysts repeatedly to review or reconsider judgments. (Did this signal that there was only one correct answer and that officials would watch until analysts got it?) Perhaps the senators who did not believe that such actions constitute "pressure" have never worked in a large bureaucracy, taken an exam from an opinionated teacher, or faced a manipulative parent.

I have seen this pattern dozens of times in companies. The big boss wants board approval for a controversial investment that he or she is already publicizing. Your department is asked to run the numbers. Before you have done much work, the big man himself comes by to thank your group. You provide a draft assessment, including some concerns, and send it to your manager. The boss returns it with red question marks on the negative sections and deploys another analyst to rerun the data. The big boss visits again. You know the costs of letting the boss down. So you convince yourself to set aside doubts. You present only the positive case.

Or the chief executive plugs a new product in various speeches before it has been tested fully. You're in product testing. There are signs suggesting that the product will not be ready as soon as the CEO claims and that it could have serious flaws. But then again, there is other evidence you could use to override these concerns. Your manager jokes that you don't want to get a reputation as a wet blanket who delays the mission. You get the message. You decide to emphasize the fastest, flaw-free scenario.

In short, powerful officials do not have to issue direct orders. People who succeed in bureaucracies are so attuned to bosses that a wink and a nod will do. Zealous workers can overinterpret their bosses' preferences and set in motion events that even those bosses later regret. Consider the "Murder in the Cathedral Problem," which I have named after T. S.

Eliot's play *Murder in the Cathedral,* about King Henry II of England. King Henry's plans were often blocked by Thomas Becket, the archbishop of Canterbury. When the king wished aloud that something could be done about that "pesky priest," aides took it upon themselves to murder the archbishop. Henry spent the rest of his life in penance.

No one says that the White House ordered the CIA to find evidence of WMD in Iraq. But the White House did not have to; their pressure was felt anyway. The Senate report accused the CIA of interpreting ambiguous evidence as conclusive, ignoring or discounting conflicting information, failing to consider alternatives, and blurring the line between fact and theory. Evidently, even agents in the field had the impression that their job was to support claims of Iraqi weapons programs. In everyday life, we know that when someone who has already made a decision asks your honest opinion, he or she doesn't want the truth; the person wants confirmation. As my teenage friends would say, "Duh."

When those who tarnish their offices by crossing ethical or legal lines are exposed and respond with public relations campaigns intended to mitigate their errors without addressing their causes, contempt is reinforced. An already-cynical public sees public officials responding with "spin" and becomes even more cynical. At stake is not individual actions—everyone makes mistakes—but respect for the institutions and instruments of government themselves.

Some observers have compared President Bush's problem of restoring public trust to the problems faced by former President Clinton. Bush supporters took this as a hopeful sign that he could bounce back from that string of abuse of power accusations because Clinton recovered from personal scandal and impeachment hearings to leave office with high approval. But there was a big difference between the Bush and Clinton situations. People trusted Clinton's desire to carry out his official duties with the highest professional standards because of his belief in the positive role of government. This was reflected in the signature Reinventing Government initiative, which was premised on criticism in the service of improvement. In that sense, dissent in the workplace is not a sign of disrespect; it makes clear one's respect for the integrity of the mission and the importance of the institution. That's the tone leaders must set at the top.

### Ideology, Competence, and Contradictions: John Roberts's Confirmation

Politicians who play loose with the facts sometimes get trapped by their own words, but meanwhile, irresponsible statements chip away at trust and respect. A case in point involves a coincidence of events around the time John Roberts was appointed to the Supreme Court. Periodically, some politicos have tried to undermine the court's integrity (contempt for court?) by trying to nominate unqualified people who supported their agendas. ("Even the mediocre deserve representation on the court" was Senator Roman Hruska's refrain accompanying President Richard Nixon's failed nomination of Harold Carswell in 1970.) The eminently qualified Roberts followed inexperienced Harriet Miers, but meanwhile a member of the president's party was lashing out against the same institutions that helped make Roberts so qualified.

Chief Justice Roberts might not even have known about his lucky escape from attack by partisan pit bulls when President

Bush nominated him to the Supreme Court. The growling could have begun when a member of the president's party, then–U.S. Senator Rick Santorum (R-PA), focused on what could have been Roberts's background flaw—that Roberts spent his formative years getting educated in *BOSTON*. At *HARVARD!*

Boston, Santorum said, was responsible for abusive pedophile priests in the Catholic Church. "While it is no excuse for this scandal," he wrote in *Catholic Online* in 2002, "it is no surprise that Boston, a seat of academic, political and cultural liberalism in America, lies at the center of the storm." Despite the fact that cases of child abuse committed by priests were found in Louisiana, Ireland, Latin America, and elsewhere, Santorum continued to blame Boston for tainting people. Just a few weeks before Roberts's nomination, Santorum refused to back off. His aide Robert Traynham explained, "It's an open secret that you have Harvard University and MIT that tend to tilt to the left in terms of academic biases. I think that's what the Senator was speaking to."

Those comments bring us back to Roberts, who is as Harvard as you can get (Harvard College 1976, Harvard Law School 1979). Seven years as an impressionable youth being molded in the Boston crucible! See the taint? In a photo with other *Harvard Law Review* editors, the young John had—gasp—long hair. Does that mean that Santorum should have led a charge against Roberts's confirmation? If he wanted to be consistent, he would have. After all, isn't consistency a Republican virtue and "waffling" the label some party members pin on Democratic opponents?

Though it would have been fun to see Santorum squirm in the confirmation hearings, consistency is not all it is cracked up to be. With Roberts ensconced on the Supreme Court a few years later, it is not too late for Santorum to apologize to Boston and tout the virtues of a Harvard education. Learning from experience and changing one's mind is a characteristic of great leaders, and an honorable American tradition. "A foolish consistency is the hobgoblin of little minds," Ralph Waldo Emerson declared in his essay "Self-Reliance." Similarly, Walt Whitman, poet of American individualism, wrote in *Leaves of Grass,* "Do I contradict myself? Very well, then I contradict myself. I am large, I contain multitudes." In his early decisions, Chief Justice Roberts demonstrated the large mind that got him to Harvard in the first place by avoiding the hobgoblin of foolish ideological and partisan consistency. He put long-term national interests first and decided against the president who appointed him in the matter of presidential prerogative.

Leaders are not the sum of their past actions and opinions; they respond to changing circumstances and weigh the matter at hand. Harry Truman grew in office when he succeeded FDR as president. Former Mayor Rudy Giuliani morphed from mean politician to emotional healer after September 11. On the Supreme Court, former Chief Justice Earl Warren was the quintessential example of a supposed conservative moving in a surprisingly liberal direction because he supported the civil rights movement in the 1950s. Senator John McCain, known for strength of character after surviving five years in captivity in Vietnam, showed similar openness of mind; an early staunch opponent of President Clinton's proposal for AmeriCorps, he became one of its strongest supporters and co-sponsored re-authorization legislation.

When seeking top leaders, companies do not expect them to repeat exactly what they did in their last job (except get great results). The best searches involve probes into ways of thinking about decisions, not the decisions themselves. One savvy CEO said his favorite screening question for any candidate for a top position is to ask about instances in which the candidate changed his or her mind from an initial position. In short, he preferred learning, flexibility, and responsiveness to context, not consistency.

A concern with the facts and a willingness to change one's mind based on the evidence should be a main criterion for choosing leaders. The Katrina failure can be attributed, in part, to dismissal of science—echoing a problem I discussed in Chapter 1. For purposes of governing, in contrast to campaigning, we rely on leaders' commitment to judgments based on evidence, not on assertions about what they think ought to be true because of their religious values or political ideologies. That's why science and politics are separate and sometimes conflicting pursuits, as the great sociologist Max Weber observed a century ago in his classic essays "Science as a Vocation" and "Politics as a Vocation." Politicians are advocates who passionately push their point of view, forcing facts into their frameworks. Scientists are supposed to be dispassionate, led by the facts to findings that could disprove their hypotheses. That's why political speech is colorful and fun, not to mention glib, while scientific writing is often full of hedges, qualifications, and long excursions into methodology before ever drawing a conclusion. That doesn't mean we should let politicians get away with ignoring the facts. Quite the contrary, we should push them to be more scientific once they are in office. Indeed, distorting science to fit political ends increases the public's cynicism and mistrust in public servants.

Judgment is the essential consideration. The best judgment is based on the facts.

## Leadership to Restore Confidence: What High-Performing Teams Have in Common

In the search for models of leadership, Bill Belichick, Andy Reid, Anson Dorrance, Gordon Bethune, and Jim Kilts can teach us a thing or two. Under Belichick, the New England Patriots won three out of four twenty-first-century Super Bowls and achieved a record winning streak. Reid coached the Philadelphia Eagles to win more regular-season games between 2000 and 2004 than any other NFL team (though losing the Super Bowl to the Patriots before an estimated global audience of 1 billion people in 222 countries). Dorrance has led the University of North Carolina women's soccer team to victory for over twenty-five years. Bethune became CEO of Continental Airlines after the company experienced ten losing years that included two bankruptcies and ten CEOs; he propelled the company to a ten-year winning streak. Kilts, Gillette's turnaround CEO, reversed a cycle of decline and restored Gillette's culture of success.

Government is bigger and more complex than sports teams or even 30,000-employee businesses, but there are many leadership lessons that translate well—which is how former entrepreneur and media mogul Michael Bloomberg transformed himself into an effective mayor of New York City. I've studied hundreds of coaches and captains of industry who routinely produce high performance despite daunting challenges. Their actions tell us what questions to ask about leadership in government and what items to put on the job description for the CEO of America.

The Patriots and the Eagles stressed the meaning of "professional" in professional sports, recruiting for "character" as well as raw athletic ability and holding everyone to high standards of conduct. Andy Reid was a largely unknown assistant coach when the Eagles hired him to lead a turnaround. Under a tough but not strategic predecessor, the team was running downhill fast. Reid fostered disciplined implementation of a clear and focused long-term strategy, but with the openness to admit mistakes and the flexibility to try new tactics. When the Eagles lost the first two games last season, he returned to fundamentals, dropping tactics that were too hard to execute, but he stuck with the overall long-term strategy, and the team resumed winning.

Reid's leadership approach stands in contrast to questions raised about President Bush's war on terrorism. Was it leadership by President Bush to start a war against terrorists in Afghanistan, neglect to follow up aggressively there, and shift to Iraq without a plan for what to do next? It neither inspires confidence nor engenders respect when the CEO changes his mind about whether winning is possible. It's the top person's job to define appropriate goals and achieve them.

"A promise made is a promise kept," Jim Kilts liked to say. Kilts became CEO of Gillette in 2001, after market share, sales, and stock price had slipped. Too many managers offered unrealistic sales forecasts, and they scrambled to meet these forecasts by cutting prices, which caused further losses. Kilts restored accountability by insisting on honest numbers—that forecasts are supported by facts. Moreover, departments could no longer coast on empty while blockbuster products such as Mach3 shaving systems carried the company. Each department was required to meet highly specific targets with abundant performance metrics.

In a different setting, but in a similar vein, Anson Dorrance modeled accountability. "We don't whine" was the first item on his championship soccer team's values statement. Dorrance measured many aspects of the women athletes' performance and discussed the data openly. He encouraged making improvements rather than excuses.

Hiding or distorting information, whether in the examples already discussed or by manipulating the accounting reports from the war in Iraq, would be unacceptable to the leaders just mentioned. Should the nation's CEO allow his team to distort information to justify ideological preferences, neglect external allies, or duck responsibility for big mistakes (such as Abu Ghraib)? And at every level of government, are targets and goals clearly stated and results measured and reported to the public?

Showing respect was part of Gordon Bethune's formula for teamwork and customer service at Continental. When Bethune, an outsider, became CEO, he cultivated allies. His team went so far as to call customers to apologize for Continental's past behavior—even when they personally had nothing to do with causing it. Bethune took another step that is sorely needed in most levels of government and certainly among the rival agencies making up the new Department of Homeland Security. He replaced turf wars with widespread commitment to a common mission involving service to the public (in this case, on-time flight arrivals). Respect was an explicit value; he treated all employees with dignity and expected them to do the same, to customers and one another. He personified this by making a memorable video with comedian Rodney "Don't Get No Respect" Dangerfield.

Leadership is not about personality. It is about actions. Great leadership shapes a culture of professionalism that makes it possible to achieve goals. Eagles President Joe Banner said, "The skill of an athlete is irrelevant until the right culture surrounds him." In the Eagles' headquarters and fitness center, the front lobby features photos and tributes to Martin Luther King, Mother Teresa, and Jonas Salk—heroes "whose lives embodied the essence of leadership, vision, determination, conviction, and courage."

In the performance-driven worlds of sports and business, CEOs must deliver results or they are replaced. (Well, eventually.) Today there is a healthy trend toward increasing performance tracking in government, too, particularly at the local level. Perhaps that's why the survey of confidence in leaders that I mentioned earlier in this chapter found that the public has more confidence in local officials than in any other level of government. The functions performed by local government are tangible and visible—the garbage gets collected or not, the police keep the streets safe or not, and so on. Cities such as Baltimore, St. Louis, San Francisco, and Boston have added tracking systems for citizen complaints and requests, similar to package-tracking systems for Federal Express, to use data to both speed and measure performance. (One result is reduced costs of overtime and absenteeism.) Technology, including handheld computers to communicate with workers in the field, gives people the tools they need to do their jobs—that's one of the most important signs of respect. And this helps managers to maintain high standards.

Accountability and professionalism also require vigilance in terms of finding, discussing, and dealing with ethical lapses. Performance standards must be supported by open discussion about whether standards are being met, particularly in areas that are less objective and subject to interpretation.

## The Best Decisions: Dialogue and Inquiry

In 2005, after Abu Ghraib but before Katrina, I thought I had finished writing about politics and could return to business. Then I heard the news that congressional Republicans were trying to make ethics inquiries harder to begin. That year, the new congressional session opened with a House vote requiring majority agreement of the ethics committee before investigating members of Congress. With a committee of five Democrats and five Republicans, that would mean that a member of the proposed investigative target's party would have to vote in favor of probes, rendering already rare ethics inquiries even less likely. No wonder the survey of confidence in leaders put Congress and other federal officials near the bottom of the barrel (the one with more than a few rotten apples).

Since I am a member of a profession that has been attacked for graduating some M.B.A.s with the ethics of a flea, I can only thank those distinguished U.S. representatives for making business-school professors—who want ethics discussed more openly—look good by comparison.

House Republicans also tried to pass another controversial ethics proposal: limiting ethics complaints to violations of specific rules or laws, eliminating inquiries about conduct that creates the appearance of corruption without actually breaking the law. It was ironic as well as appalling that anyone in Congress would weaken ethics inquiries, since one of the most effective ethical-problem-exposers is an arm of Congress: the Government Accountability Office, which changed its name from the General Accounting Office to make clear that its audit and inquiry function extends well beyond accurate numbers to broader aspects of living up to promises and standards.

The desire to narrow ethics discussions in 2005 was provoked by rebukes to then–House Majority Leader Tom DeLay for political tactics that were still under investigation in Texas—in essence, changing procedures to benefit one person. Had this succeeded, I was ready to argue for exempting other powerful interests from ethics inquiries. Imagine an Enron Exception: "Any company whose CEO appears on the cover of *Fortune* magazine for innovation, thus reflecting a business bestseller's advice to 'first break the rules,' is exempted from any legal liabilities associated with breaking said rules." Fortunately, even DeLay's cronies realized that appearances matter, and they backed off. Still, what they eliminated is the essence of ethics. Ethics are all about the inquiries. Ethics require raising questions about actions that raise eyebrows.

The temptation to skirt the truth, cover up mistakes, and deny problems has long infected public life in many countries. Sex and spy scandals in Britain in the 1960s started with War Minister John Profumo's denials and ended up bringing down the Tory government. The Watergate scandal in the 1970s eventually caused U.S. President Nixon to resign. Senior members of government in Japan in the 1970s and 1980s were implicated in denial-ridden bribery scandals in which they tried to recast bribes as "donations." Denial of an affair led to U.S. President Clinton's impeachment hearings in the 1990s. Financial scandals provoked the resignations of Japanese Prime Minister Yoshiro Mori, Economic Minister Fukushiro Nukaga, and others in the early 2000s. In the spring of 2004, both President George W. Bush's administration in the United States and Prime Minister Tony Blair's government in the United Kingdom were under investigation for allegedly misleading the public in their intelligence reports about the existence of weapons of mass destruction in Iraq.

We have plenty of law but not enough inquiry. Definitions of good conduct cannot stop at the letter of the law, cannot be tweaked to exclude the peccadilloes of people in power, and, most of all, cannot be understood or embraced without inquiries. This is important to effective decisions well beyond the domain of ethics—especially in large institutions that concentrate power at the top and confine most people to isolated silos with only a limited view. In those cases, no one asks, and no one tells. That leads to shoddy decisions of all kinds that undermine not only integrity but also performance.

In our bottom-line-focused country, results are important, which is why we must meet a higher standard for public service. But inquiry is necessary to look beyond results and ask how they were achieved. For example, as I have indicated, it is common practice for some manufacturers concerned about meeting quarterly sales targets to push additional products on retailers whether or not consumers will buy them. Not exactly unethical, but it is a practice that would not withstand inquiry, either. Krispy Kreme, a former Wall Street darling, tried this with doughnuts, and its stock tanked as its business decayed. Overloading retailers with paper towels is one thing, but food that gets stale? Hard to do more than once before finances suffer. Didn't anyone inquire?

Cutting off any form of inquiry subverts the ability to identify problems while there is still time to find solutions, correct mistakes before they do permanent damage, or make improvements. Prior to Enron et al. and the subsequent Sarbannes-Oxley requirements, corporate board meetings were notorious inquiry-eliminators (and perhaps some still are). Many of them run on tight time frames with information provided by management and pressure to get on with the vote. Asking questions, especially those that challenge a CEO's desires or probe a CEO's motivations, is considered impolite. Directors have been fired for this, just as dissenting employees are fired for not being "team players"—perhaps one of the fears of those CIA staffers who could be so easily pressured.

Unfortunately, failures of leadership to confront problems honestly occur even in sectors dedicated to teaching morality, such as schools and religious institutions (e.g., the child abuse scandals in the Catholic Church). In the 1970s, some public school officials in some parts of the United States were accused of hiding data on declining enrollments or on school dropouts in order to protect their budgets. More recently, the Houston school district, once a national model whose superintendent was named secretary of education, became mired in scandal when it appeared that test scores were significantly lower and student dropout rates were significantly greater than had been claimed (even by that well-known superintendent). Administrators were said to push out children who would skew test scores, and then enter codes indicating that those students had transferred somewhere else. This reduced the official dropout rate to near zero not by real actions but by false data. In another scandal, this time in my home state, the superintendent of the highly regarded Everett, Massachusetts, school system was indicted in March 2004 for bid-rigging and illegal kickbacks of school construction and maintenance contracts.

Some argue that ethics start with a personal conscience—with an individual's own values. But the best way to get an inner voice to yell "Stop!" is to make sure that enough outer voices ask questions. I sometimes joke that the true benefit of rising to the top of a large organization is not money or perks. Rather, it is never again having to listen to anyone who disagrees with you! That's really not very funny. When leaders don't want to hear criticism or dissent, the joke is on the rest of us. Stifling disagreement makes for poor decisions. When anyone in public service takes a step in this direction, the quality of our government and our nation will suffer.

During the long run-up to the millennium, pundits were being asked to make predictions for the year 2000. Renowned sociologist Daniel Bell said that the only thing he was sure of was that in 2000, the United States would hold a presidential election and have an orderly transition of power. Look how close we came to proving the esteemed professor wrong. In the 2000 election, Vice President Al Gore won the popular vote but George W. Bush ascended to the presidency based on the decision of five Supreme Court justices who awarded him Florida's electoral votes, amid outcries over Florida's voting practices.

Is American democracy more fragile than we would like to think, sometimes hanging on a few hanging chads? We cannot take the system for granted and assume that it will run without inquiry, investigation, and multiple checkpoints against neglect, ineffectiveness, or corruption.

## Toward Respect and Competence

In the 2006 midterm congressional elections, the Republicans lost their majorities in both the House of Representatives and the Senate. One of the first moves by the new Speaker of the House was to support an ethically challenged but senior and loyal congressman for the number two post. Fortunately for the hope expressed in this chapter, the Democrats chose Maryland's untainted Representative Steny H. Hoyer instead. Clearly, restoring respect for government is not a matter of replacing one party with another. It requires a deeper, longer-term commitment to excellence and high standards at every turn.

Much of this chapter has dealt with inadequacies of elected officials and political appointees in Washington. I have argued that those inadequacies represent distortions rather than inevitabilities because of a larger problem—those twenty-five years of right-wing contempt for government. Those given the public trust must believe in public purpose and respect the people and institutions that they serve. Accountability and professionalism as well as dialogue and inquiry stem from institutions that promote them and from leaders who believe in them.

How can we stop people running for office who run against the very thing they are running to get? The answer is that we can't. But we can enlarge the pool of talented people who are willing to serve. To encourage outstanding people, we can start early in life: civics education in schools, internships in public-sector organizations, and public service fellowships to forgive undergraduate or graduate student loans for people who take government posts. The human capital crisis will not be solved by civil service reform alone, although pay for performance, administered fairly and with transparency, with help to attain standards and decent pay, could go a long way to change the profile.

Maintaining mechanisms for accountability is essential: performance standards, reporting, disclosure, transparency, and consequences for poor performance. Judges can easily declare someone in contempt of court; it would be wonderful to have such instant consequences for contempt of office. We should also applaud independent watchdog authorities such as the Government Accountability Office, whose head is appointed for eleven years, making the person virtually political-pressure-immune. We can support a free press, whose journalistic courage should not be subverted. Of course, if scrutiny turns into prurient interest and investigation into witch-hunts, those extremes keep good people out of government, so some media soul-searching is also in order.

Innovation is as important in the public sector as in private industry, and fortunately, there are award programs to reward excellent examples. Government agencies with fresh ideas and leading-edge practices bring respect—whether using the Internet to streamline tax refunds or offering iris scans at airports. And change is definitely possible. It is not a waste of taxpayers' money to give public employees the best tools; it helps ensure a faster and better return on taxpayers' investment through better service by more highly motivated people. In addition, innovation champions, such as the British prime minister's Strategy and Innovation Unit in the United Kingdom, can provide vehicles to propose and test new ideas. Innovation awards by organizations promoting better public service publicize accomplishments, help spread role models of best practice, and ensure that the good in government permeates public consciousness, not just the bad.

The most important factor is leadership. To restore respect for government, leaders need to argue the positive case—that government carries out meaningful and beneficial functions, that public service can be a high calling, and that government services can be (and should be) provided with impartial professionalism. Political moderates of both parties should avoid the temptation to gloat over the other side's latest scandal and should counter the extreme right wing's contempt for government by articulating a compelling alternative view.

If democracy-building is considered so important abroad, shouldn't we care more about who staffs the institutions of democracy at home?

The positive case for government—that its functions create value for the public and that it can govern least only when governing best—should be on the agenda for the American electorate. As long as antigovernment rhetoric goes unchallenged and voices of respect are silent, Americans will never get good government back. The barrel will continue to rot from within, spoiling even the best apples.

# FIVE

# Engaging the World

## Globalization, Leadership, and the Rule of Thirds

The Oprah Winfrey Leadership School for Girls opened in January 2007 in Henley-on-Klip, South Africa, with a celebrity-studded launch featuring Oprah herself. American investment in girls' education, especially with an emphasis on building future leaders, was such an important milestone that even the ailing Nelson Mandela, South Africa's first democratically elected president, made an exceptional public appearance there.

My thoughts that day turned to some less-heralded people who had contributed to Winfrey's achievement and South Africa's development several years earlier. Greg Ricks, an African American, had worked for Winfrey's foundation on initial rounds of planning for her leadership school. He was living in Johannesburg at the time, having just completed his work leading the formation of another American-inspired youth organization for South Africa. Ricks seemed to know everyone and how to connect them. His relationship talents included a special touch with young people. He believed strongly in classic American values, and he liked to explain the meaning of opportunity to those who had never seen it in action. He encouraged poor black youth to work together to take responsibility for HIV-AIDs prevention, and he helped some promising students travel to America.

Eventually Ricks returned to the United States to become the director of multicultural affairs for the Taft School in Connecticut. But before he left, he took me to visit the poor black township of Kliptown and, in 2002, introduced me to Brother Bob. Brother Bob became a fount of lessons about how Americans can and should engage with the world.

Kliptown is a dirt-poor section of the black township of Soweto, just a hop across the superhighway from Sandton, an affluent suburb of Johannesburg that resembles Beverly Hills. Dirt tracks wound their way through Kliptown. There was no pavement, sewer system, running water, indoor plumbing, or electricity other than what was generated in battery shops drawing power from car batteries. To get to school, Kliptown children crossed railroad tracks and a field of electric poles— poles that were mysteriously unable to power Kliptown.

Ricks, in a bright green dashiki, and his multiracial entourage brought my family in a van to the edge of Kliptown, where we met the leaders of SKY—Soweto Kliptown Youth. These community workers, themselves young and mostly unpaid, included Brother Bob, a program assistant noticeable for his long thick hair and serious manner. We began to stroll through the village, attracting a growing number of smiling small children in our parade, which by now included other visitors, such as Grace, an advocate for the elderly from nearby Alexandra Township, another black settlement. The SKY staff knew we were Americans and that American democracy had been a model for President Mandela and the new South African constitution. They seemed to hold us personally responsible for whatever our country had done, or not done, for their country. As I walked alongside Brother Bob on the dirt paths, he waved his arm toward the faucet outside a cluster of tiny houses that was the only source of running water and then toward the lines of people in front of a half dozen portable toilets. "Tell me as you look at this what democracy has brought to South Africa," he said. Clearly Brother Bob didn't think a new political culture had done much for the people. I mumbled something about how Americans needed to know the situation and would certainly want to help.

That chance came soon. The next time I saw Brother Bob was a few years later, at a posh home in Wellesley, one of Boston's wealthiest suburbs. He had been busy in the meantime solidifying SKY's ties to America. By the time I encountered him in Wellesley, he had created a set of youth projects to which Americans could contribute, having received help from Kristen and Jim Atwood, Marsha Feinberg, Corrine and Tim Ferguson, and other well-to-do families that had taken Greg Ricks's Kliptown tour and encouraged their children's private schools to "adopt" Soweto schools. There were e-mail contacts, class projects, the collection of supplies to donate, fundraisers for education, South African students being brought to America, and the organization of trips for Americans to participate in community service projects in South Africa.

With a broad smile on his face, Brother Bob gave me a warm bear hug and shrugged off any hint that he had once been disdainful of the American system. He and other leaders of his youth organization mingled comfortably with the group of forty-something venture capitalists and money managers in Wellesley. With African drummers in the background, Brother Bob spoke passionately about the difference Americans were making to the aspirations and education of children in Kliptown.

Without knowing it, Brother Bob had taught me about a growing opportunity for America in today's troubled, conflict-ridden world. Americans who form ties that enhance prospects for people in other parts of the world represent an active force of citizen-diplomats who can support the development of future leaders with positive views of America.

A few celebrity philanthropists make headlines with enormous commitments, especially to Africa—Bill and Melinda Gates, Bono, Angelina Jolie, Brad Pitt, and, of course, Oprah Winfrey. They also attract criticism, of two sorts. First, that they handpick projects to fund with enormous sums—some said that Winfrey's $40 million was too much to spend on one school—and, second, that they neglect many grass-roots organizations that could use small amounts to achieve a wider impact. That makes the work of the larger army of citizen-diplomats like Greg Ricks or the Atwoods that much more important. They play a quieter but increasingly important role in America's engagement with the world. Their connections with other citizen-diplomats on the ground can augment (and sometimes even improve upon) government foreign policy. After all, there are only 12,800 career officers employed by the U.S. foreign service, but potentially hundreds of millions of other citizens who might care to help in a small way. While each effort can seem minor in light of huge issues such as war or terrorism, small acts effectively pursued can augment official acts to make a difference.

This chapter explores that opportunity for American engagement with the world, especially in light of new global realities. With so much of world affairs dominated by conflicts and quagmires in the Middle East, and so much unease in America over the rise of Asian economic superpowers, there is a natural tendency for Americans to look to Washington to find solutions or keep us safe. Military and defense expenditures are enormous—about $578 billion in the fiscal year 2006 federal budget. Even the smaller federal allocations for diplomacy and foreign aid, including everything from embassies to the Peace Corps and disaster and famine assistance at about $31 billion for 2006, swamps private-sector contributions combined—individual, corporate, or foundation efforts. Of course, it's interesting that military and defense spending represents 21.37 percent of the federal budget, whereas the twenty-five programs we counted as involving State Department and international assistance programs accounted for a mere one-sixteenth of 1 percent. Official budgetary priorities have been war, not securing peace by winning friends. The approximately $8 billion per month the Bush administration planned to spend on the war in Iraq in 2007 greatly overwhelmed the $20 million estimated for the year to help 2 million Iraqis fleeing their war-torn country (and not being admitted to the United States).

Private spending looks minuscule by comparison to government expenditures, however we feel about their allocation. The top ten U.S. foundations by total giving gave only $4.78 billion together in 2006, and far from all of it was for international efforts. Yet, despite the money gap, the role for grass-roots contributions seems greater than ever. Private philanthropy can be leveraged to make a big difference. For example, in 2000, Bill and Melinda Gates committed to give $750 million over five years for childhood immunization, which persuaded seventeen governments to increase their own contributions to what became a powerful campaign for change, with the U.S. government the second-biggest financial contributor. As a result, immunization reached record highs, and 2.3 million lives have been saved so far, according to a World Health Organization report in January 2007.

I want to stretch the definition of foreign policy to encompass what citizens do, not just what politicians do. I want that definition to include contributions to the development of leadership in other countries. I want it to go beyond dealing only with immediate military, terrorist, or economic threats (although of course the acute always demands attention) to include steps to enlarge our circle of friends and improve the state of the world. That could help take the edge off current threats today, and for tomorrow, it could create better opportunities for our nation and the world.

## Grass-Roots Diplomacy and the Change Agent Rule of Thirds

International public opinion in the opening years of the twenty-first century contains a great disconnect: *love Americans, hate America*. That states it too starkly, of course. Still, polls in a range of friendly to unfriendly countries tend to show a gap between positive views of American people and negative views of American government policy under the Bush administration. For example, in 2006, 69 percent of British respondents to a poll held a favorable view of *Americans*, but only 56 percent had a favorable view of *America*. In

France, 65 percent liked Americans, but only 39 percent liked America. In Germany, the gap was 66 percent versus 37 percent; in Japan, 82 percent to 63 percent; and in Spain, a much less friendly 37 percent to 23 percent. Gaps also appear in feelings about the generosity of the American people, which respondents considered a positive influence on their countries, and the sensationalism of American pop culture, which respondents considered a negative influence.

I experienced this firsthand on several trips to the Middle East in 2006. In Egypt that May, on a research trip for a project that examined how exemplary multinational companies, such as the good companies described in Chapter 3, apply their standards in developing countries, I spoke to business executives, young professional women in head scarves, shopkeepers, tour guides, and students at the American University in Cairo. Each had a story about Americans they knew or about an act of kindness during a visit to America, but I found a similar disconnect between views of government and views of people with respect to contentious issues in the Middle East itself. (The Egyptian gap between views of Americans versus America was 37 percent to 30 percent, showing a low proportion favorable even to the American people.) One large multinational company (whose norms include no discussions of politics at the office) has a large research center in Cairo that cooperates quietly and effectively on a personal basis with a similar center in Haifa, Israel. The universal language of technology and the power of human relationships transcend vitriolic official government-to-government antagonisms.

Another experience was equally interesting. In Abu Dhabi in September 2006, I was warmly received and my remarks were listened to attentively at a leadership conference sponsored by the all-Arab police, despite being an American Jewish woman (three strikes right there) who specializes in business, not security forces. I was followed by former Malaysian Prime Minister Mahatir Mohammed, whose inflammatory anti-Western, pro-Islam rhetoric was unchanged since the last time I heard him speak ten years earlier. I expected him to sway the Arab participants and be the most influential speaker at the conference. But leadership messages with an appeal to universalist human values were the ones that got the buzz at the conference.

I hope that this doesn't sound like there's a Disneyesque chorus of "it's a small world after all" in the background. I simply want to put on the table the potential value of multiple small acts of engagement by Americans with the world, as individuals and in their business or nonprofit organization roles. If the old 1950s image of the "Ugly American" can be replaced by a 2000s image of the "Generous American" or the "Principled American," then we are fortunate that people in other countries separate the American people from the American government. That provides an opportunity to lay a foundation for better forms of engagement with the world than military swagger.

A starting point for understanding this issue is a lesson from efforts to change large systems, whether complex organizations or communities. I call it the "change agent rule of thirds." In any change effort, start by assuming that roughly one-third of the people are with you, one-third are against you, and the remaining third are on the fence. Your mission is to find that first group of allies and get them working for you, isolate the second group of enemies and try to starve them of support or destroy them, and concentrate on converting the remaining neutral or open-minded moderates by offering them some benefits for jumping to your side of the fence.

Ah, how many Americans wish that the rule of thirds had been in play before the war in Iraq! There were three groups, for sure, but hardly divided evenly. The Bush administration pursued the war with a trivial number of foreign allies. There was a large group opposed and, outside of the United States, a growing set of enemies willing to fight. As the war progressed, the ranks of the moderates diminished; within Iraq, they flooded to enemy camps and fought vociferously with one another, while public opinion elsewhere turned increasingly against the United States.

How we failed became the topic of endless debate and a major investigation by former Secretary of State James Baker and others, but it's not my intention here to repeat it or critique it. My point in invoking the rule of thirds is to identify a missed opportunity then and a positive opportunity for the future. The moderates or neutrals in the middle are key. Winning over the moderates occurs through actions felt at the grass roots: by improving daily lives, educating their children, developing their leaders, and investing in their economic opportunities.

Such commitments to moderates can isolate and undercut extremists while moving the moderates toward the ranks of friends and keeping Americans connected to the opportunities that the moderates create or control. It is interesting to note that a strategy of appealing to the moderates and neutrals had been used by our official enemies: The anti-Israel/anti–United States violence-approving Palestinian party of Hamas won their first election because of services to people at the grass roots, such as efficient garbage collections. The terrorist group

Hezbollah won favor in Lebanon after the brief war with Israel in 2006 by offering to rebuild bombed-out houses. But America can do better, and we have done better. After World War II, the warm sentiments for Americans held by Europeans were not merely because of cultural similarities and were not primarily because America had been instrumental in winning the war, but because America won the peace. That true victory occurred through big investments in rebuilding communities, via the Marshall Plan, and through numerous acts of kindness at the grass roots by individuals, including GIs stationed in Europe.

Today, we have not committed to a Marshall Plan on the huge scale that only the federal government can provide, although former Secretary of State Colin Powell had suggested this. But we are fortunate to have the Gates Foundation Plan and the Oprah Winfrey Plan and the Kristen-and-Jim-Atwood Mini-Plan and numerous others that can start adding up— especially if this citizen-diplomacy becomes matched by government investment. It works both ways. Citizen-diplomats like Oprah Winfrey, Greg Ricks, and the Atwoods can augment foreign aid and government programs to reach people directly, community by community. As a diverse crossroads nation with people from every other nation on earth represented among our citizens, we can also build on international social networks to strengthen positive engagement with the world. Then government investments can leverage and spread the work of private citizen-diplomats.

Former President Clinton has called a so-called war on terrorism a futile misnomer because unlike conventional wars, this one is unwinnable. He said that we can't ever eliminate all terrorists, but we certainly can make it very hard for

them to thrive. Of course, if there are real threats by opponents clearly out to get us, and efforts at diplomacy don't
bring peaceful resolutions, then we should be ready to pull
out the weapons. As the saying goes, "Even paranoids have
real enemies."

Paranoia, however, is not a sufficient basis for policy. Americans need to add some positive psychology. To repeat, if we
befriend and empower moderates by meeting them in their
communities, helping develop their leaders, and investing in
their economic futures, we can isolate and undercut extremists, ensuring that those on the fence jump to join our allies
rather than fleeing to our enemies.

Throughout this chapter, I will explore some ways to act on
this principle. First, I will argue for the importance of grass-
roots community development—a departure from the traditional aid programs that went to governments, often corrupt
ones, and involved big infrastructure, not human-scale social,
educational, and economic development. Then I will discuss
leadership and the opportunities that could stem from our involvement in educating leaders of the future—from Oprah
Winfrey's girls in South Africa to emerging leaders in the Middle East and Eastern Mediterranean. Finally, I will take us to
China and India to see how challenges such as competition for
jobs can be converted into better opportunities through the
cultivation of human networks.

## Globalization's New Questions:
## Coming Down from the Mountain to the Grass Roots

I was standing on a mountaintop in 2006 looking up at even
higher peaks in Davos, Switzerland, but all I could think of

was the ocean. Appropriately named a summit, the World Economic Forum (WEF) was all about the discontents of globalization. My mind kept returning to a classic British poem by George Gordon, Lord Byron:

Roll on, thou deep and dark blue Ocean—roll!
Ten thousand fleets sweep over thee in vain;
Man marks the earth with ruin—his control
Stops with the shore. . . .

Like Lord Byron's ocean, the global economy rolls on. It rolls on despite backlash, despite efforts to close borders, and despite clashes of civilizations. International interdependence is a fact of life. How can leaders whose control stops at their countries' or companies' shores steer their fleets wisely? And what can American citizens do to urge our leaders, or how can we act ourselves, to ensure that the world ahead contains expanding opportunities?

The World Economic Forum was founded in 1980, at the dawn of the computer-led global information age, to discuss the global economy. But the forum soon found itself filling a void, as Davos, Switzerland, became one of the few places where government officials, corporate executives, and social sector leaders could meet on neutral territory to deal with the tidal waves from the globalization ocean.

My first invitation to speak at the World Economic Forum was in the early 1990s. "Davos" was not yet a household name, but the world economy had just taken a dramatic turn toward free markets. During this period, the fall of the Berlin Wall effectively ended communism in Eastern Europe, Asian financial markets had opened, Latin American countries were democratizing, and plans were afoot in South Africa to release Nelson Mandela from prison. Global capitalism's proponents, thinking history was on their side, exuded moral superiority.

Today—humbled by corporate scandals and excesses, conscious of the ravages of global climate change and persistent poverty, and sobered by protesters, terrorists, wars, clashes of civilizations, and forces of nature—the members of the global elite gathered in Davos manifest moral earnestness. There is less grandiosity about globalization's promise and more attention to globalization's downsides. The expressed Davos desire is not to ruin the earth (as Lord Byron's poem had it) but to repair it.

Business has always been the WEF's main business. Every year, Davos is thick with purveyors of airplanes, software, management consulting, and investment banking—and companies cementing or rehabilitating their reputations. Buses, bodyguards, and barriers dot miles of town streets, facilitating behind-the-scenes gatherings for diplomacy or deal-making at dozens of hotels.

Speeches by heads of state—presidents of France, Brazil, Poland; chancellors of Germany; or prime ministers of Britain and Iraq—get international media attention. So do comments of celebrity CEOs (Bill Gates, Carly Fiorina, Ted Turner, and so on), officials such as SEC Chairman William Donaldson, and a bipartisan bunch of U.S. senators. Buzz surrounds Hollywood luminaries promoting social change: perhaps Angelina Jolie, starring as the United Nations' refugee commission goodwill ambassador, or Richard Gere, president of his own foundation.

But formal meetings are not the real story. Around 2005, the messages of Davos—and the challenges facing Americans as we connect to the world—were conveyed in subtle shifts of emphasis.

- **Less United States, more China** The United States is still the sole remaining superpower, and American multinational companies are still the biggest and most influential, so other countries are naturally preoccupied with American policies and America's role in the world. Still, China is the first topic on the minds of global leaders. They wonder how China's growth can generate the fewest shocks and greatest worldwide benefits. Chinese leaders now attend meetings such as the World Economic Forum in droves, listening to simultaneous translation but with the younger generation of rising leaders speaking excellent English—including government officials, airline and television executives, scientists, entrepreneurs (the head of Alibaba.com Technology Corporation), and the director of *Rural Women Knowing All* magazine.

- **Less government, more grass-roots social change** The International Monetary Fund and World Trade Organization get attention on the international stage today, but so does the Global Alliance for Vaccines and Immunization. Davos in 1990 was almost exclusively for those at the lofty peaks of business and government; the assumption was that policy from on high determined the state of the world. At Davos 2006, central bankers mingled with a global patchwork quilt of community activists, including social entrepreneurs from Teach for America and City Year (United States), Women's Initiative for Self-Empowerment (Ghana), National Slum Dwellers Federation (India), Youth Network for

Development (Senegal), Association of Craft Producers (Nepal), Committee for Democracy in IT (Brazil), and Seeds of Peace (Middle East youth). The mainstream agenda now includes women's empowerment and citizen peacemakers. Brother Bob and his peers are no longer outsiders; their concerns are at the center.

- **Less economics, more religion** Religion and science, religion and politics—religion pops up everywhere today, as prayer credentials are now as important as business titles. By around 2005, a forum once dedicated primarily to trade ties and business deals "got religion," too. Clergy began populating Davos—and from many countries. Now value systems get equal time with financial systems. Among recent Davos participants were a California Islamic Society director, the Russian Federation's chief rabbi, head minister of Manhattan's Won Buddhist Temple, and the former archbishop of Canterbury. Clergy from outside the United States or Europe are in special demand.

- **Less "what's good for business," more "what's good for people"** The forum's advice sessions continue to cover bread-and-butter business growth strategies, marketing tactics, and profitability, but the impact of business is also debated. Leaders of consumer federations and trade unions (John Sweeney of the AFL-CIO and counterparts from Norway, England, Barbados, and Australia) challenge global capitalists to their faces. Critics are at the table to stay.

- **Fewer answers, more questions** Experts still prognosticate, but even Davos has turned democratic and opened the dialogue. At large town-hall meetings, all views count. Session descriptions reflect uncertainty: What is the weak link in global networks? Will income disparity always be with us? Is religious tolerance possible? Such questions acknowledge globalization's downsides and trade-offs—as well as limits to elite power.

As we find an agenda for America in this changing and more uncertain world, another message can be found in Lord Byron's poetic ocean, which is bounded by decayed civilizations:

Thy shores are empires, changed in all save thee—
Assyria, Greece, Rome, Carthage, what are they?

Empires rise and fall; the ocean rolls on. That alone should help us gain some perspective and some humility. Humility, indeed, is more often associated with citizen-diplomats than with government officials.

At the most recent WEF I attended, it was heartening to see the summit participants coming down from the mountain to undertake the challenges of nurturing the people at the bottom—the people whom Brother Bob is championing in South Africa. Globalization has made more visible the gaps between its rich beneficiaries and those left behind—and there are groups that don't like what they see. The world hasn't flattened for everyone.

## The World Is Still Lumpy

During one short period in 2005, violence erupted in an unexpected range of places.

- Rioters in Bolivia, demanding more power for Bolivia's poor and nationalization of the nation's oil and gas companies, brought down the government.

- Mobs took to the streets in Argentina during the Summit of the Americas to protest against President Bush, while Brazil, Argentina, Uruguay, Paraguay, and Venezuela rejected the Free Trade Area of the Americas that the United States had desired.

- Riots in France revealed unrest in poor neighborhoods, where young people of North African origin told reporters that they just want jobs and inclusion.

- Terrorists in Jordan bombed three United States–based chain hotels—Radisson, Days Inn, and Grand Hyatt.

The common thread was this: Radical extremists—and not just radical Islamists—fanned the flames of discontent among poor people who felt left behind by global capitalism. We can write off each event as the actions of young hotheads or the violence of crackpots led by despots. But honestly, with the gap between rich and poor growing in many places, do sensible people really think that the poor and disfranchised will sit still and take it any longer?

Of course, poverty doesn't cause crime (or not directly and not always). Of course, we should punish violent extremists to the max. But let's not give them excuses, either, or help them find a willing pool of recruits who have nothing better to do.

Take Latin America. The region has the world's largest disparities between rich and poor—between highly educated and barely literate. Youth unemployment in big cities hovers above 20 percent. Rio de Janeiro is said to have the world's highest murder rate. On a recent trip to São Paulo to work with a large company, I was met by two security guards and helicoptered to the roof of downtown offices, where another large security contingent stuck by my side every minute. Affluent Latin Americans, like the well-to-do in Johannesburg, Paris, or Miami, can barricade themselves in gated communities only so long before the violence hits home. National borders are also not safe barricades. South Africa's high rate of violent crime is often attributed to Nigerians stealing into South Africa. The best fortification tends to be community development; Soweto and Kliptown are just across the highway from Sandton, the Beverly Hills of Johannesburg, but the youth of SKY, the community service program, are nonviolent and motivated to achieve.

A Palestinian-Israeli, born and raised an Arab in a poor village but who eventually attended college in the United States, gave me his conclusions after talking to a Hamas terrorist who later blew up thirty-eight Israelis and himself:

> The only way to battle extremism and terrorism (the major block to peace) is by creating a society with opportunities available to people on the ground. The simple person needs to have something to hold on to, needs hopes and aspirations, needs to taste a better life in order to aspire to building a better life. It is so easy to destroy peace—it only takes one hungry or angry man. I truly doubt that we will reach true peace without first tackling the most basic human needs of water, food, health, education, and simply job creation. The lowest rate of suicide bombings coming out of Gaza occurred during the

time when Israel opened the joint industrial zones where
it mostly employed Palestinians from Gaza.

If we don't care about helping the poor struggle out of
poverty because it's the right thing to do or in the long-term
interests of our nation, how about poverty reduction in the
name of safety?

For businesses, it is imperative to be seen as part of the solution, not part of the problem, or the backlash against free markets and trade will turn uglier. In 1995, when globalization
was trumpeted in headlines declaring, in effect, that "Capitalism Has Won," I warned my audience of business leaders at
the World Economic Forum to be careful. If they didn't pay
attention to social needs and help close the gap between top
and bottom, the headlines a decade later could read "Socialism
Returns." And it did.

Socialism is back in vogue in Latin America. Whatever one
thinks about Venezuelan president Hugo Chávez's outra-
geous political pronouncements, Chávez enjoys support from
poor *barrios* because he has expanded access to educational
and social services. Chávez called former Mexican President
Vincente Fox a "lapdog" of U.S. imperialism for backing
Washington's trade policies at the Summit of the Americas.
Perhaps Chávez's example reinforced Cuba's socialist stub-
bornness, as the Cuban government soon raided farmers' markets in what Reuters called an "anti-capitalist crackdown."

An exception to that trend is Álvaro Uribe Velez, former
mayor of Medellín and current president of Colombia. On
May 28, 2006, Uribe won a second four-year term in a land-
slide, achieving the first reelection of a sitting president in
over a century. The *Washington Post* called this a win for the

United States, too. Because Uribe restored safety by cracking down on paramilitary groups, with the help of aid from President Bush, he has sometimes been called "right-wing." But when I shared the platform with him in Cartagena on March 4 of that year, at a conference organized by a local university, I heard him express the views of a democrat (with a small "d") who saw that his country would not move beyond violence unless all citizens had increased economic opportunity. Naming him 2005's Leader of the Year, the *Latin Business Chronicle* cited his achievements in raising investor confidence in Colombia, rebuilding tourism to the country, and helping his nation jump seven places in the World Economic Forum's ranking of countries by their national competitiveness. The *Chronicle* attributed this in part to his "unique leadership style—combining hard work, a sharp mind, humor and humility—that has won praise from businesspeople and ordinary Colombians alike." He reached out to poor peasants and often appears in shirtsleeves instead of a suit. However, scandals involving Uribe's political allies continued to plague him, inhibiting progress.

Colombia is surrounded by socialist regimes and itself still faces a poverty rate of 54.9 percent. It still needs to find economic alternatives for farmers, to stop the drug trade, and to root out corruption in the form of ties between drug lords and politicians. As Uribe acknowledged in our dialogue, unless the great social divides are bridged in his country and the poor see a brighter economic future not just in national statistics but in their own lives, Colombia could go the way of its neighbors.

Political leaders can be helped by enlightened business leaders. Some large companies in the region are rising to the challenge of finding solutions to poverty. ABN AMRO Banco Real in Brazil is offering micro-finance to poor entrepreneurs in urban shantytowns. CEMEX in Mexico created an innovative program to finance housing materials in rural areas, bringing jobs as well as better housing to poor villages. These kinds of projects reflect exactly the kind of focus the United States should bring to foreign aid: programs that spread economic opportunity at the grass roots. Americans should urge more efforts like these, and potential citizen-diplomats should get involved in more of them. Believers in a free-market economy (and I'm among them) had better be prepared to do even more to help lift the poor out of misery. Otherwise, markets will not be free enough or our cities safe enough for any of us.

For all the talk of a flat world with a level playing field, the world still seems pretty lumpy to me. When those at the bottom of the hill get tired of being trampled, they can easily erupt. What holds them back in some places, such as Colombia, is confidence that leaders, such as Uribe, want to do the right thing for them.

### Protest Is Not Terrorism

As we ponder twenty-first-century forms of grass-roots engagement, one important distinction must be made. Those who complain about the conditions of their communities, as Brother Bob did in South Africa, those who lead demonstrations to bring attention to the plight of the disadvantaged, or those who behave in disruptive ways to express their disapproval or opposition to global capitalism, are dissenters whose voices deserve to be heard. They are concerned enough to make noise while hopeful enough to envision change, so under the rule of thirds, they fall into the middle third as candidates for befriending, like Brother Bob. They are not terrorists, who belong squarely in the camp of enemies to be isolated and punished. Yet sometimes events occur in such close juxtaposition that the distinction can appear to blur. Here is one example of an unfortunate conjunction of events in mid-2005.

Just as I was about to leave for a trip to Great Britain in July of 2005, the e-mail grapevine spread the horrifying news of four terrorist bombings in the London subway system. This disaster, called the worst in British history since World War II, brought heartbreaking deaths and injuries to both commercial and residential areas. "Be careful," friends whispered to me through cyberspace before I boarded the plane.

Echoing the World Trade Center tragedy of September 11, 2001, the targets of the July 7 attacks were emblems of globalization. London, a cosmopolitan capital of international finance, had just been named as the site for the 2012 Olympics. The G-8 Summit of leading industrialized nations, hosted by British Prime Minister Tony Blair, was meeting a few hundred miles north in Gleneagles, Scotland, to hammer out principles for dealing with global warming and African debt relief. Before British commuters went to work that morning, global institutions appeared to be on course toward long-term goals to improve the state of the planet. Then came the explosions.

A backlash against globalization had already emerged in Gleneagles and elsewhere in Scotland, in the form of hundreds of thousands of protesters using the G-8 meeting to press their causes. Antinuclear activists from the Campaign for Nuclear Disarmament demonstrated outside Clyde Naval

Base, trying to draw the link between "the industrial war machine" and poverty around the world. More than 225,000 protesters organized by "Make Poverty History" formed a human chain around Edinburgh in a demonstration CNN described as "festive."

Security personnel were out in full force, on the ground and in helicopters. In the small town of Gleneagles alone there were 10,000 police, because of reports that panicked locals were convinced their town would be the site of a terrorist attack. That's not what happened. Scotland attracted protesters, while London suffered from terrorists. Clearly, protesters should not be confused with terrorists. But the symbolism implied by the terrorists' timing in the London attacks was misleading and unfortunate. It falsely associated legitimate protest with the outrage of terrorism.

In the wake of a vicious terrorist assault, politicians can be tempted to repress civil liberties and ban demonstrations (which always annoy them) by citing the threat of terrorism. This temptation makes it even more important, in the aftermath of London and Gleneagles, to keep the difference between protest and terrorism firmly in mind:

• Protests affirm democracy. Terrorism is antithetical to it.

• Protesters have values, an agenda, and a belief that their actions can rally public support and sway leaders to make better decisions. Terrorists have none of the above—no values, no agenda, and no trust in leaders.

• Protesters are exercising their rights to speech and assembly and are living within the law. Terrorists are violating rights— the rights of others—and are ignoring the rule of law.

- Protesters are critics operating within the system, even as they challenge the mainstream and the establishment. Terrorists operate outside the system, and no one is safe.

- Protesters support some policies, reject others, and can distinguish issues (which arouse their concerns) from leaders (whom they might otherwise like). Terrorists see only extremes, and they can turn on their own.

- Protesters can be avoided. I could heed my friends' e-mail exhortations to take care by rerouting travel to bypass organized demonstrations. But who really knows when terrorists will strike or where they plotted? (Coincidentally, the terrorists involved in the London attacks plotted in Leeds, my destination.)

- Protesters sometimes should be invited to the table to discuss their cause. Terrorists should be isolated and frozen out. We can tolerate protesters (even if we feel we must hold our noses) as long as they obey the law. We should punish terrorists to the fullest extent permissible by law.

The distinction between protesters and terrorists is vitally important to the future of democracy. Longer security checks and more police are OK. A crackdown on critics is not OK. Let's remember to preserve the right to legitimate protest even as we react to the horror of terrorism. That's another lesson Brother Bob taught me on our walk through Kliptown a few years ago. Brother Bob at that time was radical and angry, but he was not destructive. And he reminded me that former South African President Nelson Mandela, now considered one of the great leaders of the twentieth century, was once branded a terrorist by the U.S. government—despite his democratic values and desire to gain freedom and opportunity for all communities in South Africa.

Cultivating a new crop of leaders with democratic values and a desire to open opportunity for the poor should be an American priority. That's the standard set by Nelson Mandela in South Africa, and that's the standard America should encourage other regions to meet. American engagement with the world, whether through government action or citizen-diplomacy, must aim to develop leaders dedicated to grass-roots development and empowerment.

### Cultivating Leadership: Where's the Mandela for the Middle East?

Yasser Arafat's death in 2004 temporarily renewed hopes for Middle East peace talks and a Palestinian state. Then Hamas won the elections, and the battles continued. Terrorist incidents became armed combat spilling across borders, such as Israeli retaliation again Hezbollah by bombing their bases in Lebanon. The Middle East was once the crucible of civilization, giving rise to three major religious traditions. Today it remains on fire, as the trouble spot most likely to put America in jeopardy. The Middle East needs a Nelson Mandela. So far, there are no contenders.

Mandela, South Africa's first democratically elected president, shows what is possible when a leader of character looks beyond his own group to embrace what will bring peace and prosperity to many groups. Mandela made an inspiring transition from revolutionary to statesman. His twenty-seven years in prison provided ample time to plot revenge against black

Africans' white oppressors. Yet he emerged in 1990 to unite a divided land—well before his election in 1994.

Mandela mastered challenges that echo in the Palestinian situation: fear-ridden enclaves of prosperity surrounded by resentful and impoverished native majorities, a history of suppression of communication and dissent, suspicion and violence across racial groups, and political schisms within groups. Mandela showed deep commitment to democratic dialogue, including a free press. "It was the press that never forgot us," he said upon his release from prison. As president, he declared, "I don't want a mouthpiece of the government. The press would be totally useless then. I want a mirror through which we can see ourselves."

Mandela encouraged voice along with votes. Public input helped frame a new constitution—unprecedented for any country in the last century, let alone one rebounding from racial separation and information restrictions. Newspaper ads in late 1994 proclaimed, "You've made your mark [having voted], now have your say." People could call talk lines, submit written statements, or speak at town hall meetings. Nearly 1.7 million submissions were received. Surveys showed that a majority from all walks of life felt involved; a quarter of adults discussed issues with friends or family.

He sought to stop violence, not to fuel it. In April 1993, a year before Mandela's election, a popular black leader, Chris Hani, was murdered outside his home near Johannesburg. A white woman reported the license number of the perpetrator's car. Police captured him, a Polish immigrant. The National Party, still officially in power, feared violent retaliation against all whites. Mandela televised a message that saved South Africa from chaos: "A white man full of prejudice and hate came to our country and committed a deed so foul that our whole nation now teeters on the brink of disaster. A white woman, of Afrikaner origin, risked her life so that we may bring to justice this assassin."

Mandela continually emphasized that "whites are fellow South Africans. We want them to feel safe and to know that we appreciate their contribution toward the development of this country." He delivered speeches in Afrikaans, the language of his oppressors. In 1995, he visited the ninety-four-year-old widow of former Prime Minister Hendrik Verwoerd, an architect of apartheid. Mandela patiently sipped tea while she urged racial separation. Such gestures to former enemies were based on his belief that people would "come right in the end." The remarkable hearings of the Truth and Reconciliation Commission, a national inquiry about the abuses of apartheid, were designed to foster "the need for understanding, not vengeance; the need for reparation, not retaliation; and the need for ubuntu [humanity], not victimization."

Mandela reversed white flight, inspiring talented expatriates to return. David Munro, a successful banker, was working in London in 1996 when Mandela spoke during a state visit to Britain. Munro heard Mandela envision a nation of opportunity and hope and express his wish to carry South Africans home in his pocket. Munro, like many, returned. So did foreign investment.

Could a Mandela emerge in the Middle East? Recently I led a discussion about Mandela's presidency with senior business and government officials from many Arab-Muslim countries across the Middle East. I began by asking if anyone could improve on Mandela's leadership. When I posed a similar question to my Harvard M.B.A. students, who usually can second-guess a saint, they fell silent; they had no improvements to suggest. Not the Middle Easterners. The all-Muslim group faulted Mandela for being too lenient to his former enemies and too trusting of the people, allowing too much participation.

Oops. If that's a reflection of the values of more people than my small sample of executives and government officials, no wonder the Middle East remains conflict-ridden and resistant to change.

Unless Palestinian leaders embrace Mandela's premise that democracy and progress require healing the wounds of the past, there will be no improvement in the situation—because peace must precede prosperity in the region. And the key to peace lies not in the formal trappings of democracy but in the soul of leadership.

Developing that leadership soul for trouble spots around the world is an activity in which Americans can participate. We can support the work of institutions that educate a new breed of cosmopolitan leaders. We can mobilize citizen-diplomats to become educators. That's what my friend Akin Ongor is trying to do, and he wants to do it in a country that itself spans several clashing civilizations.

## Bridging, Not Clashing, Civilizations

In the beautiful Aegean port of Bodrum, Turkey, on a high piece of land with a stunning view across the wine-dark sea from Turkish cliffs to the Greek islands, Akin Ongor envisions establishing an international institute for emerging leaders of the Eastern Mediterranean. For Americans, "Eastern Mediterranean" encompasses a sweeping strategic swath from the Balkans to the Persian Gulf and from Bosnia to Baghdad to

Bethlehem—sites of our post–Cold War wars and conflagrations. Still, as I stood there with Ongor talking about the role
American professors could play in his vision, I could feel the
potential for healing.

This region's path to peace and prosperity is cluttered with
ongoing obstacles. But Ongor, a former Turkish national bas-
ketball star whose leadership skills were honed at General Electric, is not afraid of challenges. As CEO of Garanti Bank from
1991 to 2000, he built it into "the best small bank in the
world" (*Euromoney* magazine) and one of Europe's "50 most
respected companies" (*Financial Times*) by emphasizing technology, teamwork, and talent development. Ongor's leadership during Turkish monetary crises generated offers for him to
become his country's Alan Greenspan after leaving the bank.
He preferred to pursue his dream of training the next generation of leaders to build bridges between Islam and the West,
and doing it in a strategically positioned country.

A secular republic with a population that is 99 percent
Muslim, Turkey borders Iraq, Iran, Syria, Georgia, Armenia,
Bulgaria, and Greece. In 1492, the Turks of the Ottoman
Empire welcomed tens of thousands of Sephardic Jews ex-
pelled from Spain by Ferdinand and Isabella, a population
that prospered in Turkey. Turkey has long been a friend to Israel, although disagreeing about the treatment of Palestinians.
Israeli diplomacy helped overcome the rift between Turkey
and the United States over the war in Iraq, when the Turkish
parliament refused entry of troops through Turkey for a war
opposed by the Turkish population.

On October 3, 2005, negotiations began for Turkey's bid
to join the European Union (EU) in 2015. Secretary of State
Condoleezza Rice expressed strong support for Turkey's EU

membership, which the BBC's William Horsley called an "epoch-making change, a merger of Christian Europe with the major Muslim power on its doorstep."

Before Germany's election of a new chancellor, Turkey's largest trading partner was expected to oppose Turkish membership. Some analysts argued that French and Dutch voters recently rejected the EU constitution because of Turkey's bid, fearing the loss of jobs to lower-paid workers and the costs of helping a poor country. But Wolfgang Ischinger, German ambassador to the United States, gave me a more encouraging response at an informal gathering: He mentioned that East Germany was absorbed successfully, so he believed that attitudes toward Turkey would also change eventually.

Europe demands much of Turkey. First, democratic reforms that have already been put into practice under Prime Minister Recep Tayyip Erdogan must accelerate, with extra proof of protection of human rights. Next, Turkey must recognize Cyprus (a possible deal-breaker because Turkey is the only nation supporting a Turkish Republic of Northern Cyprus). Finally, limitations will be imposed on Turks' rights to live and work in other EU nations.

Negotiations started at a delicate moment. Tension has been growing in the souls of many Turks between the Westernized world and Islamic fundamentalism, as depicted in *Snow,* Nobel Prize–winner Orhan Pamuk's widely acclaimed novel. The image of snow symbolizes the religious veil (secular Turkey opposes head scarves in schools while fundamentalists use head-scarf-wearing girls as political weapons) and also a periodic barrier isolating Turkey from Europe. In his book, Pamuk indicates that many Turks flirt with the West but feel degraded. "Most of the time it's not the Europeans who belittle us. What happens when we look at them is that we be-little ourselves," a character says.

It is in America's interest that Turks feel valued and em-braced by Europe, especially if Turkey then encourages the development of cosmopolitan leaders able to build bridges be-tween warring factions within and across Muslim nations. The prospect of peace is why Turkey's president and prime minis-ter endorsed Ongor's vision of a leadership institute for the whole region. But Ongor wanted their endorsement, not their participation. In the best tradition of citizen-diplomacy, he felt that the involvement of any government, from any of the countries from which he hoped to recruit, would interfere with the ability of people to form social networks unencum-bered by politics. His mission was citizen diplomacy, and he wanted Americans to play the role of educators.

An institute on a beautiful piece of land, even one over inter-national waters, cannot by itself heal centuries of conflict. But if we keep Turkey on our mental maps, cheer on its European as-pirations, and applaud its private-sector leaders such as Ongor who offer visions for change, then there is hope for ending ter-rorism and finding peace. Efforts similar to Ongor's vision for an institute in Bodrum to develop emerging leaders are worthy causes for American citizen-diplomats to support, ones that offer the opportunity to improve the state of the world.

Grass-roots engagement to address the social needs of poor communities, develop leaders, and build networks of relation-ships transcending national borders and government activities is one aspect of dealing with the middle group in the rule of thirds. A related issue is how to find opportunities through networks and private-sector involvement with emerging eco-nomic superpowers China and India. How can Americans deal positively with the countries that appear to be taking American jobs? How can connections be made in ways that build opportunities? Those questions took me first to China, and then to India.

## Connecting with Consumer China

From my ultramodern room on the seventy-seventh floor of the Grand Hyatt Pudong in Shanghai ("the world's highest hotel"), only the won-ton soup for breakfast told me that I was in China. The spiky metal-and-glass towers on the skyscape go beyond the twenty-first century; they resemble *Star Trek*'s rendering of planetary capitals of the twenty-third century.

I came in search of the many thousands of U.S. jobs recently lost to offshoring. After prowling Shanghai streets, visiting a premier industrial park, going backstage at a retail chain, and dialoguing with participants at Harvard Business School's Global Leadership Forum, I found those lost jobs—but I can't bring them home. They've been snared by what I term Producer China. Producer China brings benefits to Americans in the form of lower prices and efficiencies for American manufacturers, but that's little consolation to the people who see high-wage manufacturing jobs disappearing and their remaining prospects stemming from selling those cheaper goods as retail clerks. So we must look elsewhere for opportunities. The hope for American domestic jobs lies in a different side of China—in Consumer China.

American companies are making goods for world markets in Producer China—and profiting. That terrifies traditional American workers. China's manufacturing taps an abundant pool of rural youth putting in their six years at low-paid factory jobs before marriage or buying a farm—a labor situation resembling that of nineteenth-century New England mill workers. Docile workers, well-educated engineers, and advanced technology give Chinese manufacturing a growing advantage in both cost and quality.

When I was first invited to tour the Suzhou Industrial Park, I imagined a small suburban development with a circular drive containing a handful of buildings—not the new city for millions that China means by that term. Even before it was completed, many dozens of multinational corporations located facilities in the one-hundred-square-mile Suzhou Industrial Park, an attractive new city complete with a man-made lake, high-end housing, and a five-star resort developed jointly by the Chinese and Singaporean governments, one of many world-class economic zones in China.

Producer China might be too far ahead to catch (although my recent interviews with employees of IT companies in China leave me still unconvinced of that, except that Chinese companies are learning quickly). But it is clear that the emerging opportunity is Consumer China. Though only about 10 percent of China's population is middle class, that growing segment represents 130 million eager consumers—equivalent to the United States halved. For Consumer China, grass-roots citizen diplomacy is embedded in business outreach and business brands.

Shanghai's 17 million residents love shopping. On Nanjing Lu, a wide avenue turned pedestrian mall, shops feature bands playing American rock music. Despite a legacy of puritanical communism (hotel brochures forbid "solicitous" material—i.e., pornography), one finds every consumer excess, including a bar with a women's night so that, ads proclaim, "women can prove they can drink men under the table."

China has more people under the age of twenty-four than the entire U.S. population. The young, lacking memories of Mao jackets, want fashion and beauty, sometimes to an extreme. During one of my trips, I read in the *Beijing Morning Post* of a woman from Jilin Province in northeast China who has undergone fourteen body-perfecting plastic surgeries, including breast enlargement, thigh reduction, and height enhancement. Models pictured in apparel promotions are invariably Western. Except in high fashion, dominated by European brands, U.S. products are sophisticated status symbols. In Suzhou's old city, a few miles from the Industrial Park, bicycle rickshaws carry McDonald's ads.

While the United States had a $213 billion trade deficit with China by the end of November 2006, American food processor Cargill ran a trade surplus, sending soybeans and orange juice to China from the United States. Executives credited the superiority of American agriculture in scale and in its use of technology, a head start that China cannot match.

Chinese consumers are growing users of information and communication services, which are American strengths. China was second to the United States in Internet users (at 132 million, or 10 percent penetration, as of the end of 2006), but it should surpass the United States by 2007 or 2008. On any given day, nine of the world's twenty-five busiest websites are situated in China. Yahoo! and eBay are coming on strong in competition with locally entrenched portals. Even before establishing China-based offices, Google attracted 40 percent of China's search users, although it has since dropped to 33 percent in 2006, and Baidu, a local company, was much more successful than U.S. transplants.

Content exports to China include American football. In the

fall of 2003, the National Football League (NFL) signed a deal with China's CCTV, reaching 300 million households, many of them Super Bowl watchers. NFL China Flag Football is introducing tens of millions of schoolchildren to the game. Is American football an example of citizen diplomacy?

China's industrial growth brings a demand for business services in which American firms predominate, including management consulting, marketing, investment banking, and venture capitalism. Then there's our unmatched higher education. A book by the mother of a youth admitted to Harvard College (entitled *Harvard Girl* in English) sold 1.5 million copies and brought a flood of inquiries about college in the United States, according to former Harvard Faculty of Arts and Sciences dean William Kirby, clearly a citizen-diplomat in his role as a China expert making Harvard University attractive to the Chinese.

American strengths lie in creativity, flexibility, and diversity—the attributes that bring the innovation I tout in Chapter 1. America's ethnic diversity helps us invent things for our own market that easily go global—even reaching China. American ingenuity can create new jobs, in which what we manufacture is not hard goods but great ideas.

The Chinese character for change combines both threat and opportunity. If we focus only on the threat, we could miss the opportunity. That truth also holds for India. And India offers the further promise of valuable alliances struck inside the United States.

## India: The Power of American Connections

In Mumbai, the City-Formerly-Known-as-Bombay, the fastest computer networks coexist with the slowest traffic jams. The sound heard everywhere is the beep. Drivers leaning on automobile horns honk their way through streets packed with bicycles, buses, mini-cars the size of a phone booth, urchins pressing their noses against car windows, and an occasional cow.

However slowly, India is on the move and making noise. Americans who once viewed India as a land of ashrams and incense need to see India's reincarnation as a global business player, where the "gurus" are of the management type.

Contradictions abound. India has a booming economy with more than a billion people, but 400 million still live in poverty. India's BPO ("business process outsourcing") industry is flourishing, fueled by educated high-tech talent; yet, in villages without electricity, computers must be powered by hand-cranks or bicycle generators. India reveres elders but has the world's youngest population, with 65 percent below age thirty-five. Women executives prefer saris to Western-style business suits.

Though culturally exotic, India should feel familiar to Americans. The world's two largest democracies share a language and experience with British institutions. The business leaders I met are savvy about American enterprise and eager to apply American techniques. Their knowledge of us is not reciprocated. Americans' attention in recent years has focused on two of India's neighbors: Pakistan (making political news because of Afghanistan) and China (making economic news). We know relatively less about India—except that our credit-card bills might be processed there and our telephone information calls might be answered there and that India refused to send troops to Iraq. But India has enormous potential as a U.S. partner, and Indian companies are even creating jobs for Americans.

By 2030, India's population will overtake that of China, five years earlier than previously forecast. According to Tarun Khanna, a Harvard colleague specializing in emerging markets, India could even outpace China's economic growth because of its homegrown entrepreneurs, greater transparency, and relative lack of government interference.

India values property rights, enjoys active private-sector competition in media and banking, has long had first-rate business schools producing professional managers, and features an educated population with high savings rates. Those stabilizing factors should make India an attractive place for American investment. "India is the place to be," Funds World India has proclaimed as it promotes international investment into the burgeoning Indian funds market. "While funds growth has reached a maturity level in the developed markets of Asia such as Hong Kong, Singapore and Japan, India offers financial institutions an enticing mix of strong economic fundamentals, a strong and stable political system and a market that is largely untapped," its website argued.

Sophisticated Indian companies are on the move. Tata, a conglomerate that grew as the local partner for such global giants as IBM and Mercedes-Benz, now earns over 22 percent of its sales outside India. An industrial pioneer that built India's first steel mills and hydropower stations and has been involved in information technology since 1968, Tata now aims to compete on a world stage. Tata Motors already exports cars to Europe. Tata has the potential to be the next Hyundai or Honda.

The American global giant IBM is now India's largest information technology company, with over 45,000 employees in India, a feat of growth attributed to India's recent market liberalization. BPO companies, such as Wipro and Infosys, are growing so quickly that they are exhausting the talent to be found in India and are hiring Americans based in America. That is, American companies are sending work over the Internet to be performed in India. That work is being sent to the United States to be performed by Americans. Indian firms then bill their U.S. clients. Can you follow that global chain?

Increasingly, the noise from India is inside the United States. In Washington, the Indian American Center for Political Awareness has spent ten years giving Indian Americans a political voice. In April 2005, the Confederation of Indian Industry sent leaders to major U.S. cities for a ten-day blitz. In Seattle, India's science and technology minister met with 200 Indian employees of Microsoft. In New York, officials launched the Indian American Council to connect Indian Americans to opportunities in India.

Indian Americans are impressive: about 2 million U.S. citizens or permanent residents, 62 percent with some college (compared to 20 percent of the general population) and 35 percent holding graduate or professional degrees. Their median income is the highest among ethnic groups (over $71,000, compared with a national average of about $40,000). Nearly 200,000 Indian Americans are millionaires.

Chinese Premier Wen Jiabao recently suggested that India and China join hands to lead the world's IT industry. That would hurt U.S. interests. Americans should be the ones partnering with India. The Indian economy is hotter than its curries, so let's educate ourselves about India as a market and investment opportunity—and educate our children to such high standards that we keep American jobs in America.

In an ideal world, entrepreneurs and investors would be the leading edge of foreign relations, not military troops or even foreign aid workers. Those investors would understand the principles of the best alliances and partnerships: that all parties must benefit and that they must grow in order for us to grow.

## Toward Broader Diplomacy: Acting on the Principles

Baseball player Yogi Berra's twisted-but-true saying that "the future isn't what it used to be" is especially appropriate in the complex international arena. As is the usual case in a world of flux, most predictions that were made twenty years ago have been proven wrong. For example, it was thought back then that the number of sovereign nations would shrink, as Europe moved toward unity and regions discovered common interests. Today, after the breakup of the Soviet Union and splintering in the Balkans, there are more independent nations than in previous decades, and separatist movements continue to surface. The Cold War was replaced by hot battles in Iraq and throughout the Middle East, with religion invoked as often as politics or economics to explain them. And though the United States remains the last political superpower and strongest economy on the planet, American-style free market capitalism faces a backlash in our hemispheric backyard of Latin America, and U.S. jobs are threatened, some think, by the rise of China and India, as I have indicated.

These kinds of complexities form the context for the tour I've taken in this chapter. The world is too big, and events are moving too quickly even as I write, to extract a single set of foreign policy prescriptions. But in any event, my goal is not to set foreign policy directions for Washington officials. I have explored another opportunity for ensuring a bright American future—involving support for dense networks of positive ties through citizen and business connections that can form a collaborative nongovernmental infrastructure to deal with the rule of thirds: more friends, fewer and more-isolated enemies, and fence-sitters jumping over to our side. Each Oprah Winfrey Leadership School for Girls, each set of American friends of Brother Bob, each Indian American business association, and each potential leadership institute for the Eastern Mediterranean with the support of American educators increases the opportunity for America to continue to be strong and respected. Citizen diplomacy can help encourage a more positive stance toward Americans, while at the same time the multiple ties that Americans and American businesses build with other countries augment official actions by government.

There are signs that business leaders are beginning to embrace citizen diplomacy. In May 2006, a group of communications and marketing executives, headed by the retired chair of advertising giant DDB Worldwide, created Business for Diplomatic Action. Its mission is to mobilize American multinational companies to address perceptions of America, arguing that a growing trend of anti-Americanism, unchecked, can threaten future economic competitiveness as well as national security by eroding our ability to engender trust and recruit talent. Reaching out to business leaders in strategic world markets, members of the group say, can build new bridges of mutual respect and understanding.

There is one other vehicle for grass-roots change and citizen involvement: the Internet. Advanced technology and Web-savvy citizenry now make it possible for open source information gathering to rival, if not surpass, the clandestine intelligence produced by government agencies. While motivated citizens and academics have often been able to generate analysis that rivals that of government experts, the difference today is that technology such as wikis and blogs allows thousands to contribute to an analysis. Diffusion of the Internet itself has the potential to change politics at the grass roots; research on Internet café use in Jordan and Egypt showed that users became more open-minded, better informed, and more likely to talk with people outside their usual social networks, including Americans.

The business of America at home is the creation of opportunity, and that should be the business of America abroad. Economic opportunity brings hope to those at the bottom. Trade that results from the growth of enterprises enhances cross-border encounters and personal relationships. Trade doesn't necessarily prevent conflict, but it should give more people a larger stake in a peaceful world and enlarge the pie. The preponderance of the evidence is that trade increases communications and promotes peace among nations. But there are some caveats here. Scholars are divided about whether trade always reduces conflict; some argue that it generates conflict even as it is intended to facilitate conflict avoidance. And some people in some cultures don't want the pie of modernization enlarged if it means "Westernization" to them. Still, I think that a combination of trade-spawned business networks and grass-roots citizen diplomacy is our best hope. The alternatives—doing nothing or crossing swords—are unpalatable. They could make us less, not more, secure.

Let me end by repeating the principle that pervades this chapter: If we befriend and empower moderates by developing their leaders and investing in their economic futures, we are more likely to isolate and undercut extremists, increasing the likelihood that those on the fence jump to join us as allies rather than fleeing to our enemies. Whatever short-term issues the American government must resolve, the American people can insist that our relationships with the world are principled—that we offer hope and opportunity to those at the bottom, support the development of more cosmopolitan and inclusive leaders, and strengthen the networks of business and personal ties across our borders.

# SIX

# Building Community

## Service and the Spirit of Summer

On a sunny October day a few years ago during the period New England calls "Indian Summer," the colors were particularly vivid on Boston Common. The foliage was at its peak, and the varied hues of the hundreds of young people from every imaginable ethnic and racial group formed a sparkling rainbow of people. They were wearing bright red jackets to signify that they were corps members of City Year, an urban variant of the Peace Corps. They handed out T-shirts and maps to the army of thousands who had just warmed up with exuberant calisthenics on the Common and were now ready to march into service in over a dozen Boston neighborhoods. The City Year corps members were organizing teams consisting of families with young children, college students, school groups from suburbia and exurbia, proud relatives of corps members, and energetic citizens attracted by the idea of community service.

City Year, which mobilizes participants from the ages of

seventeen to twenty-four for a year of full-time community service, was started in Boston in 1988 by two then-recent Harvard Law School graduates, Alan Khazei and Michael Brown, who wanted to demonstrate what national service could mean for America. City Year received encouragement from the first President Bush, and it expanded dramatically when it became the model for President Clinton's AmeriCorps national service program. By 2007, City Year operated in sixteen U.S. metropolitan areas and Johannesburg, South Africa. I joined the national (now international) board in 1994.

Similar scenes were familiar in other City Year sites—a diverse geographic array including Seattle, San Antonio, Chicago, Philadelphia, and Columbia (South Carolina), among others. One year I served in Columbus, Ohio, among dozens of volunteers and corps members building a playground for an inner-city school; my brigade included a big-deal CEO and a high school dropout who had earned his GED during his time with City Year. He was thinking about college and wanted advice from a Harvard professor while we sawed and hammered.

That Indian Summer morning in Boston, as the crowd on the Common dispersed, my group drove to a neglected city park to join my friend Mike Boston, a City Year technology staff member, who was one of the day's service leaders and would organize the clearing of brush and debris. Mike had graduated out of the City Year youth corps as one of its stars, serving as a patient and warm mentor to younger children. Like other corps members, he often told his story in public as a testimonial to how City Year had saved his life, and he was happy to tell it again to the volunteer landscapers.

Mike, a tall African American with his hair in neat cornrows, had joined the corps after serving a short prison sentence for gun violence, which was common in the neighborhood in which he grew up, where "gang-banging" was the norm. A number of people advised him to apply to City Year when he left prison; to his surprise (because only about one in four people make the corps), he was accepted. He was assigned to a diverse team that included white female college graduates from the suburbs, Asian Americans, and urban youth who had interrupted a year of college in order to serve. They worked in a primary school in a run-down neighborhood whose principal was determined to move it from worst to desirable. They tutored children, organized after-school programs, assisted teachers, and helped parents make it to school for conferences. This work freed teachers to focus on the classroom, connected parents to the school, kept children off the streets at a vulnerable time, and gave the students a set of inspiring role models to whom they could relate more easily than to their teachers. (City Year now calls this approach "whole child/whole school," seeing its role as surrounding the core teaching functions with a community support system.)

During his national service year, Mike Boston bonded with the children in his care and felt he could never let them down by returning to street ways. He wanted to stay with City Year for an additional year and hoped to increase his computer skills, so he was given a job in the technology group. He was then in his mid-twenties.

A City Year leader had first brought us together. I wanted to learn something about rap and hip-hop and wondered if someone could help, figuring that an urban youth corps was the right place to ask. The City Year leader directed me to Mike, who aspired to create and produce music. After telling me that I had no feel for the rhythms, he proceeded to teach me as patiently as he had tutored fourth-graders in math. Soon we were connecting on physical service days, clearing parkland or painting classrooms. Eventually my husband and I included him in parties, met his fiancée, and cooed over their newborn daughter.

The day we spruced up the park, a great deal of visible work was accomplished—and so was some invisible work. Thousands of people touched one another across wide social and economic divides, including partisan ones. Though later called "President Clinton's favorite social program," City Year was supported by prominent Republicans, including the second President Bush and Mitt Romney, who joined the national board when I did, serving until he went to Salt Lake City to rescue the Olympics; he was later elected governor of Massachusetts and joined the Republican presidential hopefuls for 2008.

When Mike Boston stood shoulder to shoulder with shovel-wielding, clipper-grasping, hoe-handling volunteers of every color, he was not just helping to build a park. He was helping to build a community.

## Social Capital or Social Isolation?

Civil society, the realm of voluntary action by people with shared interests, produces everything from nonprofit organizations and advocacy movements to book clubs and neighborhood potlucks. Long an American specialty, it is a source of both social connections and social solutions. It fills gaps where business and government don't quite meet every need—just as City Year's "whole child/whole school" helps with the extras that teachers are not paid to do.

Leadership from civil society is especially vital today, when many Americans feel they cannot count on government officials or establishment figures to fix the mess in the world—indeed, as we have seen, flawed leaders are sometimes part of the problem. Complaining doesn't help. The partisan divide in politics has been at its widest, meaning ugliest, in living memory. Recent elections have unleashed enough anger, complaint, and criticism to spread the raw sewage to states not hit by floods or hurricanes. But acrimony produces nothing except a collective bad mood.

The national mood has already been dampened by an eroding sense of community. In recent years, the evidence has mounted about the loss of traditional "social capital" in America—that dense network of relationships that connect people to opportunities, information grapevines, and shared purpose. In twenty years, between 1985 and 2004, the number of people who have no one to talk to doubled, and the number of confidants of the average American declined from three to two, a national survey showed. "If you're feeling isolated, you're not alone," syndicated columnist Ellen Goodman proclaimed.

Electronic screens—not face-to-face—are increasingly the way people interact. Blogs are the new soapboxes and chat rooms and instant messaging the new street-corner hangouts. They enable free-flowing, liberating expression—and less engagement with real people. We know the wonders of the Internet for business: working remotely (which can be good for working parents), sharing documents with colleagues elsewhere and editing them in real time, arranging trips, checking-in for flights, finding data fast, buying books, getting maps, and so on. . . . Pick your favorite, and I'll continue to tap

Google, numerous websites, and my network of remote research assistants as I word-process this chapter.

But on-screen interactions can sometimes move from useful tools to dangerous obsessions that undermine relationship skills, let alone a larger sense of community. How much are children engaging with the real world? Half of all preschoolers between the ages of four and six have played video games—and a quarter play regularly. Is screen life more compelling than real toys? These days, young children request cellphones and electronic gadgets for birthday and holiday gifts instead of trucks or dolls. Yale psychologist Jerome Singer complained that "plopping kids in front of a TV or computer cuts away a whole aspect of development" that requires interaction with the physical, not the virtual. For adults, virtual intimacy, especially when spelled S-E-X, jeopardizes relationships. According to ProtectKids.com, there are more than 1.3 million porn websites. Sex is the number one topic of Internet searches, and 40 percent of all website visits involve sex—if true, an alarming statistic. Virtual adultery often turns into actual cheating. One survey found that a sixth of all those logging on to the Web were doing so to find sexual partners; two-thirds of them successfully initiated contact, a higher rate than offline. Clinical psychologist Michael G. Conner (www.crisiscounseling.com) argued that those seeking sex online risk low productivity, marital problems, and depression. And, of course, screen-fixated couch potatoes contribute to the national obesity epidemic.

We need to get up, get out, and get connected. Rebuilding community—the kind with a face-to-face component—will not only reduce social isolation and improve the national mood, it will get more people engaged in solving problems. A virtuous chain reaction will open more opportunities for more people, guided by a greater sense of common purpose.

This chapter points in some positive directions. After offering a parable about what lies behind partisan divides, I argue that democracy in America can proceed from the grass roots up—and the self-organizing potential of the Internet can even help us. Philanthropy and community service can bring us together, under leaders who inspire and engage us. We can find new sources of leadership among a generation of young social entrepreneurs and the older generation of baby boomers who refuse to "retire"—they want to stay active and make a difference in the world. We can build on the current national service movement to enhance dramatically the infrastructure for service, which includes companies engaging employees in service, service learning in schools, new educational opportunities for people in later life, and full-time national service for young adults. If we do this, we can regain a spirit of hope that will make it feel like summer in America year-round.

### Country Mouse/City Mouse:
### A Fable About What Divides Us

After the 2004 elections, red-state/blue-state distinctions entered the national vocabulary. But before *Electoral Color Coding for Dummies* becomes our permanent playbook, I propose another way of understanding current divides in America—this one based on Aesop's classic fable "The Country Mouse and the City Mouse."

The story is simple. City Mouse visits Country Mouse and feels sorry for his rural friend's humble existence, where the only fare is plain barley and grain. So he invites Country

Mouse to experience the richness and variety of the city. Country Mouse is instantly enthralled by urban life. But no sooner than the two mice start nibbling happily on brown sugar and other cosmopolitan delights, numerous dreadful dangers arise to terrorize them, in the form of humans, cats, and mousetraps. Country Mouse quickly decides to return home. Forsaking the excitement of the city for his simpler country existence, he declares that he would rather eat barley in peace and comfort than have brown sugar and be frightened to death all the time.

The fable suggests that the countryside offers a life of greater purity. It certainly provides isolation from enemies who are "different." Country Mouse does not want to deal with complex problems or live in fear of encountering strangers. City Mouse, in contrast, chooses the delicious pleasures and tempting possibilities of city life despite the menacing creatures and deadly traps lurking around every corner.

No wonder Country Mouse voters picked Republicans for morality and national security in 2004, while City Mouse identifiers preferred the Democrats' more urban-oriented agenda, involving domestic investments in school reform and help for working families. Republicans have become the Country Mouse party, while Democrats are associated with City Mouse problems, such as opportunities for minorities and affordable housing. When the U.S. map is colored red or blue by counties rather than by states, the Country Mouse/City Mouse divide is easily spotted. In November 2004, urban counties in major metropolitan areas tended to vote Democrat and rural and exurban counties tended to vote Republican. For example, New Hampshire, once Country Mouse red, is increasingly urbanized and attracting migrants who bring City Mouse values; urban influences in southern counties turned the state blue in that election.

This divide has resonated throughout American history. The ideal of the countryside as a place for attaining moral perfectibility shaped American ideology from the beginning of European colonization. Early settlers included religious groups establishing congregations in homogeneous communities. Throughout the nineteenth century, religious sects came to the American countryside to create their version of Utopia, forming closed communities that lasted decades as one-group towns. After World War II and as soon as they could afford it, families escaped from cities to new suburbs infused with pastoral images. Pretending that urban problems would not reach their children, suburban parents shaped the quintessential baby boom experience. It might have been a suburban legend, but it entered the American experience as an ideal, supported by a booming auto industry, cheap gas, and, soon, the interstate highway network. More recently, Utopian impulses have flowered in small towns that have become openly Christian enclaves in Colorado, Minnesota, and elsewhere, with church and state indistinguishable in the parish hall or city hall.

Cities, on the other hand, are complex and contradictory, cosmopolitan and diverse. As transportation centers, they connect people to the rest of the world, making it hard to retreat into isolationism. Cities are rich in cultural attractions, entertainments, amusements, and diversity of choices and people. Ideas clash in many languages. People of varying religious persuasions or ethnic customs live side by side, constantly aware that there are other competing claims to know the one right way. Cities are dangerous to orthodoxies, if not physically dangerous.

Major social problems are also more visible in cities: unemployment, violent crime, traffic congestion, air pollution, low-performing schools, lack of affordable housing and affordable health insurance, issues concerning gay rights, illegal immigration, and illegal substances. Those who live in and around cities want solutions urgently; they support social innovations. They are likely voters for City Mouse agendas.

Never mind that many social problems are common in rural areas—teenage pregnancy, illiteracy, youth unemployment, and drugs. In Country Mouse habitats such as gated suburban developments, these problems can be ignored as someone else's failing. In cities, it is hard to wish away such problems because they are so visible. Big-city mayors, regardless of their political party, tend to work on these problems rather than toeing a party line about taxes.

Country Mouse/City Mouse tensions are ancient, but more straightforward to resolve than the artificial color war between the states. Elections force us to take sides, but there are other ways that democratic institutions can bring us together across habitats to find common ground. Let's start with an ethic of philanthropy and service, because those honorable American traditions that stem from the grass roots have the potential to arouse generosity of spirit across partisan divides.

## Big Citizens: How Democracy Trickles Up

In the fall, in most of America, hurricane season and Halloween are followed by election day (which some find the scariest of all). Campaign rhetoric in election seasons makes elected officials, and especially the president, seem responsible for the personal happiness of each and every American. Certainly The Big Guy in Washington looms large, especially on national security. But the national mood is shaped by all citizens. Both country and city mice have chewed holes in the social fabric, and those holes need to be repaired community by community.

Elections, like sports, produce winners and losers. But unlike sports, the real game gets started only after the contest. That's when passionate partisans should take off their party hats to collaborate with the opposing team. For starters, winners should try not to gloat. For them, the hard work is really just beginning. They are responsible for solutions to the problems of job creation, health care, quality of public education, affordable housing—you name it. That demands creative thinking instead of knee-jerk ideology. Constructive change requires patience to work through differences and gather broad support. Winners must remember that we Americans are all in this together. At the same time, losers should get over it. They must resist the temptation to sulk, whine, or remain angry, and they must get back in the game. The issues that motivated the losing side to support their candidates should motivate them to do something about those challenges, especially when the candidate can't do it for them.

In declaring the end of big government, President Clinton called for the rise of Big Citizens. We need not focus on the State House or the White House to put our own house in order in every community. Even without joining the Peace Corps or today's domestic equivalent, AmeriCorps, we can heed John F. Kennedy's inaugural plea: "Ask not what your country can do for you; ask what you can do for your country."

There are countless ways to make a difference, neighborhood by neighborhood. That important work shapes American life regardless of who is the president.

In 1831, French aristocrat Alexis de Tocqueville toured the young American nation seeking the essence of democracy. He found its meaning neither in the design of the federal government nor in our voting procedures but in grass-roots activism. In his book *Democracy in America,* he expressed amazement at our penchant to form voluntary associations:

> Americans of all ages, all stations of life, and all types of disposition are forever forming associations. . . . In democratic countries knowledge of how to combine is the mother of all other forms of knowledge; on its progress depends that of all the others. In towns it is impossible to prevent [people] from assembling, getting excited together and forming sudden passionate resolves.

Tocqueville found America riddled with contradictions— contradictions that remain with us today. He viewed Americans as being simultaneously religious and materialistic; individualistic yet deeply involved in community affairs; isolationist and interventionist; and pragmatic and ideological. I wish we could add another item to his list: being partisan until election day and cooperative afterward.

In our spiritual-while-secular society, it's appropriate to invoke late theologian Reinhold Niebuhr's nondenominational prayer. "Grant me the serenity to accept the things I cannot change, the courage to change the things that can be changed, and the wisdom to know the difference." We cannot change the results of elections. But we do not have to wait for elections to change America ourselves. Let's start with philanthropy, to create communities of the generous.

## Generosity Can Unite Us

Warren Buffet set a new standard for philanthropy when he (finally) decided to give away much of his $40 billion fortune to the Bill and Melinda Gates Foundation before he died, affirming what others (such as George Soros of Open Society Foundation fame) know: Philanthropy is for the living, to express values and fill gaps. It cemented a partnership between Buffett's and Gates's partnership. Can philanthropy also bring communities together?

Total annual giving in the United States is a relatively constant $250 billion, though it rose from $245 billion in 2004 to $260 billion in 2005 due to increased disaster relief giving after the Asian tsunami and Hurricane Katrina. Roughly three-quarters of the annual total comes from individuals, not corporations or foundations. And half of all annual giving by individuals occurs in the weeks between Thanksgiving and Christmas—which is not surprising, since philanthropic donations appear high on lists of year-end tax-saving tips. Is charity just a chance for a tax deduction, or can we make it something more?

Individual philanthropy has become a mass market fueled by direct marketing campaigns and payment options (installment plans, credit cards) resembling arm's-length commercial transactions. Giving on the Internet makes checkbook philanthropy even easier. This impersonal character creates opportunities for occasional abuses. My current candidate for least-necessary trust violation is the phony newspaper profile of a nonexistent ten-year-old boy created by Texas state social workers to solicit donations for a charity serving foster children in a town outside Houston. The boy's story of separation from his mother while he lived in a posthurricane emergency shelter was heart-tugging. It was also fictitious, as a newspaper reporter discovered when he could not locate the boy for an interview. Fortunately, cynicism about a few scandals does not spread to all charities. But there has been a rising chorus of complaints from donors about the commercialization of philanthropy. Disgruntled donors resent slick or aggressive fundraising techniques, intrusive telemarketing, and duplicate appeals.

Between tax planning and direct marketing, what remains of the original meaning of philanthropy as love of the human community? Philanthropy should unite us as a community of the generous—a grand fraternity or sorority whose special handshake is a helping hand. But giving is too often done in isolation. When all we do is insert checks into envelopes or click through a website, we don't get to meet our fellow members—donors, organizers, and recipients alike.

Small donors deserve naming rights like big contributors, instead of seeing their money disappear into undifferentiated pools or their names in small print on throwaway dinner-program booklets. Nonprofits should do for the living what Washington's Vietnam Memorial does for the dead: Etch every name in a visible place. In the Cape Cod town of Sandwich, Massachusetts, community members sponsored boards on a new boardwalk over wetlands and marshes, proclaiming their love for specific people while becoming known to one another. The Miami Children's Museum invited donors to put messages on artist-designed ceramic tiles for permanent installation.

"Everyone has idealism in them, but they need a community to bring it out," said Michael Brown, co-founder and now CEO of City Year. Giving circles are one small-scale example of community in philanthropy. They connect individual donors and increase their impact, while cementing friendships. Residents of Fisher Island, near Miami Beach, created a philanthropic fund with Miami-Dade United Way, visiting nonprofits together while discussing their values and choices and then committing both funding and service time. In another example, a midwesterner started a giving circle of Jewish professional women. Some circles are informal. Every year, a family I know turns their Christmas tree into a "giving tree" for a cause they champion personally to their friends. At their holiday party, ornaments are joined by envelopes, while gifts for homeless shelters circle the tree.

At 5.3 percent of the total estimate for charitable gifts, corporations accounted for a slightly larger slice of the pie in 2005 than the average of 5 percent given by corporations in the past forty years. Employer matching contributions give arm's-length charity a boost, but some companies go further by making philanthropy a more active part of work life. Weaving community service into their organizations builds teams that share values. Timberland offers employees forty hours a year of paid time for community service and includes service opportunities in sales meetings and supplier conferences. CEMEX, the global cement company, deployed 300 international managers to rebuild a rural school near Cancún, Mexico, as part of its worldwide executive conference. IBM offers employees a suite of Web-based tools (called On Demand: Community) to use to help their favorite nonprofits. Procter & Gamble, in Egypt of all places, offers employees two hours a week to tutor at a school.

Active engagement is educational. Those who serve learn about problems that are otherwise only textbook abstractions, they come to see more dimensions of people who would otherwise be cardboard stereotypes, and they are provoked to think about innovative new solutions. These are among the reasons that service learning is an increasingly important part of education at all levels. For colleges, Campus Compact, a coalition of over a thousand college and university presidents, promotes models of community service that can help students work off education loans, among other virtues. Service projects are built into high school graduation requirements in states such as Maryland. In other places, such as communities in Michigan, schoolchildren are helped to start their own giving circles that screen and choose charities to which they want to contribute from a young age.

Local community service makes charity a meaningful part of everyday life. It builds social bonds among those who serve, reducing social isolation and cementing new relationships. It provides a bridge to connect people from across social, economic, and racial divides—the way I connected with Mike Boston. When country and city mice get involved in active philanthropy, they become more aware of one another's problems and perspectives, which doesn't mean that they agree about everything, but it does help them argue with less acrimony and more understanding. Direct service also offers a check against abuses because the recipient organizations' people, activities, and impact become visible to those working with them. And—to get back to those checks and tax deductions—personal contact with a cause is likely to inspire financial contributions. Those who volunteer the most time also give the most dollars (and demand the greatest accountability), studies show.

It has been said that philanthropists are people with more money than time. But it is worth taking the time for active involvement rather than only writing a check. Generosity can unite us. That's an addition, not a deduction.

## The Positive Passion of Social Entrepreneurs

One step beyond passive philanthropy is active service, and a step beyond that is leadership to mobilize others to serve, creating new solutions and inspiring people to believe in them.

Though U.S. happiness scores have trended down, I find that the happiest people around, or at least the most cheerfully optimistic, are social entrepreneurs who spring into action when they see problems that need solutions. They are not happy about the problems, of course; they become happy when they assemble, as Tocqueville observed, and form passionate resolves to Just Do Something.

Americans' can-do entrepreneurial spirit, so important in the business world, has taken hold in the nonprofit world, especially among young adults bringing fresh eyes to old dilemmas. For every problem, there is a potential social entrepreneur ready to innovate—to create a promising new solution through a new organization: Citizen Schools, offering after-school apprenticeships for middle school children; Jump Start, a literacy program matching college-student mentors with preschool children; and New Leaders for New Schools, which recruits and trains experienced managers from business to become public school principals in New York, Chicago, Memphis, and elsewhere.

In America, and internationally, social entrepreneurs are increasingly seen as the vanguard for making change. Geoff Mulgan, a top adviser to former British prime minister Tony Blair and former head of the Prime Minister's Strategy and Innovation Unit, is leading the United Kingdom's Young Foundation to develop "social Silicon Valleys" around the world, to produce more social entrepreneurs and social innovations. Singaporean Member of Parliament Penny Low aspires to make Singapore a global role model for incubating social entrepreneurs, such as her friend Elim Chew, who started a successful chain of punk clothing stores called 77th Street and then founded several charities dedicated to helping young people stay in school and go on to college. Her community work landed Chew a seat on the board of trustees of the prestigious National University of Singapore.

The kaleidoscope thinking behind innovation, which I described in Chapter 1, guides social entrepreneurs to breakthrough solutions that challenge orthodoxy. Consider the creativity of my friend Cindy Laba, one of City Year's first staff members in Boston, whose work in leading corps members in the public schools helped her realize how much talent was wasted when middle school students started lowering their aspirations. Laba and co-founder Marsha Feinberg have received national praise for starting Beacon Academy in 2005: a school that offers an extra fifteen months of education between eighth and ninth grades to help low-income public school students compete for entry to elite private and public high schools, a concept endorsed by the Boston School Committee and embraced by prep school admissions offices. In conventional wisdom, spending an extra year in school is a punishment for failure to make the grade. In the Beacon Academy vision, spending an extra year in school is a reward for demonstrating high potential, an investment in the students with the greatest potential, and an opportunity for them to transform their lives.

In conventional wisdom, if urban kids plan to leave the public schools, they are potential dropouts. In the Beacon Academy vision, if urban kids plan to leave the public schools, they might be heading for something even better. In 2006, Beacon Academy had graduated its first class and had moved on to the next.

Social entrepreneurs are at the vanguard of community building in times of disaster, too. Post-Katrina floods had barely subsided in September 2005 when City Year began strategizing about how to assist with relief and recovery. City Year founders Alan Khazei and Michael Brown quickly secured a commitment from former President Clinton for support from the Bush-Clinton Katrina Fund to open a Louisiana program within a few months of the disaster. In January 2006, fifty City Year corps members were sworn in to assist families and support children.

Ideas seeded by social entrepreneurs like Khazei and Brown gain traction when they trickle up into public consciousness and gain support from businesses and government. Federal support through AmeriCorps was key to City Year's expansion from a small Boston program to a national (and international) force. It's a win-win. Local voluntary action creates new possibilities that mayors, governors, legislators, and the president can turn into programs and policies. Grass-roots demonstrations become national models in partnership with both business and government. For example, YouthBuild USA, supported by both Home Depot and the federal government, teaches at-risk youth construction skills; they earn high school credentials while building affordable housing for the poor.

These social entrepreneurs believe in a classic children's tale, the starfish story, about maintaining idealism and taking action even against daunting odds. It's one of City Year's founding legends. Hundreds of starfish have washed up on a beach and are dying for lack of water. A young girl is carefully putting one starfish and then another back into the sea. A man on the beach, observing this with amusement at the naiveté of children, tells her that her effort is futile because she can't possibly save all of them. She proudly holds up a starfish and replies, "But I can make a difference to this one."

Making a difference, step by small step, separates long-term winners who have the confidence to achieve their goals from those who always seem to fall short. Instead of feeling over-whelmed by the magnitude of the problem, social entrepreneurs identify achievable actions and get started. Small wins are not as dramatic as big bold strokes, but they can be more effective and more fulfilling because each success increases confidence.

America has an abundance of potential social entrepreneurs for causes large and small. Consider these examples, to pick a few stories out of millions, culled from among my own friends: Dr. Gloria White-Hammond, an African American pediatrician-minister who had gone to Sudan on many errands of mercy, and Kenneth Sweder, a Boston lawyer long committed to human rights as head of the Jewish Community Relations Council, wanted to take a step toward ending genocide in the Darfur region of Sudan through an awareness and letter-writing campaign, so they met over numerous breakfasts to form a coalition. Lisa Foster, a Los Angeles English teacher married to a Hollywood feature film producer, started One Bag at a Time as a step toward reducing dependence on foreign oil by increasing reuse; her fast-growing venture imports reusable shopping bags she discovered in Australia when she and her daughters accompanied her husband to shoot a movie in Melbourne. In

Albuquerque, New Mexico, Joanne Ashe, daughter of Holo-
caust survivors and mother of three (including an adopted
Russian orphan), created Journeys in Film to increase international understanding in middle schools, to provide curricula to
accompany foreign films that offer insights into other cultures,
and—in her grand vision—to help heal a conflict-ridden
world. Not every vision is grand; some start out more modestly
but contribute to neighborhood-building. Cheryl Batzer, a
dancer and arts manager for other performers, had followed
her husband's career from New York to Dallas and was so
happy when they moved back to New York that she planted
flowers around four trees in front of her high-rise co-op apartment at her own expense when the co-op board didn't want to
spend the money. Soon, this simple act, and her daily tending,
began to transform a cold neighborhood. People began to stop
to say hello, watered the flowers when she was away, and
picked up litter. Batzer might have a Manhattan street garden
program in her future.

Those who become great leaders know they don't always
have the answers themselves. They believe that everyone can
make a difference, however small. Maybe that's what we need
from elected officials in a messy world—to encourage and
support the rest of us to get involved. The exhilaration from
accomplishing something valuable to the nation could potentially make Americans happier, too.

## The New Demographics of Service:
## Senior Boomers Still Want to Change the World

Young people are not the only American idealists eager to rebuild community. Americans of all ages increasingly express

their desire to perform some sort of service to their communities and nation. But those who came of age in the 1960s lead the charge among mature adults, according to a recent survey by the MetLife Foundation and Civic Ventures. A majority of Americans between the ages of fifty and seventy want to benefit their communities by helping the poor, elderly, those in need, or children, or by improving quality of life through the arts or the environment, the survey shows. Leading-edge boomers, from the ages of fifty to fifty-nine, are the most emphatic about this. Many say they want to change to a career in service now, not just in retirement. Among those who say they will never retire, nearly two-thirds are interested in a service career.

World, get ready! As the once-radical student baby boomers become the "senior boomers," they want to change the world again, but now in more benign ways. Could the generation that marched militantly in Washington in the 1960s soon stroll into schools, hospitals, and homeless shelters seeking opportunities to serve? The activists who staffed the civil rights and women's movements four decades ago say that today they want to eradicate diseases, raise literacy rates, create ventures to produce peace in the Middle East, or alleviate global poverty—there's no cause too big.

Baby boomers' parents were the first to use post–World War II child-centered philosophies, which made boomers feel they could be anything and do anything. Dr. Spock's influence was said to be one of the reasons that the first wave of boomers so naturally felt like world-changers in the 1960s. People who were told from birth about their own significance aren't ready to stop being significant just because they've hit a career ceiling called "retirement age."

Retirement options for healthy seniors once ran the whole

gamut from A to B (&B). The two most common pictures were a life of aerobics and athletics or running a bucolic bed-and-breakfast. These were the choices of former President Gerald Ford (a devoted golfer) and failed presidential candidate George McGovern (proprietor of a country inn). Now a more appropriate aspiration is to be a Bill—Clinton or Gates—and start a foundation to champion social causes. New models include retired Chrysler CEO Lee Iacocca's campaign to find a cure for diabetes, actor Paul Newman's business venture to raise money for charity, or former Paramount Pictures head Sherry Lansing's foundation for cancer victim advocacy.

If you want to be a Bill, Civic Ventures can show you many paths to service. Civic Ventures was founded by the late John Gardner, who was U.S. secretary of health, education, and welfare under President Lyndon Johnson and founder of Common Cause, and Marc Freedman, author of the book *Prime Time*, to be a national advocate for civic engagement in later life. To find and honor senior social entrepreneurs, Civic Ventures established the Purpose Prize, an annual award of $100,000 each to five senior social entrepreneurs who established significant community ventures after the age of fifty. (Sherry Lansing chaired the first panel of judges, on which I served.) There was an outpouring of nominations and an even more impressive set of accomplishments. Consider just two finalists:

- Former Florida official Conchy Bretos became the driving force behind the nation's first public housing project—the Helen Sawyer building in Miami—to bring assisted living services to older adults who just need a little help to stay in their homes. Her consulting company has helped forty public housing projects in a dozen states bring assisted living services to their residents.

- James Ketelsen created Project GRAD (Graduation Really Achieves Dreams) in 1988, when he was CEO of Tenneco, a Fortune 500 manufacturer of heavy equipment. When he retired, he turned his full attention to doing more to help minority and low-income youth graduate from high school and attend college. Early efforts focused on tutoring and summer jobs, but Ketelsen wasn't satisfied with the return. Today, Project GRAD includes college scholarships, rigorous new K–12 reading and math curricula, teacher training in classroom management, and a partnership with Communities in Schools, a nonprofit that coordinates school-based community resources. To date, 135,000 students in eight states have been served.

Of course, not everyone has the means or time to start a whole new social venture, so one of Civic Ventures' early signature programs was Experience Corps, which engages several thousand retirees a year—blue-collar and white-collar alike—in such service activities as tutoring at public schools. Still, traditional volunteering is not what many of the leading-edge senior boomers have in mind. They want to be leaders and have a significant impact. Respondents to the MetLife/Civic Ventures survey who think they can have a big or moderate impact in their community are much more likely to want service opportunities than those who feel their impact would be small (at 55 percent vs. 38 percent, a noteworthy gap). The educated and affluent are more likely to want postretirement service positions. About half of them are very or somewhat interested in taking a paying job (albeit part-time or flexible); a paycheck is a proxy for significance in a nation in which income is equated with success and only paid work is taken seriously. "Connection" and "sense of purpose" loom large as reasons that people aged fifty to seventy want to get involved in their communities—even more so for women of the boomer group. These motivations drive boomers toward roles with leadership potential.

Yet, for all the talk about what senior boomers want to contribute, there are practically no ways to help more of them do it. How do they gain the knowledge and refresh their skills to apply them to ending childhood hunger, curing Alzheimer's, or combating poverty in Newark, New Jersey (among the desires senior boomers have voiced to me)? When and where do they define a path that will get them started and make the right connections? And how can we ensure that community institutions are ready for them? IBM's Transition to Teaching, which I mentioned in Chapter 1, is one new vehicle, aimed at helping the company's experienced engineers and professionals gain teaching credentials and placements as math and science teachers. Many more social innovations are needed. Colleges and universities, which are increasingly embracing a community economic development role in their communities and engaging students in service, could take on this task of helping experienced leaders use their knowledge to build community.

## Institutional Change: Even Higher Education

What if former lawyers, business managers, retired military officers, or aging scientists gathered on a college campus for a semester or a year of advanced study to prepare for serving their communities in new ways for the rest of their lives? Decades ago, when they were eighteen or twenty years old, boomers honed their zeal for change (however youthfully excessive) on college campuses. Now in their fifties and turning sixty, those same boomers could return to college campuses to develop their next steps into mature leadership to improve the state of their communities or even the nation and the world.

To make it possible, colleges and universities could design advanced leadership schools around the interests and life situations of accomplished adults who want to make the transition from their primary income-earning careers to their years of flexible community service. They could also design programs for people who never went to college earlier in life or who want to switch fields. Corporations could include tuition for these schools in their retirement packages and support scholarships through their foundations, the way IBM supports Transition to Teaching. The federal government could offer tuition grants and tax breaks for attending universities after age fifty to support new forms of philanthropy and public service that truly solve problems. Social Security, pension funds, and retirement monies from 401(k) plans could also be tapped in a more flexible way when invested in education or re-education, as I suggested in Chapter 2.

It's time to turn experience into significance and help aging boomers find opportunities through new higher education initiatives. This isn't going *back* to school. It's using school to move forward.

That's the vision I'm developing with Rakesh Khurana, David Gergen, David Bloom, Charles Ogletree, Fernando Reimers, and our colleagues from five professional schools at

Harvard University. The idea is a new stage of higher education—call it even higher education. Higher education later in
life could produce a large pool of much-needed leaders to
improve communities, nations, and the planet. Higher education could redefine later life as a time for social entrepreneurship and public service, which is the goal of Pace
University's new program for corporate executives in New
York City and its suburbs who want to transition from business to nonprofits.

The educational model shouldn't resemble the lecture
halls, know-it-all professors, and musty textbooks of college
memories. Sessions would be more like think tanks, in which
faculty facilitate discussions among these leaders about how to
tackle major social needs, while participants brush up on recent developments in the sciences or add a language skill.
Their "dorms" could be two-bedroom apartments, with their
spouses or partners as not just roommates but co-participants
in the program. Participants wouldn't exactly be "students";
they would be more like contributors, themselves mentoring
undergraduates or leading seminars for graduate students.
And they could use the time to develop their plans for a foundation or a new social enterprise or business venture with a social purpose, or they could develop a fresh approach to take an
existing nonprofit to the next level of effectiveness. They
could enter politics, as Michael Bloomberg did in journeying
from media mogul to mayor of New York. They could write a
book or initiate a national awareness campaign.

Imagine the benefits from boomers-in-service. Seniors
would get meaning and purpose as well as potential income,
as Social Security funds fewer life necessities. Community and
public-sector organizations would get new talent and ideas

from experienced professionals. Hospitals, public schools, museums, and community agencies could find an experienced workforce. This could supply urgently needed leadership to make the world a better place, while turning an aging population from a burden to an opportunity.

Perhaps the senior boomers' biggest impact will be on eliminating the term *retirement* and inventing a new stage of life—one with community service at the core. They could unite with giving circles, social entrepreneurs, corporate volunteers, and full-time AmeriCorps members to restore the spirit and ethic of community. That could indeed change America—and possibly the world.

## Points of Light to Laser Beams: Why America Needs National Service

"Everyone can be great, because everyone can serve," the late great Dr. Martin Luther King Jr. declared. Community service is universal and inclusive, and it can sometimes spring up spontaneously in those local American assemblies Tocqueville saw so early in our history. But to have impact, individuals need a platform to organize and aggregate service, to get more people involved, to build more relationships across partisan divides, and to make a bigger difference.

As a big fan of letting a thousand flowers bloom, how could I not love the thousand points of light that the first President Bush praised so highly? The more lights the better, I say! But the points are only a starting point. Scattering a little service here, a small action there, is not enough to build strong communities or to unite enough people in common purpose. Imagine dividing the military into hundreds of small, new organizations instead of four big branches. Would national defense still be strong?

Fragmented national service would lack impact. Instead, a national platform for service should focus those points of light like a laser beam at some of our biggest problems. National service, even if it takes place community by community, turns service into a responsibility of citizenship. Democracy in America, as Tocqueville noted, is not about voting. It is about doing. (Happily, it turns out that those who have served in an AmeriCorps program also vote in much larger numbers than their peers, according to national surveys.)

Teach for America, one of the best-known programs started by the younger generation of social entrepreneurs, would not be where it is today, placing 4,400 teachers in 1,000 schools in under-resourced low-income communities in twenty-five regions, if it were not for AmeriCorps and a federal and state commitment to national service. Teach for America, which was founded by Wendy Kopp after she conceived the idea as a Princeton undergraduate, is a national corps of recent college graduates who commit two years to teaching in public schools with low-income students. After a determined push to recruit more math, science, and engineering majors to address the shortage of science and math teachers, Teach for America found nearly 500 of them to start in 2006 and was awarded a $5 million grant from biotech company Amgen to expand further. There is sufficient hunger among college students to serve that the organization received 19,000 applications for 2,400 slots; it was the single most popular recruiter on many college campuses, including Notre Dame in Indiana, where 11 percent of all seniors applied.

That hunger to serve went inadequately fed in the first six

years of the century because a Republican-dominated Congress starved AmeriCorps. While Americans worried in recent years about our young people in military service in Iraq, they were less aware of another army of young people—the ones engaged in civilian service in America. The 75,000-plus members of AmeriCorps, the national service program developed in 1993, are fighting a different kind of war—against illiteracy, AIDS, or school dropouts. Dedicating at least a year to their nation, they don uniforms and report to bases in inner-city schools, homeless shelters, or community health clinics. They build playgrounds instead of battlegrounds, helping ensure peace on city streets through constructive alternatives to drugs and violence.

Like their military counterparts, some young people find a ticket to a better life through AmeriCorps, gaining skills and college scholarships. Others expand their worldviews and become leaders of diverse groups spanning races and backgrounds.

For City Year, diversity is an important value; its corps members serve in teams mixed by gender, race, ethnicity, and social class. High school dropouts serve next to college graduates (but getting a high school diploma is a requirement of the service year), city youth next to country youth. Morever, City Year corps members empower even younger people. To recount just one of thousands of stories, from just one of the hundreds of disadvantaged inner-city schools that City Year serves, a City Year team organized a group of fifth-graders to plan a day of service for their neighborhood, drawing participants from an ongoing lunch discussion group that City Year corps members led. The lunch group included some of the school's most troubled kids, who gradually let go of dysfunctional behavior and learned to become child-leaders. One student in particular emerged as a leader over the course of the planning. His conclusion about how City Year changed him was the proud declaration that "Now I have a voice."

Compared to the widely known Peace Corps, AmeriCorps is not yet a household name, but its numbers are impressive. About 187,000 Americans in total have served in the Peace Corps since its inception in 1961. Nearly twice that number have served in AmeriCorps, founded in 1993, in just its first ten years, with a total of nearly 500,000 by the end of 2006. In 2006, about 7,700 Americans worked abroad in the Peace Corps, but over 73,000 served domestically in AmeriCorps, nearly ten times as many. The cost per Peace Corps member per year is $40,886. For AmeriCorps, the cost is only $12,208 (plus an education award added at graduation).

The idea for civilian national and community service was seeded in the first Bush administration through the Commission on National Service. It blossomed in the Clinton administration, which launched AmeriCorps under the auspices of the Corporation for National and Community Service. Initial critics such as Republican senators John McCain and Rick Santorum became staunch supporters, as AmeriCorps brought tangible benefits to both communities and young people. President George W. Bush promised expansion as part of his call for every American to serve the country. But continuing opposition from some Republicans in Congress meant that funding was uncertain, and proponents had to fight each year for barely adequate resources to meet the demand.

AmeriCorps members, like the soldiers in our all-volunteer army, are "volunteers" only in the sense that no one forces them to join. They serve as full-time workers performing direct service to communities—including organizing community service events for thousands more people. Members can afford to dedicate themselves to service regardless of financial situation because AmeriCorps provides a living allowance, health care, and child care benefits, and, at the end, an education award. These pittances have been periodically criticized as "paying people to volunteer," a charge that is clearly incorrect. Without those small stipends, national service would become a luxury for the affluent, not an expression of democracy that gives everyone a chance to serve. We don't want a two-class system in which the poor sign up for military service because they have few choices and the rich join civilian service programs.

Federal funding has helped large service programs flying the AmeriCorps flag create innovative solutions to community problems, as Citizen Schools has done in its models for after-school learning that make a longer, richer school day possible. National service could also bridge military and civilian service and make America safer at home—say, a civil defense corps to help communities recover from disasters. Senator Barbara Mikulski has called the innovations in national service "the highest and best use of taxpayer dollars." But periodically, congressional critics have tried to establish a time limit and ceiling for federal funding. That would punish the most successful models, such as Teach for America and City Year, and prevent their expansion.

When AmeriCorps was threatened with deep cuts in 2004, strong support was voiced on the SaveAmeriCorps website by 79 senators, 233 members of Congress, 44 governors, 148 mayors, 190 college and university presidents, 1,170 community organizations, and numerous CEOs of corporations that sponsor portions of AmeriCorps programs. But the very fact of widespread backing was twisted to justify cuts. Then–House Majority Leader Tom DeLay implied that if private-sector groups are so enamored of strong AmeriCorps programs, they should pay for more of their work. Corporations are certainly doing their part; City Year generally gets 60 percent of its funding from the private sector. But insisting that private companies fund public service in its entirety is like requiring corporate sponsorship of Army tanks, Navy ships, or Marine outfits. Ralph Lauren Green Berets, anyone?

National service should be expanded to engage all young people and to do even more for America. Let the young and the generous of all generations lead all of us (whether country or city mice) to find common ground through service.

## Toward Summer in America

In summer, the Country Mouse and the City Mouse are likely to exchange visits. Summer brings people out onto the streets, trails, beaches, city parks, and bike paths, encountering one another. Long days of sunlight are proven mood elevators, and when people are in a good mood, they are more likely to be generous, active, and engaged.

Ronald Reagan coasted to the presidency in the 1980s by declaring that "It's morning in America." I would prefer to make it summer in America, year-round. We couldn't be on vacation all that time (see the vacation woes in Chapter 2), but we could enjoy the spirit of community that makes dreams seem achievable. If winter is the season of discontent, summer is the season of contentment and generosity that reminds us of our common ground.

In summer, people can focus on little things. Grains of sand. Tiny orchids on a forest floor. Catching a ball in a corner of a park or quiet street. The flicker of birds' wings. Spotting the currents where the fish are feeding. Monarch butterflies. Stepping carefully to avoid the poison ivy while hiking. Cotton candy and carousels at county fairs. Bright, red farmstand tomatoes that haven't been bred for shipping containers, so they can grow in any shape they please. A schoolyard where many generations play. There are small children everywhere. Summer is when many families gather across generations to delight in playing with the children. Even the hardest-driving professionals forget pressured careers (though checking into the office occasionally) to remember what it is like to be a child again.

Summer is physical, visceral, and wild. It smells like flowers, piney woods, or low tide. In summer, cities empty out, and Americans return to the land. Those remaining in cities start urban gardens and talk to their neighbors. Small towns are in their element, their remoteness connecting us to wilderness. Summer is the ultimate off-road experience. Big world events seem far away—not just in miles, but in time.

In summer, commercial interests and consumer interests are least aligned. Merchants pray for rainy days to force people into shopping, while everyone else craves sun. (Was the record retail spending in the summer of 2006 due to bad weather or state tax holidays?) In the stretch between June weddings and back-to-school season, even credit cards can take it easy. Summer has none of those Hallmark holidays that require buying something (who sends Fourth of July cards?). Instead, many summer pursuits cost little to nothing. You can live off the land and waters, catching dinner and surrounding it with backyard-garden salad. You can toss the antidepressants—seasonal affective disorder melts in the sun. There is so little profit in special-for-summer garb that many department stores have stopped carrying swimsuits. Newspapers slim down in July and early August just like our exercise-improved bodies.

Summer is also the great leveler. The ubiquitous summer uniform of T-shirts, faded jeans, and flip-flops makes ethnicity, occupation, and age disappear. Americans didn't invent the picnic, but surely we've democratized the art. Parks, whether urban or rural, are open for grilling, with picnic tables ready to receive families of vastly different incomes, who are united in their burgers and corn. Lakeside cottages, campgrounds, and cabins in the woods are still within reach of working-class families. The rich can't monopolize the simple pleasures of summer, despite their starter castles in chic overpriced summer resorts. And the trust that exists on public beaches always amazes me—that we spread our blankets near complete strangers, yet, surprisingly often, we leave our belongings unguarded when we go for a swim or a stroll. When we ask strangers to watch our things, scientists have shown, those beach neighbors might even be willing to chase thieves on our behalf.

When summer ends in sober September, the big things command attention again. Algebra. The Middle East. College applications. Partisan squabbling in Congress. Third-grade homework. The pricing and marketing of prescription drugs. Global warming. Global poverty. The list goes on . . . People go inside, slamming doors on their communities. When preoccupied with the big things, it is tempting to lose sight of the little things that comprise the sensibilities and the generous, inclusive impulses of summer. If only we could hold on to summer a while longer—the hope and promise and sense of life and possibility that summer arouses. Keeping summer in the hearts and minds of Americans could provide a guide for dealing with the big issues of the rest of the year.

Summer sensibilities can help improve national health. If you like your leaner look from summer activities, keep walking. Nutrition and exercise are alternatives to some high-cost prescription drugs. Then think about children. Lobby for universal childhood immunization, more nutritious school lunches, and enhanced exercise programs. Tell businesses that their workers are much more productive and healthier after quality time with their families.

Summer experiences can increase environmental awareness. Surely the extreme weather of recent summers should raise interest in getting the U.S. government to deal with global warming more effectively. Surely the beauty of beaches and mountains should make more people want to protect our natural treasures.

Summer activities can offer new experiences that open minds. Travel. Camp. New encounters on the streets or at the beach. Volunteering. Summer memories can help us feel more generous toward strangers. The spirit of summer is the spirit of community. It feeds the spirit of service.

## The Spirit of Service:
### What Unites Us Can Be Stronger Than What Divides Us

All of us can take actions to bring people together, produce more leaders with idealism who value serving communities, elevate the national mood, and make it seem like summer in America again. Social capital need not decline; it can grow through a new breed of social enterprises that engage people rather than merely count their checks.

We must build the service infrastructure to help Americans of all ages, whether country or city mice, work together across habitats and leave both city and countryside in better shape. We can do the following:

- **Continue to make philanthropy an active endeavor** Encourage companies to provide time for employees to engage in service together. Increase service learning in schools so that little citizens learn to be big citizens. Recognize and applaud those who contribute time as well as money in permanent donor walls or floor tiles or wherever their names will be noticed. Name names and honor those who honor community.

- **Invest in social entrepreneurs** Offer public challenge grants for new solutions to high-priority problems that potential social entrepreneurs can use to seek private-sector support. Create social investment pools to support graduates of national service programs and members of the military who have a promising "change the world" idea. A new GI Bill for the twenty-first century—an idea floated by City Year's Brown and Khazei—could help alumni of any service program earn full college scholarships, matching the size to the magnitude of service (e.g., higher benefits for military than for civilian service).

- **Make civic engagement and local, national, or global service a prestigious alternative to retirement** Define the new "third stage of life" as the time for giving back. Encourage colleges and universities to take on the role of transitioning people from their first occupations to new lives of service and add educational investments akin to older student loans. Make pensions more flexible so that people can start a social purpose venture. For those who cannot live on Social Security or pensions alone, offer stipends for vital community service.

- **Expand national service** Keep full-time service at the core because it has catalytic effects, as full-timers become professionals leading others into service. Add opportunities for civilian service with training and benefits akin to military service. Consider a rich menu of specialized service corps—tutoring groups, health aides, civil defense corps for disaster relief, neighborhood beautification crews . . . there are numerous positive possibilities. Ask why it is not mandatory for all young people to serve—perhaps at least for a summer.

And to establish summer as a time of idealism and civic contribution, here's an idea that could become big everywhere fast: a summer of service. As envisioned by Shirley Sagawa, a former founding official of AmeriCorps and chief of staff to then–First Lady Hillary Rodham Clinton, a summer of service could be a rite of passage for young people who are too old for summer camp and too young for significant paid work. Summer of service programs could be run inexpensively by existing national and local organizations. And social entrepreneurs of all ages could tap this talent pool to help seed other great social innovations.

The act of service often makes Americans forget about grand theories, religious battles, or ideological positions. In my travels across America, I have seen that the desire to help a particular human being transcends arguments about what's wrong with humanity in general. Republicans and Democrats tend to check their partisan identification at the door when joining to tutor third-graders or build a Habitat for Humanity house. We must find that what unites us in terms of values can be stronger than what divides us. That's the spirit of summer and the spirit of America.

---

# Seizing the Six Opportunities

Threat and opportunity can be two sides of the same risk-reward coin. "Open" means honest, trustworthy, and transparent, or it means open to new possibilities. It also means exposed and vulnerable, with openings that might let in things we fear. Still, the rewards of openness can more than compensate for the risks. An open society populated by people of open minds remains an ideal worth supporting and a risk worth taking for the rewards that follow from innovation, accountability, and shared civic responsibility.

This book has proposed that six items form the agenda for restoring American strengths. We can do the following:

- **Secure the future by nurturing innovation** Innovation fuels economic prosperity. Innovation can provide solutions to current vulnerabilities. These solutions could include increasing alternative energy sources to reduce dependence on foreign oil or finding better and less-intrusive technology for transportation security. To ensure that innovation flourishes, ideas must keep flowing in an open dialogue. We must value fact-based inquiry and discovery, develop homegrown scientific brainpower, mount science and math campaigns in schools, and deploy technology faster to underserved areas in education and health care, using them as laboratories and showcases while enhancing their role as foundational institutions out of which innovation springs.

- **Help people pursue happiness by getting the work-family balance right** To forge better, more productive connections between work and family, we should rethink the organization of work. *Portable, virtual,* and *flexible* should be watchwords for the twenty-first-century workplace. Employers should be required to make vacations a priority, pay adequate wages, and remove unnecessary stressors. Valuing family enough to consider it in the design of organizations would help close the gender gap that keeps women just enough behind men to prevent opportunity from being quite equal and causes organizations and the nation to lose women's contributions unnecessarily.

- **Encourage good companies by demanding transparency and rewarding contributions that go beyond the bottom line** A new conception of the role of businesses as corporate citizens has been growing alongside the wave of financial and accounting scandals. We should keep the heat on the latter and elevate public awareness of the former. The voice of the public can be effective in reducing the number and power of imperial CEOs while applauding progressive leaders.

- **Restore respect for government and the public sector by insisting that leaders set high standards and meet them** Leaders who value public service and treat it honorably would help reduce cynicism and help make public-sector careers appealing to the best and most competent people. Government could then be reinvented to be more efficient and better run. There is a great deal of work to be done, as the need to rebuild a whole city after Hurricane Katrina showed us—repairing aging infrastructure, upgrading the public-health system to anticipate disasters and minimize human suffering, or just keeping us safe and educated.

- **Engage with the rest of the world in ways that maximize opportunities for the many** Our foreign policies should always work through the change agent rule of thirds: to stay close to allies and never take them for granted, to isolate and shrink the pool of enemies, and to invest in winning over the fence-sitters by improving their prospects. Aid programs should focus on grass-roots empowerment, poverty alleviation, education, and health care for the masses. American institutions of higher education could be mobilized for partnerships to develop a pool of cosmopolitan national leaders in troubled regions. Ethnic diversity within America can help us form profitable market connections with rising economies such as those of China and India so that they become engines for new American business ventures and not merely threats to current American jobs.

- **Unite in circles of generosity to serve our communities at home** We should get serious about national service for all young people and find creative ways to use their energy,

such as a civil-defense corps under AmeriCorps, for neighborhood organizing, disaster relief, and first aid, and an expansion of existing programs such as Teach for America and
City Year. We should tap the aging baby boomer generation
and help them find new careers in public and community
services (such as education or health care) or as social entrepreneurs and civic leaders.

Behind these prescriptions are a set of principles that can
guide choices about how to take action—the shared commitments and responsibilities that come with working, living, and
doing business in America. But first we should be clear about
what America is and can be.

## America as an Idea

For America the Beautiful to be restored to America the Principled, we should proceed with a theory of who we are as a
nation and how we are positioned in the world.

Positioning is a term straight out of marketing. Nations are
increasingly being seen as "brands"—one more sign of increasing commercial creep, as private-sector analogies sweep
the world. New Zealand has played with branding itself and
its products as "green." Early into Tony Blair's government in
the United Kingdom, there was a campaign to rebrand stuffy
England as "cool Britania." Appropriately, the first U.S. State
Department official for public diplomacy was former advertising executive Charlotte Beers.

If we are not fully satisfied with what our national brand
stands for, we can refresh it. Brands are intentional and imagined, and they are established through communication and

action. There is nothing inevitable about what is happening to America. Our future will be shaped by the assumptions we make about who we are and what we can be.

Let's start with a rather negative assumption about America's role in the world. "Failed empire" is one conception of America as a world power. This idea is floated by thinkers of all political persuasions, although they disagree about whether the "empire" is "failing" through overreaching or "failing" by under-utilizing national strengths. To some center-left thinkers, America has veered in the 2000s toward "neo-imperial unilateralism." By not involving allies who would help legitimize American power, especially regarding the war in Iraq, our political leaders could no longer achieve their objectives. Bullying has its limits, this perspective suggests. Yet, to others, turn-of-the-century America has not gone far enough in using its power, holding back out of misguided concerns that we must pretend to listen to others rather than do what we think is right. For a third group, America's current troubles reflect the long-term decline of a great power. In this view, the United States had increasingly become greedy and arrogant throughout the twentieth century, and thus it would inevitably lose power and prominence to the next rising civilization (or two) in Asia.

Who we are outside depends heavily on who we think we are inside—a truth for individuals as well as institutions and nations, and one based on authenticity. Theories about our place in the world will come true, or not, depending on our theory of who we are within our own borders. So let's look for more positive frameworks. We can find those positive conceptions in open-society ideals reflected in the spirit of summer. We can find them when we try to understand American history before we became a superpower.

America has been said to be the world's first "new nation." That is, the United States is the first nation where occupancy of shared space formed the idea of nationhood, instead of shared history or ethnicity. This positive conception of America rests not on who we are by origin or race or faith but on what we decide to do with the space we occupy together. That by itself opens doors to new possibilities; the very definition of America involves creating the future. Americans of any stripe or color can become something more or different than the prospects of their ethnic counterparts elsewhere by the opportunities that arise in our shared space. At the time of our nation's founding, that space once seemed limitless, and it could be expanded through land grabs and land purchases. Manifest destiny might not have been the proudest idea in American history, but that doctrine, and the fight to keep a divided nation together through the Civil War, kept alive the idea of nation as an intentional act of self-determination.

## Village Squares and Public Beaches: Finding Common Ground

In a sense, then, America was a society founded on trust. Villages and then cities arose around the "commons," a place where people could let their animals graze and where members of the community encountered one another. Today, summers on the beach, where strangers leave their belongings in sight of other strangers, are a reminder of the trust that can emerge simply from co-occupancy of the same space.

America's best principles stem from the idea of common ground occupied by extremely diverse people. For philosopher John Rawls, America is a community of communities, a social union of social unions. To political scientist Michael Walzer, Americans can embrace differences while having a common way of life. We are simultaneously the most devout and the most religiously diverse nation on earth. Even our economy is diverse, encompassing enormous regional variation and a federal system that devolves power to the provinces. Centuries before Europe's common market or international trade blocs, we created, in a sense, the world's first common market of distinctive economic regions.

Continuing contentiousness comes with the territory for a place that values freedom of speech, hosts many divergent traditions, and finds links that smooth commerce across many distinctive areas. But disagreement on specifics can help us find creative syntheses, as long as we remain firmly on common ground.

Our diversity requires finding a common denominator without destroying the depth that differences imply. Often it's a lowest common denominator, something superficial. I have often said that American pop culture has swept the world not because we won World War II and occupied defeated nations or because American companies are large, but because pop culture is designed to be grasped quickly by people of highly diverse backgrounds—and American companies can grow globally because they have already been tested in a home market that is a microcosm of the world. American pop culture must appeal to people who are otherwise unimaginably different. Similarly, American-style English became the universal language of commerce because it is so easy to speak badly and still be understood. American openness and inclusion required finding a common touch-point that floated above (or below) deep cultural or religious traditions.

We can do better than always reverting to the lowest common denominator. We can find a highest common denominator in our principles of openness, inclusion, and civic responsibility. These principles help us master the future by renewing our population, reinventing our institutions, and adding to our stock of new ideas that produce innovations.

We no longer graze cattle in the village square, but we share a common infrastructure and national defense; we breathe the same air and move freely across the same roads. We need a new definition of the commons for this new century so that we might rediscover what it means to share public space and responsibility. The need is urgent. The commons could dissolve into our iPods as we create iWorlds with segment-of-one markets of iIndividuals. Mass markets have morphed into niches and customization. Mass media (the so-called MSM, for mainstream media) are disappearing quickly. Will Wikipedias unite us? The public interest is often seen as the sum of private interests and actions, not as a whole that is worth more. Interest group politics are strong largely because of the role of money in campaign finance. So the public interest writ large is never quite articulated, and many people are suspicious that everything is self-interested anyway, however altruistic it appears.

Even some excellent movements can stress the I over the We. Social entrepreneurship, for example, is a highly effective method of helping communities and solving social problems. Still, even good causes can contribute to fragmentation under some circumstances—for example, when starting a new organization consists of a noble but narrow purpose and is bereft of connections to an organizing framework or a theory of change and is independent of other action by other groups. Even community service can focus people too narrowly on one activity without provoking them to think about their responsibilities for a larger whole. "Why vote?" asked a young Harvard College student in October 2006 at a Kennedy School seminar with former senator and 1980s presidential candidate Gary Hart. "Why is voting a better mark of citizenship than volunteering for the PTA?" he asked. The answer is that voting shapes the commons, and after that there are many forms of service that can enhance it. City Year, the organization that deploys young people for community service (described in Chapter 6), makes registering to vote a requirement for graduating from the program.

We should return to the idea of America as common ground occupied by diverse people. We can seek not the lowest but the highest common denominator when we use noble, traditional principles to guide actions of varied, diverse kinds. To do this will take an informed citizenry, civic institutions to connect people to service locally and nationally, a strong articulation of public purpose, and frequent convening across institutions and sectors to examine problems and issues that can't be handled by any single sector or group acting alone.

Call this pluralism with a common vocabulary. A national conversation on values would be a cliché. But perhaps we can have a common set of questions to ask every potential leader (a questionnaire for applying for the job) and a scorecard to see how he or she performs. Is the person a divider or a uniter? Does the person show favoritism or favor inclusion? Does he or she appear to scorn those with the least or call for those who have more to do more?

## Who Should Act?: The Change Process

Years ago, when I was first studying innovation and strategic change in companies, I came to a surprising conclusion about the change process. Often, all of the elements for a significant change were already in place before the ostensible time of change (before the historical markers used to note the change), but they had been unrecognized or unacknowledged. Every nation, like every organization (and, I suspect, every person) contains multiple coexisting tendencies. At any particular time, leaders tell stories about those tendencies, trying to make sense out of them. Some are called core; those mainstream items are encouraged, rewarded, publicized, and used to justify actions. But there are many other tendencies or capabilities latent in the situation that are so peripheral they can languish unnoticed or be written off as deviant. Sometimes change consists merely of redefining what is core and what is periphery. Indeed, sometimes the deviant actions turn out to be innovations that open new possibilities.

To initiate change, we can ask potential leaders to tell us a different story—one that builds on better parts of ourselves—by revisiting core principles, taking principled stands, and using that strength to take new steps. Former President Clinton often repeats (and so do I) that there is nothing wrong with America that can't be fixed by what's right with America.

Who should take action? Societies are complex and multi-layered. Change takes place at three broad levels: policies, projects or programs, and behavior. Government policymakers and corporate decision-makers can set frameworks. Entrepreneurs and social entrepreneurs can create demonstrations of new ways of operating. Individuals can reshape norms at the grass roots by using the power of voice.

We can demand change from leaders (or potential leaders competing for our votes), and we can get started ourselves, wherever we are located. But first we have to believe in the possibility of becoming better—that the game isn't over and that we're only stuck in the middle.

Americans were once known for being a people who responded to circumstances, however seemingly adverse, by saying, "Yes, we can." How do we return to that positive "yes"? That's hard. "No" is always an easier answer than "yes." Being against seems easier than being for, and doing nothing requires no heavy lifting. But there is too much nay-saying in America. Given the national mood studies cited throughout this book, I think my country needs a pep talk.

## A Pep Talk for America

If you are among the professional cynics predisposed to poke fun at sunny optimists, or frothy images like "summer," or self-help books, do I have a speech for you! Moviemaker Woody Allen once proposed an all-purpose graduation talk, with lofty advice parodying Reinhold Niebuhr's serenity prayer. It went something like this: *More than ever in history, humanity faces a crossroads. One path leads to despair and utter hopelessness. The other path leads to total oblivion. Let us pray that we have the wisdom to choose the right one.* Funny, but some days will feel like that—between Iraq and a hard place.

Any pessimist can put down pep talks, because despair-mongers have a great deal of truth on their side. The world is indeed troubled, with a recent history of riots in Bolivia, murders in Mexico, genocide in the Darfur region of Sudan, North Korean nukes, avian flu outbreaks, and continuing Middle East conflagrations in Iraq and beyond. We're reminded of dangers every time we go through airport security or read about job losses to China and India.

But when has the world not faced troubles? Even in supposedly good times, troubles are always lurking. It's just that in times defined as "good," people feel better about their ability to handle the troubles. In every endeavor—whether in politics, business, sports, or the game of life—Kanter's Law kicks in: *Everything can look like a failure in the middle*.

Surprising events, unlucky breaks, or unfortunate injuries can pop up at any time, coming between us and our goal. If we give up in the middle, by definition we've failed. Find the will to keep going and to make adjustments, but stick with it, and the likelihood of success grows. Winners of the game often come from behind.

What separates long-term winners from perpetual losers is the confidence to bounce back from troubles. Confidence stems from productive habits that are the foundation for problem-solving—the kinds of habits that restore American strengths:

- **Take responsibility** Don't waste time assigning fault or pointing fingers; anger and blame are unproductive emotions. We must analyze problems and face our role in them head-on. My sports and business studies show that winners indeed work harder. They don't whine or deny problems; they seek ways to improve.

- **Rely on relationships** It's easier to do together what seems impossible alone. We must avoid the losers' temptation to slink away and withdraw. Better yet, support someone else first. People who reach out to help others increase their own self-confidence.

- **Get moving** Doing something, anything, is always better than doing nothing. Losers tend to feel helpless and passive. Winners favor action. They prefer looking ahead to looking back. When problems seem overwhelming and when circumstances seem uncontrollable, that's when winners focus on whatever it is they *can* control.

- **Celebrate small wins** Championships are won a game at a time—one play at a time. City Year, the national youth service corps, begins every meeting with "ripples": personal stories about recent accomplishments, however modest, that send out a "tiny ripple of hope" (in the late Robert Kennedy's words). Small wins produce confidence to tackle bigger issues.

Americans have been on top of the world, so change can make us feel down in the dumps. Yet we will never be utterly helpless. Even if we don't control our circumstances, we can control our responses to those circumstances. When things don't go our way, we can refuse to slip into losers' negativity. Anyone who looks positively at his or her strengths and faces truthfully his or her deficiencies is likely to grow stronger. If we view other people positively, they're likely to come through for us. If we look for opportunities in any situation to take small steps now, we're likely to achieve bigger things later.

That's not a guarantee, but it shifts the odds. Often, what makes us successful is not which road we choose. It's how we decide to handle the bumps in it.

## Self-Fulfilling Prophecies and the Promise of America

A popular Americanism advises people to wait for the final score before declaring the result of the game, although it's usually posed in musical terms: "The opera isn't over until the fat lady sings." In these opening years of the twenty-first century, the fat lady hasn't even opened her mouth—let alone burst into song. Yet, too many people are thinking about leaving their seats early by giving up on the promise of America.

In politics, pundits and handicappers like to declare it all over when it's just getting serious. Certainly the 2006 midterm elections brought a few cliff-hangers and surprises. Here's another case in point from my hometown: In a recent primary election for sheriff of Boston, the pundits got it wrong, and voters defied expectations. The heavy favorite, an experienced politician who even looked the part of sheriff, lost to an underdog political novice, the appointed incumbent Andrea Cabral, a woman who is part African American and part Native American. The surprise was high minority turnout.

Many candidates say they ignore the polls, just as professional athletes say they ignore media hype surrounding their games, and corporate leaders say they ignore the analysts and simply focus on executing their plans. Don't believe it for a minute. Forecasts and predictions shape a mood, an emotional climate, which affects the ability to attract fans, money, talent, volunteers, or positive press—let alone keep insiders' spirits up. The danger for any effort is if polls lead to a self-fulfilling prophecy in which supporters give up because they assume it's hopeless. In the 2004 Olympics, a star British runner who thought she couldn't win dropped out of the race before it ended. That failure to even try set her up to lose in her next match.

The difference between winning and losing often lies in the confidence to persist—or not. In the heyday of Notre Dame football, fans stayed glued to their seats to the bitter end, knowing that their team could triumph in the final seconds. In contrast, during the nine-year record-holding losing streak of a southern college's football team, the team's own cheerleaders often left games after halftime. Assuming that losing is inevitable can make it so. Assuming that winning is possible even from behind keeps people playing at their peak.

In politics, business, sports, and life, momentum influences treatment by those whose support matters. Teams on winning streaks, whose numbers seem to be heading up, get the benefit of the doubt. Their fumbles get treated lightly. Those on losing streaks find their every move criticized. Their stumbles, not their successes, are the story. Premature celebration is always a mistake, because a surefire recipe for losing is to let being ahead go to one's head. But so is premature burial. "Reports of my death are greatly exaggerated," humorist Mark Twain once said. It's not over until it's over. We cannot take success for granted, as some Americans once did when they felt entitled to a great deal more than people in other countries, but neither should we count ourselves out.

Could it be as simple as the politics of hope versus the politics of fear—a contrast posed in the 2006 congressional elections? Maybe it is. So much of life is shaped by self-fulfilling prophecies. Our best guess (or worst fear) about the future directs what we do today, and then we act in ways that make our prediction come true. From the vantage point of 2006, it is interesting that the politics of fear have been offered by conservatives who claim to represent mainstream values, while the politics of hope have been conveyed by American politicians who came from outside the mainstream yet believe in the promise of America, such as Senator Barack Obama or newly elected Massachusetts Governor Deval Patrick. Hispanics indicate the strongest belief in the American dream of any group on some surveys. Perhaps those from groups once shut out can most appreciate the meaning of open doors.

America's future is still to be determined. By definition, an open society is always a work in progress. But at least let's start a new season. Let's declare that the winter of our discontent is over! With the spirit of summer surrounding us, we can open our doors and our minds, take a deep breath, go outside to find common ground, and work on restoring American strengths.

# Notes

Introduction
page

2    **resonated with the public**  One manifestation is the popularity of Barack Obama's book *The Audacity of Hope: Thoughts on Reclaiming the American Dream* (New York: Crown, 2006).

4    **"bleeding ulcer conservatives"**  For evidence that this might be more than a caricature, see John T. Jost et al., "Political Conservatism as Motivated Social Cognition," *Psychological Bulletin* 2003 129 (3): 339–375. The authors find in a meta-analysis of 88 samples from 12 countries encompassing 22,818 cases that several psychological variables predict political conservatism, in descending order of strength of correlation: death anxiety; system instability; dogmatism—intolerance of ambiguity; need for order, structure, and closure; and fear of threat or loss. The authors argue that the core ideology they call conservatism stresses resistance to change and justification of inequality. It correlates negatively with openness to experience.

5    **if someone else is worse off**  Some studies in social psychology and economics show that this might be a long-standing propensity. For evidence about relative status and status envy, see Robert H. Frank, *Luxury Fever: Why Money Fails to Satisfy in an Era of Excess* (New York: Free Press, 2000). But others are beginning to question the inevitability of status envy, finding that there are circumstances in which people applaud the well-being of others or are uncomfortable with huge inequities in status or large reward differentials. For example, researchers found that individuals, playing the

ultimatum game, actively avoid one-sided offers in the interests of fair play. Subjects in an experiment were given $20 and asked to allocate it to another subject in one of two ways: by splitting the money evenly or by keeping $18 for themselves and giving only $2 to the other subject. More than 75 percent of the subjects chose the fifty-fifty split, showing a concern for unequal outcomes, even among strangers. See Daniel Kahmenman, Jack Knetsch, and Richard Thaler, "Fairness and the Assumptions of Economics," *Journal of Business* 59 (1986): S285–S300.

6   **America can no longer assume**   See Thomas Friedman, *The World Is Flat: A Brief History of the 21st Century* (New York: Farrar, Straus & Giroux, 2006 edition).

8   **religious and secular utopian communities**   The dissertation became a book. Rosabeth Moss Kanter, *Commitment and Community: Communes and Utopias in Sociological Perspective* (Cambridge: Harvard University Press, 1972).

8   **woman who wanted to break barriers**   That concern about women's opportunities that started with personal career concerns later led to a policy monograph and another signature book published the same year. See Kanter, *Work and Family in the United States* (New York: Russell Sage Foundation, 1977); and Kanter, *Men and Women of the Corporation* (New York: Basic Books, 1977, updated 1993).

8   **French aristocrat Alexis de Tocqueville**   Alexis de Tocqueville, *Democracy in America* (New York: HarperCollins paperback edition, 2006). The book was originally published in 1835. Tocqueville observed firsthand some of the nineteenth-century communities I studied through historical archives in my doctoral dissertation.

9   **management principles**   See Kanter, *The Change Masters* (New York: Simon & Schuster, 1983); and Kanter, *Confidence: How Winning Streaks and Losing Streaks Begin and End* (New York: Crown, 2004).

9   **importance of the Internet**   See Kanter, *Evolve!: Succeeding in the Digital Culture of Tomorrow* (Boston: Harvard Business School Press, 2001).

9   **global economic competition**   For an analysis of the tension between the globalization of business and the needs of local communities and how these might be resolved, see Kanter, *World Class: Thriving Locally in the Global Economy* (New York: Simon & Schuster, 1995).

## Chapter 1: Securing the Future
page

12   **education of children in Union City**   I visited Union City and its schools several times in 1997 and 1998, and I then returned in 2003. Extensive interviews were woven into a five-part educational case series, a video, and a follow-up case. See Rosabeth Moss Kanter and Ellen Pruyne, *Bell Atlantic*

*and the Union City Schools (A): The Intelligent Network; (B): Education Re-form in Union City; (C1): Project Explore; (C2): Project Explore; (D): Results and Replication.* Harvard Business School cases #9399029, 9399043, 9399065, 9399066, 9399084 (Boston: Harvard Business School Publishing, 1998, 1999). The follow-up case study, based on visits in 2003, is Rosabeth Moss Kanter and Ryan Leo Raffaelli, *Union City Schools: Sustaining the Turnaround.* Harvard Business School case #9303137 (Boston: Harvard Business School Publishing, 2003).

17   **raise money for their project**   The example was featured in the *Boston Globe* "Prototypes" column on December 25, 2006.

20   **regions can succeed in a global economy**   Rosabeth Moss Kanter, *World Class: Thriving Locally in the Global Economy* (New York: Simon & Schuster, 1995).

22   **"kaleidoscope thinking"**   See Chapter 9 of Rosabeth Moss Kanter, *Evolve!: Succeeding in the Digital Culture of Tomorrow* (Boston: Harvard Business School Press, 2001).

23   **Innovation is the result**   Richard Lester and Michael Piore, *Innovation: The Missing Dimension* (Cambridge: Harvard University Press, 2004).

23   **the innovation process**   I showed this in the case of companies innovating around the Internet in Rosabeth Moss Kanter, *Evolve!: Succeeding in the Digital Culture of Tomorrow* (Boston: Harvard Business School Press, 2001).

24   **presence of colleges and universities**   When Carnegie Mellon professor Richard Florida announced the rise of the creative class a few years ago in a book by that name—*The Rise of the Creative Class* (New York: Perseus, 2002)—he found a receptive audience among economic development officials around the world who were eager to fuel the next high-tech job creation engine. Florida found a correlation between the concentration of scientists, engineers, and other knowledge workers in certain cities and the presence of musicians, performing artists, ethnic minorities, gays, and lesbians. (San Francisco; Austin, Texas; Boston; San Diego; and Seattle were his top five creative cities.) Florida urged investments in cultural amenities and progressive social legislation. His economic logic has been challenged by events, as job creation has recently occurred faster in some of his least creative (i.e., least progressive) cities, such as Las Vegas, as critic Steven Malanga showed in the winter 2004 *City Journal.* Of course, job creation can be the result of building booms in appealing climates rather than innovation per se.

24   **restricted the flow of ideas**   AnnaLee Saxenian, *Regional Advantage: Culture and Competition in Silicon Valley and Route 128* (Cambridge: Harvard University Press, 1994).

24   **"knowledge nomads"**   The label comes from Todd L. Pittinsky.

25   **biblically rooted creationism**   A University of Minnesota biologist found

that about 15 percent to 20 percent of the nation's high school biology teachers teach creationism. Constance Holden, "Creationism Edges Toward the Classroom," *Science,* 27 September 2002.

25  **the religious right**  Frances Fitzgerald, "Holy Toledo: Ohio's gubernatorial race tests the power of the Christian right," *The New Yorker,* 31 July 2006.

26  **the first human embryonic stem cells**  "Timeline of Stem Cell Debate," *Washington Post.* Compiled from Staff Reports, reported 18 July 2006. URL: http://www.washingtonpost.com/wp-dyn/content/article/2006/07/18/AR2006071800722.html Accessed: 22 August 2006 and 20 February 2007.

27  **Alzheimer's or Parkinson's disease**  Eleni Berger, "Research avenue adds fuel to stem cell controversy," CNN Health, 18 July 2001. URL: http://archives.cnn.com/2001/HEALTH/07/11/stem.cell.fact Accessed: 19 August 2006 and 20 February 2007.

28  **Many of the approved lines proved to be contaminated**  Ceci Connolly and Rick Weiss, "Stem Cell Colonies' Viability Unproven," *Washington Post.* URL: http://www.washingtonpost.com/wp-dyn/content/article/2001/08/28/AR2005033106414.html. Accessed: 22 August 2006 and 20 February 2007.

28  **States sprang into action**  All figures come from "Timeline of Stem Cell Debate," *Washington Post,* ibid. Additional commentary can be found in Maria Godoy and Joe Palca, "A Brief Timeline of the Stem-Cell Debate," National Public Radio (NPR). URL: http://www.npr.org/templates/story/story.php?storyId=5252449 Accessed: 22 August 2006 and 20 February 2007.

29  **the Newcastle Center for Life**  "Stem Cells: Policies and Players," Genome News Network. URL: http://www.genomenewsnetwork.org/resources/policiesandplayers/ Accessed: 22 August 2006.

29  **Singapore launched a major biotechnology initiative in 2000**  Wayne Arnold, "Singapore Acts as Haven for Stem Cell Research," *The New York Times,* August 17, 2006. URL: http://www.nytimes.com/2006/08/17/business/worldbusiness/17stem.html?ex=1155960000&en=d86c409a4547ac0c&ei=5087%0A. Accessed: 22 August 2006 and 20 February 2007.

30  **Two of America's most prominent cancer researchers**  Paul Elias, "Singapore woos top scientists with new labs, research money," Associated Press, April 12, 2006. URL: http://www.boston.com/news/nation/articles/2006/04/12/singapore_woos_top_scientists_with_new_labs_research_money/ Accessed: 20 February 2007.

32  **doctorates in biological sciences grew**  Calculations were based on the National Science Foundation Survey of Earned Doctorates from numbers in Susan T. Hill, "2004 Doctorate Awards Increase in Science and Engineering Fields for the Second Straight Year in a Row." InfoBrief SRS (Science Re-

sources Statistics), National Science Foundation, NSF 06-301 November 2005. URL: http://www.nsf.gov/statistics/infbrief/nsf06301/nsf06301 .pdf. Accessed: 25 August 2006 and 13 February 2007.

32 **fastest-growing category** This is based on U.S. Census Bureau data analyzed by www.wisertrade.org.

34 **science and engineering doctoral degrees** According to National Science Board, Science and Engineering Indicators 2006, Arlington, VA: National Science Foundation (volume 1, NSB 06-01; chapter 2, pg. 6). URL: http://www.nsf.gov/statistics/seind06/pdf/c02.pdf. Accessed: 25 August 2006 and 13 February 2007.

35 **U.S. higher education institutions** Christine M. Matthews, "Foreign Science and Engineering Presence in U.S. Institutions and the Labor Force," *Congressional Research Service Report for Congress,* #97-746, updated January 3, 2006. URL: http://www.fas.org/sgp/crs/misc/97-746.pdf#search= %22%25%20science%20engineering%20degrees%20awarded%20by%20Unit ed%20States%20to%20foreign%20%22. Accessed: 25 August 2006 and 13 February 2007.

35 **postdoctoral appointments at U.S. universities** National Science Board, Science and Engineering Indicators 2006. Two volumes. Arlington, VA: National Science Foundation (volume 1, NSB 06-01; chapter 2, pg. 4). URL: http://www.nsf.gov/statistics/seind06/pdf/c02.pdf. Accessed: 25 August 2006 and 13 February 2007.

36 **U.S. average income per capita** Calculations were made from data found in Bureau of Economic Analysis, *State Personal Income 2005 News Release.* Preliminary Report. 28 March 2006. URL: http://www.bea.gov/bea/ newsrel/SPINewsRelease.htm. Accessed: 25 August 2006.

36 **between upper-income and lower-income** From information supplied by the Massachusetts Budget and Policy Center, 2006.

37 **the race barrier** Underrepresented minorities (blacks, Hispanics, and Native Americans/Alaska Natives) do not enroll in or complete college at the same rate as whites, according to the NSF (National Science Foundation) Indicators 2006. The percentages of blacks and Hispanics ages twenty-five to twenty-nine in 2003 who completed bachelor's or higher degrees were 18 percent and 10 percent, respectively, compared with 34 percent for whites. Completing high school improved the odds: Among high school graduates, the percentages of blacks and Hispanics ages twenty-five to twenty-nine in 2000 who had completed bachelor's or higher degrees stood at 21 percent and 15 percent, respectively, compared with 36 percent for whites. The good news is that among those who do earn bachelor's degrees, similar percentages of underrepresented minorities and whites earn their degrees in science and engineering—from a third to a half (with Asians at the high end). See National Science Board, Science and Engineering Indicators 2006, op cit.; chapter 2, p. 4.

38    **science, engineering, and technical training**   Calculated from U.S. Labor Department figures. See also Leonard J. Bond, "Future Energy Technologies and Employment Challenges." *IEEE-USA-Today's Engineer,* November 2006. URL: http://www.todaysengineer.org/2006/nov/future_technologies.asp. Accessed: 13 February 2007.

38    **not always qualified**   "American Board Unveils Passport to Teaching Certifications in General Science & Biology." *The American Board for Certification of Teacher Excellence.* 14 April 2005. URL: http://www.abcte.org/press/press_releases?page=13. Accessed: 13 February 2007.

45    **perform no better**   According to the 2003 National Assessment of Educational Progress—the first national comparison of test scores—charter school students on average performed no better than comparable students in regular public schools. F. Howard Nelson, Beth Rosenberg, and Nancy Van Mater, "Charter School Achievement on the 2003 National Assessment of Educational Progress," August 2004, available at http://epsl.asu.edu/epru/articles/EPRU-0408-63-OWI.pdf. Accessed: 12 February 2007.

46    **Web-based leadership tools**   IBM offers these tools, which are based on my work, free to educators at www.reinventingeducation.org.

## Chapter 2: Pursuing Happiness
### page

60    **employer pressures**   Sylvia Ann Hewlett and Carolyn Buck Luce argue that certain industries breed a type of professional for whom excessive work hours are a badge of honor in their article "Extreme Jobs: The Dangerous Allure of the 70-Hour Workweek," *Harvard Business Review.* December 2006.

60    **difficult to manage**   Juliet Schor, *The Overworked American: The Unexpected Decline of Leisure* (New York: Basic Books, 1993).

61    **no vacation plans**   More than a third of the workers surveyed by the Families and Work Institute in 2004 were not taking their full allotment of vacation time. See Ellen Galinsky et al., *Overwork in America: When the Way We Work Becomes Too Much* (New York: The Families and Work Institute, 2005). At the start of the summer of 2006, the Conference Board found that 40 percent of consumers had no plans to take a vacation over the next six months, the lowest percentage in their study in twenty-eight years. See The Conference Board Consumer Confidence Survey (New York: Conference Board, May 2006). A Gallup poll in May 2006 found that 43 percent of respondents had no vacation—the Gallup Organization, Princeton, NJ.

63    **working to the max**   Elizabeth Warren and Amelia Warren Tyagi, *The Two-Income Trap: Why Middle-Class Mothers and Fathers Are Going Broke* (New York: Basic Books, 2003).

63    **chronically overworked**   On the national survey by the Families and Work

Institute cited previously, about 37 percent of those between the ages of forty and fifty-nine said they are chronically overworked, compared to fewer than 30 percent of those under the age of forty. Galinsky et al., op. cit.

64  **flexible arrangements**  Just 26 percent of employees report being chronically overworked, compared with 56 percent at companies without flexibility, the Families and Work Institute study showed. Ibid.

65  **myth of separate worlds**  Rosabeth Moss Kanter, *Work and Family in the United States* (New York: Russell Sage Foundation, 1977).

69  **We lagged behind**  Augusto Lopez-Claros and Saaide Zahidi, *Women's Empowerment: Measuring the Global Gender Gap* (Geneva, Switzerland: World Economic Forum, 2005).

70  **sex-discrimination claims**  Evelyn Murphy and E. J. Graf, *Getting Even: Why Women Don't Get Paid like Men* (New York: Simon & Schuster, 2003).

70  **"on-ramping"**  Sylvia Ann Hewlett, *Off-Ramps and On-Ramps: Keeping Talented Women on the Road to Success* (Boston: Harvard Business School Press, 2007). The book was based on a 2005 *Harvard Business Review* article by the same name.

71  **if women demanded**  Linda Babcock and Sara Laschever, *Women Don't Ask: Negotiation and the Gender Divide* (Princeton: Princeton University Press, 2003).

71  **"second shift"**  Arlie Russell Hochschild with Anne Machung, *The Second Shift* (New York: Penguin, 2003).

75  **cartoon saga**  Rosabeth Moss Kanter, *Men and Women of the Corporation* (New York: Basic Books, 1977, 1993). The cartoon DVD, *A Tale of "O,"* is available from Goodmeasure Direct (info@goodmeasure.com).

80  **unborn fetus**  David B. Caruso, "Debate revived on mother's rights," Associated Press, May 19, 2004.

84  **women were majority owners**  Florida has the fastest growth rate for women-owned firms. See *Women-Owned Businesses in 2006: Trends in the U.S. and 50 States* (Washington, D.C.: Center for Women's Business Research, 2006).

87  **greedy organizations**  Lewis Coser, *Greedy Institutions* (New York: Free Press, 1974).

89  **"seven-day weekend"**  From personal communication with Ricardo Semler, later described in his book *The Seven-Day Weekend: Changing the Way Work Works* (New York: Portfolio, 2004).

89  **checking in with the boss while on vacation**  Forty-three percent of the 700 workers across the United States surveyed by office furniture manufacturer Steelcase in July 2006 said they spend time doing work while on vacation, nearly double the 23 percent who said they did so in 1995; "The Nature of Work in 2006," Workplace Index Survey (Grand Rapids: Steelcase Corporation, part 1, July 2006). The Families and Work Institute survey

showed that about 20 percent of employees work sometimes or often on vacation; Galinsky et al., op. cit. About a third of those who worked during their most recent weeklong vacation were completing an assignment or catching up on work; 18 percent checked in with the boss, an Adecco North America study showed; "Adecco 2006 Vacation Survey," *Workplace Insights Series* (Melville: Adecco USA, July 2006).

91    **temporary-staffing industry**  The percentages come from David Autor, an economist at MIT, as cited in Michael Jones, "Lone rangers: are those in the free-agent economy just getting to the future ahead of everyone else?" *CommonWealth*, Summer 2005.

## Chapter 3: Growing Good Companies
page

96    **did not trust**  From a *Wall Street Journal*/NBC poll of trust in business. Gerald F. Seib and John Harwood, "Rising Anxiety: What Could Bring 1930s-Style Reform of U.S. Businesses?" *Wall Street Journal*, 24 July 2002.

98    **Values-based capitalism**  My Harvard Business School (HBS) colleague Lynn Paine took on this issue in her book, *Value Shift: Why Companies Must Merge Social and Financial Imperatives to Achieve High Performance* (New York: McGraw-Hill, 2002). She has also led the group developing HBS's new first-year required course on corporate accountability.

99    **lack of public confidence**  Todd L. Pittinsky et al., *National Leadership Index 2006: A National Study of Confidence in Leadership* (Cambridge: Harvard University, Kennedy School of Government, Center for Public Leadership, 2006).

99    **surveyed about trust**  Edelman's Annual Trust Barometer, a survey of opinion leaders released in January 2006. www.edelman.com/news/ShowOne.asp?ID=102

100    **public health issue**  Centers for Disease Control and Prevention, "Overweight and Obesity: Frequently Asked Questions," CDCP website: http://www.cdc.gov/nccdphp/dnpa/obesity/faq.htm. Accessed: 13 February 2007.

100    **wage ratio**  Institute for Policy Studies and United for a Fair Economy, "Executive Excess 2005: Defense Contractors Get More Bucks for the Bang," United for a Fair Economy website: http://www.faireconomy.org/press/2005/EE2005.pdf. Accessed: 13 February 2007.

104    **How much is enough?**  Harvard Business School professors Howard Stevenson and Laura Nash raised this question in their book, *Just Enough: Tools for Creating Success in Your Work and Life* (New York: Wiley, 2001).

105    **what angers people**  Public Agenda Foundation, "Where Americans and Business Leaders Agree/Disagree on Business Ethics," Public Agenda

Foundation website, March 10, 2004, http://www.publicagenda.org/press/press_release_detail.cfm?list=57. Accessed: 13 February 2007.

105    "creative accounting"  Donald C. Hambrick and Richard A. D'Aveni, "Large corporate failures as downward spirals," *Administrative Science Quarterly* 31 (1986): 274–297; Greg Brenneman, "Right away and all at once: how we saved Continental," *Harvard Business Review,* September–October 1998.

106    blinded Coca-Cola's leaders  As the late *New York Times* reporter Constance Hays told it in her deeply researched book *The Real Thing: Truth and Power at the Coca-Cola Company* (New York: Random House, 2004). (I reviewed the book for the *New York Times.*)

107    ethical eyebrow-raising territory  Ibid.

109    cover-ups and downward spirals  See Chapter 3 of Rosabeth Moss Kanter, *Confidence: How Winning Streaks and Losing Streaks Begin and End* (New York: Crown, 2004).

110    Gillette had slipped  Ibid.

117    Falling U.S. job satisfaction  A recent Conference Board report on falling U.S. job satisfaction found widespread discontent across ages and incomes, to which merger angst contributes. Half of all Americans surveyed said they were satisfied with their jobs, down from nearly 60 percent in 1995; only 14 percent felt very satisfied. In a related study, 40 percent felt disconnected from their employers, with 25 percent confessing that they were just "showing up to collect a paycheck." "US Job Satisfaction Keeps Falling," *Business Credit* 107 (April 2005): 67.

117    home to a large corporation  Rosabeth Moss Kanter, *World Class: Thriving Locally in the Global Economy* (New York: Simon & Schuster, 1995).

122    social investment  Social Investment Forum, *2005 Report on Socially Responsible Investing Trends in the United States: 10-year Review* (Washington, D.C.: Social Investment Forum, January 2006).

125    Equator Principles  Information comes from my interviews and a July 6, 2006, press release accessed from the Equator Principles website: http://www.equator-principles.com/documents/EP_Readoption_Press_Release_FINAL.pdf. Accessed: 15 February 2007.

125    BankTrack  BankTrack, "Principles, Profits, or Just PR" BankTrack website: http://www.banktrack.org/doc/File/BankTrack%20publications/BankTrack%20publications/040604%20Principles,%20Profits%20or%20just%20PR.pdf. Accessed: 13 February 2007.

131    business schools  After writing a comprehensive history of business education in the United States, Rakesh Khurana argued that business schools must deal with values as well as economics or risk becoming irrelevant. Khurana, *From Higher Aims to Hired Hands* (Princeton: Princeton University Press, 2007).

Chapter 4: Restoring Respect for Government

page

135    **residents lived in poverty** U.S. Census Bureau, "2004 American Community Survey," August 2005. http://factfinder.census.gov/servlet/STTable?_bm=y&-state=st&-context=st&-qr_name=ACS_2004_EST_G00_S1701&-ds_name=ACS_2004_EST_G00_&-tree_id=304&-all_geo_types=N&-_caller=geoselect&-geo_id=16000US2255000&-format=&-_lang=en. Accessed: 15 February 2007.

135    **Income inequality** U.S. Census Bureau, "Income, Poverty, and Health Insurance Coverage in the United States: 2004," August 2005. See also the editorial "Life in the bottom 80 percent," *New York Times,* 1 September 2005.

136    **confidence in leaders** Todd L. Pittinsky et al., *National Leadership Index 2006: A National Study of Confidence in Leadership* (Cambridge: Harvard University, Kennedy School of Government, Center for Public Leadership, 2006).

136    **Global Corruption Index** Transparency International, Berlin, Germany. "Corruption Perceptions Index 2006." November 2006. http://www.transparency.org/policy_research/surveys_indices/cpi/2006. Accessed: 15 February 2007.

137    **nonpartisan examination** This was a panel convened by Harvard's Kennedy School of Government over the course of a year, chaired by Joseph Nye and Elaine Kamarck, in collaboration with the U.S. Office of Personnel Management.

137    **private-sector jobs** See Paul C. Light, *The New Public Service* (Washington, D.C.: Brookings Institution Press, 1999).

139    **government spending** Richard B. McKenzie and Dwight R. Lee, "Government in Retreat." University of Georgia, NCPA Policy Report, No. 97. National Center for Policy Analysis, Washington, D.C. June 1991.

141    **problem of good government** Theda Skocpol argued that anti-government sentiment increased after the failure of Hillary Clinton's Health Security bill, which Skocpol called "a perfect foil for anti-government mobilization" in her detailed account. Skocpol, *Boomerang: Clinton's Health Security Effort and the Turn Against Government in U.S. Politics* (New York: Norton, 1996).

143    **Contempt often starts** Kanter, *Confidence: How Winning Streaks and Losing Streaks Begin and End* (New York: Crown, 2004).

145    **Iraq intelligence failures** United States Senate, Select Committee on Intelligence, *Report on the US Intelligence Community's Prewar Intelligence Assessments on Iraq,* 108th Congress, July 7, 2004.

149    **"center of the storm"** Quoted in Brian McGrory, "In Sanctum Santorum," *Boston Globe,* 12 July 2005.

149    **Santorum refused to back off** Ibid.

151    **Max Weber** H. H. Gerth and C. Wright Mills (translators and editors),

"Science as a Vocation," in *From Max Weber: Essays in Sociology* (New York: Oxford University Press, 1946), 129–156, and "Politics as a Vocation," 77–128, ibid.

152     **models of leadership**    The source for the stories about these leaders that follows is research for Kanter, *Confidence.*

159     **mired in scandal**    In 2003, the *New York Times* reported that Houston school administrators pushed out children who would skew test scores and then entered codes indicating that those students had transferred somewhere else. Diana Jean Schemo, "Questions on Data Cloud Luster of Houston Schools," *New York Times,* 11 July 2003.

159     **illegal kickbacks**    Ralph Ranalli and Anand Vaishnav, "Everett Schools Chief, 10 Others Indicted," *Boston Globe,* 27 March 2004.

162     **change is definitely possible**    See Steven Kelman, *Unleashing Change: A Study of Organizational Renewal in Government* (Washington, D.C.: Brookings Institution Press, 2005).

## Chapter 5: Engaging the World
page

167     **attract criticism**    See John Donnelly, "Outside Oprah's school, a growing frustration," *Boston Globe,* 20 January 2007. But the same newspaper editorialized the next day that Winfrey should be applauded in her grand gestures, even if there is a need to spread resources more widely, because many other institutions, including the U.S. government, should understand that the fate of Africa is a global responsibility and get involved.

167     **career officers**    The figure comes from the American Foreign Service Association, via an e-mail exchange between my research associate Lance Pierce and James Yorke, a labor management specialist there.

168     **$31 billion**    U.S. Office of Management and Budget at http://www.whitehouse.gov/omb/budget/2007/tables.html. Accessed: 18 January 2007.

168     **Iraqis fleeing**    Michael Kranish, "U.S. is pressed to admit more Iraqis," *Boston Globe,* 17 January 2007.

168     **foundations by total giving**    The amounts given by the top ten in 2006 came from the Foundation Center at http://foundationcenter.org/findfunders/top100giving.html. Accessed: 18 January 2007.

169     **lives have been saved**    Lara J. Wolfson et al., "Has the 2005 measles mortality reduction goal been achieved? A natural history modeling study," *The Lancet* 369 (2007): 191–200. See also "Measles Goal Achieved! Deaths Down by 60%." World Health Organization: http://www.who.int/immunization/newsroom/measles/en/index.html. Accessed: 12 February 2007.

169     **view of Americans**    Pew Global Attitudes Project, *15 Nation Pew Global Attitudes Survey* (Philadelphia: Pew Charitable Trusts, June 2006). Report is on the Pew website, www.pewtrusts.com.

183     **Leader of the Year**    "Álvaro Uribe named '2005 Leader of the Year,'"

*Latin Business Chronicle,* 11 August 2006. But despite this accolade, the country remained troubled, and early in 2007, a scandal surfaced that linked Uribe's political allies to the country's right-wing death squads and drug traffickers, according to news reports. Uribe's foreign minister was ousted and his secret police chief was arrested for murder. Indira A. R. Lakshmanan, "Colombia political scandal imperiling U.S. ties," *Boston Globe* 25 February 2007.

184    **flat world**   Thomas Friedman, *The World Is Flat* (New York: Farrar Straus & Giroux, 2006 edition).

188    **Mandela**   All facts about Nelson Mandela are drawn from the research for Chapter 10 of Kanter, *Confidence: How Winning Streaks and Losing Streaks Begin and End* (New York: Crown 2004), which was based on interviews, archival documents, and Mandela's powerful autobiography, *A Long Walk to Freedom* (New York: Holt, Rinehart and Winston, 2000).

197    **trade deficit**   U.S. Census Bureau, Foreign Trade Statistics, webpage: http://www.census.gov/foreign-trade/balance/c5700.html. Accessed: 12 February 2007. Agricultural trade with China has been in surplus for decades but has been dropping in recent years, going from a historic high of $26.79 billion in 1996 to $3.67 billion in 2005. USDA Economic Research Service, Foreign Agricultural Trade of the United States website: http://www.ers.usda.gov/Data/FATUS/DATA/XMScy1935.xls. Accessed: 12 February 2007.

197    **Internet users**   Current figures come from iResearch, China Internet Network Information Center; earlier predictions were made by Forbes Global.

197    **Google attracted 40 percent**   iResearch, CCNIC (China Internet Network Information Center). Google does not have any faith in these numbers and has disputed the methodology employed, according to my informants.

200    **India's population**   *World Population Prospects: The 2004 Revision,* The United Nations, February 2005. See also Mark Turner, "India's population 'to outstrip China by 2030,' " *Financial Times,* 24 February 2005.

201    **Indian Americans**   U.S. Census Bureau, "2005 American Community Survey," August 2006. http://factfinder.census.gov/servlet/IPTable?_bm= y&-geo_id=01000US&-qr_name=ACS_2005_EST_G00_S0201&-qr_ name=ACS_2005_EST_G00_S0201PR&-qr_name=ACS_2005_EST_ G00_S0201T&-qr_name=ACS_2005_EST_G00_S0201TPR&-reg=ACS_ 2005_EST_G00_S0201:032;ACS_2005_EST_G00_S0201PR:032; ACS_2005_EST_G00_S0201T:032;ACS_2005_EST_G00_S0201TPR: 032&-ds_name=ACS_2005_EST_G00_&-_lang=en&-format=. Accessed: 16 February 2007.

201    **Indian Americans are millionaires**   Merrill Lynch, New York, NY. "South Asian Market Fastest Growing in the U.S.," analyst press release, May 14, 2003. http://www.ml.com/index.asp?id=7695_7696_8149_8688_8579_8714. Accessed: 16 February 2007.

204 **contribute to an analysis** Douglas Raymond and Paula Broadwell, "The Wikipedia way to better intelligence," *The Christian Science Monitor,* 8 January 2007, 9.

204 **Internet café use in Jordan and Egypt** Deborah L. Wheeler, "Empowering publics: information technology and democratization in the Arab world—lessons from Internet cafes and beyond," *Oxford Internet Institute,* Research Report No. 11, July 2006.

204 **trade increases communications** See, for example: Rafael Reuveny, "The Trade and Conflict Debate: A Survey of Theory, Evidence, and Future Research," *Peace Economics, Peace Science and Public Policy* 6 (Winter 1999–2000): 23–49; Yuan-Ching Chang, "Economic Interdependence and International Interactions: Impact of Third-Party Trade on Political Cooperation and Conflict," *Cooperation and Conflict: Journal of the Nordic International Studies Association* 40 (2005): 207–232.

204 **it generates conflict** Arthur A. Stein, "Trade and Conflict: Uncertainty, Strategic Signaling, and Interstate Disputes," Working Paper, University of California at Los Angeles, May 31, 2001, presented at the Conference on Trade and Conflict, Ohio State University, September 2000.

## Chapter 6: Building Community
page

210 **network of relationships** Robert Putnam, *Bowling Alone: The Collapse and Revival of American Community* (New York: Simon & Schuster, 2000).

210 **number of confidants** Duke sociologist Lynn Smith-Lovin and her colleagues confirmed this with a face-to-face survey of 1,467 adults. Miller McPhearson, Lynn Smith-Lovin, and Matthew Brashears, "Social Isolation in America: Changes in Core Discussion Networks over 2 Decades," *American Sociological Review* 71 (June 2006): 353–375.

214 **closed communities** Rosabeth Moss Kanter, *Commitment and Community* (Cambridge: Harvard University Press, 1972).

217 **Alexis de Tocqueville** Alexis de Tocqueville, *Democracy in America* (New York: HarperCollins paperback edition, 2006). The book was originally published in 1835.

218 **Total annual giving** Estimates by the Giving USA Foundation and the University of Indiana's Center on Philanthropy, as found in Giving USA, 2005 Annual Report, Glenview, IL: Giving USA Foundation, 2006, p. 1.

218 **Thanksgiving and Christmas** Charity Navigator, "Holiday Giving Guide 2006," Charity Navigator website: http://www.charitynavigator.org/index.cfm/bay/content.view/cpid/518.htm. Accessed: 13 February 2007.

218 **phony newspaper profile** Pam Easton, "Texas Agency Spreads Phony Katrina Victim Story," *AOL News on the Web,* 10 December 2005. http://articles.news.aol.com/news/_a/texas-agency-spreads-phony-katrina/20051210044609990005. Accessed: 12 February 2007.

219    **does not spread to all charities**  Public Agenda Foundation, *The Charitable Impulse* (New York: Public Agenda Foundation, 2005), p. 23.

220    **charitable gifts**  Giving USA, op. cit.

221    **volunteer the most**  The Center on Philanthropy at Indiana University. Study of High Net-Worth Philanthropy for Bank of America. Bank of America website: http://newsroom.bankofamerica.com. Accessed: 13 February 2007.

225    **each success increases confidence**  Kanter, *Confidence* (New York: Crown, 2004).

240    **scientists have shown**  Scientific evidence for this point includes a study of staged thefts on a New York City beach to see if onlookers would risk personal harm to halt a theft of a radio on a neighboring blanket. Only 20 percent would help when they had no conversation with the person on that blanket. But if the blanket occupant asked them to "watch my things," and they agreed, then 95 percent of the onlookers became extremely active on behalf of the strangers on the next beach blanket, to the extent of chasing the thief down the beach and snatching back the radio. See T. Moriarty, "Crime, Commitment, and the Responsive Bystander," *Journal of Personality and Social Psychology* 31 (1975): 370–376.

## Conclusion

page

249    **"neo-imperial unilateralism"**  The phrase was coined by Will Marshall and Jeremy Rosner, *With All Our Might: A Progressive Strategy for Defeating Jihadism and Defending Liberty* (New York: Rowman & Littlefield, 2006).

249    **America has not gone far enough**  This perspective is reflected in Niall Ferguson's book *Colossus: The Price of America's Empire* (New York: Penguin, 2004).

249    **decline of a great power**  Historian Paul Kennedy's *The Rise and Fall of the Great Powers* is emblematic (New York: Vintage, 1989, paperback edition).

250    **first "new nation"**  Seymour Martin Lipset, *The First New Nation: The United States in Historical and Comparative Perspective* (New York: Norton, 1979, paperback edition).

250    **community of communities**  John Rawls, *A Theory of Justice* (Cambridge: Harvard University Press, 1971).

251    **embrace differences**  Michael Walzer, *On Toleration* (New Haven: Yale University Press, 1997).

254    **elements for a significant change**  Rosabeth Moss Kanter, *The Change Masters* (New York: Simon & Schuster, 1983).

254    **deviant actions turn out to be innovations**  Jerry Sternin and Richard Pascale coined the term "positive deviance." Sternin heads the Positive Deviance Initiative at Tufts University in Medford, Massachusetts.

255 **reshape norms** Rosabeth Moss Kanter, *Even Bigger Change: A Framework for Getting Started at Changing the World* (Harvard Business School Case #305099, March 29, 2005).

256 *failure in the middle* This was first articulated in Kanter, *The Change Masters,* and it was described in greater detail in Rosabeth Moss Kanter, *Evolve!: Succeeding in the Digital Culture of Tomorrow* (Boston: Harvard Business School Press, 2001).

259 **confidence to persist** Kanter, *Confidence* (New York: Crown, 2004).

260 **Hispanics indicate** This report is for Massachusetts. While Hispanics are more likely to say that the American dream is alive and well (39 percent vs. 29 percent for whites and 17 percent for blacks) and to agree that America is the land of opportunity (64 percent vs. 57 percent for whites and 49 percent for blacks), whites are slightly more likely to say that they are actually achieving the American dream (69 percent vs. 68 percent for Hispanics and 50 percent for blacks). The full report is located on the United Way of Massachusetts Bay website: www.uwmb.org.

# Acknowledgments

⎯⎯⎯⎯

This project started because Alberto Ibarguen twisted my arm, and he is one of the most persuasive people I know. Now president of the Knight Foundation and at the time publisher of the *Miami Herald* under Knight-Ridder, he encouraged me to write regularly about national affairs for his chain and other publications. My son, Matthew Moss Kanter Stein, and my husband, Barry Stein, urged me to accept it. They were both very understanding of the deadlines that this undertaking entailed—additional research and writing on top of my teaching and research at Harvard. But what resulted were the seeds of ideas from which this book eventually grew.

Juan Vasquez and Joe Ogilvy were receptive editors, as were Renee Loth, Marjorie Pritchard, Shelley Cohen, Robert Keogh, and Susan Headden at national newspapers and magazines. Numerous friends on my e-mail distribution list commented on my commentaries, especially the Rev. Dr. Ray Hammond, Kelly Craighead, Irma Mann, and Jim Stone, who always had a positive word. In addition to print, many articles were disseminated widely on the Internet, sometimes occasioning live media appearances. Thanks to all who spread the word.

I owe a major debt to the hundreds of people I interviewed over the past five years, as well as those who offered their views in public forums. Whenever I mention names and events in this book that are not accompanied by a citation to published sources, that means I was there personally or through surrogates on my research team, gathering information, observing activities, and speaking directly to primary sources. As part of my normal research process at Harvard Business School, I have checked quotes and offered private thanks to a list of people too long to include here. But I want to publicly thank Stanley Litow, IBM's visionary vice president of corporate citizenship and corporate affairs and president of the IBM International Foundation, a valued colleague for ten years. We have discussed reinventing the U.S. educational system, imagined solutions to national and international problems, created events to include other organizations in the dialogue, and explored IBM's internal changes. I also want to thank the dedicated people who serve with me on nonprofit and civic boards for conversations about entrepreneurship, civic engagement, women's issues, and American politics, especially the much-loved and, also, much-mourned Eli Segal, who made public service a high ideal and national service programs the essence of democracy.

When it came time to think about writing a book to pull my ideas together, Senator Barbara Mikulski told me that being packaged in hard covers makes ideas matter. Her advice, for which I am grateful, increased my commitment to this book project. Colleagues and informed friends read the manuscript at various stages and made helpful comments or added an important item. I especially want to thank Rakesh Khurana, who is the very model of colleagueship at Harvard and friendship outside of work. Thanks also to Jim Stone, Douglas Raymond, Alan Khazei, Michael Brown, Ande Zellman, Stephanie Khurana, and my son Matt for their deep reading and critical input on the whole book or selected chapters. AnnMaura Connolly and Shelley Metzenbaum provided useful additions.

For a long time I referred to this as "my America book," but knowing that my title consultant, Dr. Michael Wertheimer, was nearby, I tossed many titles back and forth. Michael was very supportive during the final stages, as were Laura Roosevelt, Charlie Silberstein, Phyllis Segal, Andy Spellman, and Randy Wertheimer. I owe so much to so many from whom I learned—for example, conversations over walks with Connie Borde—that I apologize to anyone whom I inadvertently left off this list, but I promise to add your name in the next edition.

Ryan Raffaelli and Lance Pierce worked closely with me as research associates during the period of thinking and writing, supplying me with facts when I needed them, intelligently and cheerfully. I owe thanks to the Division of Research at Harvard Business School for the support that allows me to entice talented people such as Ryan and Lance to work for me. Cheng Gao, a hardworking Harvard undergraduate, was also a very responsive, thorough researcher for portions of the book. Former assistant Cheryl Daigle did her usual competent job with the articles and e-mail list. My current charming assistant Klara Prachar helped greatly with the final stages.

I especially want to thank my editor at Crown, John Mahaney, and the whole Crown team. I thank the talented design team for the powerful cover, which conveys the book's message so well. Most of all, I thank John for being an editor who actually edits. That's a tradition often lost to book publishing, so I am grateful to John for his very astute and always helpful advice.

# Index

# About the Author

Rosabeth Moss Kanter holds the Ernest L. Arbuckle Professorship at Harvard Business School, where she specializes in strategy, innovation, and leadership for change. Her strategic and practical insights have guided leaders of large and small organizations worldwide for over twenty-five years through teaching, writing, and consulting directly to major corporations and governments. She has also served as editor of *Harvard Business Review.* Professor Kanter has been named to lists of the "50 most powerful women in the world" *(Times of London)* and the "50 most influential business thinkers in the world" (Accenture and Thinkers 50 research), often ranked in the top ten. In 2001, she received the Academy of Management's Distinguished Career Award for her scholarly contributions to management knowledge, and in 2002, she was named "Intelligent Community Visionary of the Year" by the World Teleport Association. Her current work continues her focus on the transformation of major institutions such as global corporations, health care delivery systems, and other organizations seeking innovative new models.

Professor Kanter is the author or co-author of seventeen books, including this one, which have been translated into seventeen languages. Her recent book *Confidence: How Winning Streaks and Losing Streaks Begin and End* (a *New York Times* business and #1 *BusinessWeek* bestseller) describes the culture and dynamics of high-performance organizations as compared with those in decline and shows how to lead turnarounds, whether in businesses, hospitals, schools, sports teams, community organizations, or countries. Her classic prizewinning book *Men and Women of the Corporation* (C. Wright Mills Award winner for the year's best book on social issues) offered insight to countless individuals and organizations about corporate careers and the individual and organizational factors that promote success. A spin-off video, *A Tale of "O": On Being Different,* is among the world's most widely used diversity tools, and a related book, *Work and Family in the United States,* set a policy agenda (in 2001, a coalition of university centers created the "Rosabeth Moss Kanter Award" in her honor for the best research on work/family issues). *When Giants Learn to Dance,* another award-winning book, showed many companies worldwide how to master the new terms of competition at the dawn of the global information age. In *World Class: Thriving Locally in the Global Economy,* Kanter identified the rise of new business networks and analyzed the benefits and tensions of globalization. It has guided public officials and civic leaders in developing strategies and skills for the economy of the future.

Kanter has received twenty-two honorary doctoral degrees and numerous leadership awards and prizes for her books and articles. For example, her book *The Change Masters* was named one of the most influential business books of the twentieth century *(Financial Times)*. Through Goodmeasure Inc., the consulting group she co-founded, she has partnered with IBM to bring her leadership tools, originally developed for businesses, to public education as part of IBM's award-winning Reinventing Education initiative. She is an adviser to the CEOs of large and small companies, has served on numerous business and nonprofit boards and on national and regional commissions, and speaks widely, often sharing the platform with presidents, prime ministers, and CEOs at national and international events, such as the World Economic Forum in Davos, Switzerland. Before joining the Harvard Business School faculty, she held tenured professorships at Yale University and Brandeis University and was a Fellow at Harvard Law School, simultaneously holding a Guggenheim Fellowship.

Her latest initiative involves the development and creation of an innovative institute for advanced leadership to ensure that successful leaders at the top of their professions who are transitioning to their next stage of life can apply their skills to help solve the most challenging national and global problems.